DM Yard Services

Accounting Capstone Project

QuickBooks®

Darlene Schnuck

CENGAGE

Australia • Brazil • Mexico • Singapore • United Kingdom • United States

CENGAGE

DM Yard Services: Accounting Capstone Project

Darlene Schnuck

Vice President, General Manager, Social Science & Qualitative Business: Erin Joyner

Executive Product Director: Michael Schenk

Product Director: Jason Fremder

Senior Product Manager: Matthew Filimonov

Content Development Manager: Daniel Celenza

Associate Content Developer: Emily Lehmann

Product Assistant: Aiyana Moore

Executive Marketing Manager: Robin LeFevre

Marketing Coordinator: Hillary Johns

Senior Content Project Manager: Tim Bailey

Production Service: Lumina Datamatics

Senior Art Director: Michelle Kunkler

Cover Designer: Tin Box Studio

Cover Images:
  Top Image: Toa55/Shutterstock.com
  Bottom Image: Jorge Salcedo/Shutterstock.com

© 2018 Cengage Learning®

Unless otherwise noted, all content is © Cengage

ALL RIGHTS RESERVED. No part of this work covered by the copyright herein may be reproduced or distributed in any form or by any means, except as permitted by U.S. copyright law, without the prior written permission of the copyright owner.

> For product information and technology assistance, contact us at
> **Cengage Learning Customer & Sales Support, 1-800-354-9706**
>
> For permission to use material from this text or product, submit all requests online at **www.cengage.com/permissions**
> Further permissions questions can be emailed to
> **permissionrequest@cengage.com**

All screen shots in this text are taken from QuickBooks software, created by Intuit. Reprinted with permission © Intuit Inc. All rights reserved.

Library of Congress Control Number: 2017941022

Student Edition ISBN: 978-1-337-56052-8
Student Edition with CD ISBN: 978-1-337-62125-0

Cengage Learning
20 Channel Center Street
Boston, MA 02210
USA

Cengage Learning is a leading provider of customized learning solutions with employees residing in nearly 40 different countries and sales in more than 125 countries around the world. Find your local representative at **www.cengage.com.**

Cengage Learning products are represented in Canada by Nelson Education, Ltd.

To learn more about Cengage Learning Solutions, visit **www.cengage.com**

Purchase any of our products at your local college store or at our preferred online store **www.cengagebrain.com**

Printed in the United States of America
Print Number: 01   Print Year: 2017

Thank you:
- To my husband, daughters and grandchildren: Mike, Tracy, Jenny, Jamie, Ben, Aaron, Kayla and Kylie for giving up wife, mom and grandma time!
- To my expert reviewer, Brian Schmoldt, Accounting and Finance Instructor at Madison College. His time, effort and sharing have added "asset" value to this project.

Thank you,
Darlene Schnuck

TABLE OF CONTENTS
DM YARD SERVICES

Preface
Project Objective / Project Highlight Features	2
Company Information	3
Using Express Start	3

JANUARY
Monthly Transactions / Activities	9
Monthly Bank Statement	20
Monthly Questions and Chapter Print / Submission Summary	22
Monthly Task List	23
Monthly To Do / Follow-Up/ Question List	23
General Journal, T-accounts, and Trial Balance Form	25

FEBRUARY
Monthly Transactions / Activities	29
Monthly Bank Statement	38
Monthly Questions and Chapter Print / Submission Summary	39
Monthly Task List / To Do / Follow-Up / Question List	41

MARCH
Monthly Transactions / Activities	43
Credit Card Services, Inc. Statement	61
Monthly Bank Statement	62
Monthly Questions	63
Chapter Print / Submission Summary	67
Monthly Task List / To Do / Follow-Up / Question List	69

APRIL
Monthly Transactions / Activities	71
Credit Card Services, Inc. Statement	101
Monthly Bank Statement	102
Petty Cash Disbursement Receipt	103
Monthly Questions and Chapter Print / Submission Summary	105
Monthly Task List / To Do / Follow-Up / Question List	107

MAY

Monthly Transactions / Activities	109
Credit Card Services, Inc. Statement	114
Monthly Bank Statement	115
Monthly Questions and Chapter Print / Submission Summary	117
Monthly Task List / To Do / Follow-Up / Question List	119

JUNE

Monthly Transactions / Activities	121
Credit Card Services, Inc. Statement	124
Monthly Bank Statement	125
Petty Cash Disbursement Receipt	126
Monthly Questions and Chapter Print / Submission Summary	127
Monthly Task List / To Do / Follow-Up / Question List	129

JULY

Monthly Transactions / Activities	131
Credit Card Services, Inc. Statement	153
Monthly Bank Statement	154
Monthly Questions and Chapter Print / Submission Summary	155
Monthly Task List / To Do / Follow-Up / Question List	157

AUGUST

Monthly Transactions / Activities	159
Credit Card Services, Inc. Statement	161
Monthly Bank Statement	162
Petty Cash Disbursement Receipt	163
Monthly Questions and Chapter Print / Submission Summary	164
Monthly Task List / To Do / Follow-Up / Question List	165

SEPTEMBER

Monthly Transactions / Activities	167
Credit Card Services, Inc. Statement	169
Monthly Bank Statement	170
Monthly Questions and Chapter Print / Submission Summary	171
Monthly Task List / To Do / Follow-Up / Question List	173

OCTOBER

Monthly Transactions / Activities	175
Credit Card Services, Inc. Statement	178
Monthly Bank Statement	179
Monthly Questions and Chapter Print / Submission Summary	180
Monthly Task List / To Do / Follow-Up / Question List	181

NOVEMBER

Monthly Transactions / Activities	183
Credit Card Services, Inc. Statement	186
Monthly Bank Statement	187
Monthly Questions and Chapter Print / Submission Summary	188
Monthly Task List	189
Monthly To Do / Follow-Up / Question List	189

DECEMBER

Monthly Transactions / Activities	191
Credit Card Services, Inc. Statement	193
Monthly Bank Statement	194
Monthly Questions	195
Chapter Print / Submission Summary	196
Monthly Task List / To Do / Follow-Up / Question List	197

YEAR END

Account Reconciliations and Year-End Analysis	199
Year-End Task List	210
Credit Card Services, Inc. Statement	211
Physical Inventory List	212
Office Supply Physical Inventory List	213

INCOME TAX PREPARATION

2016 Client Tax Organizer	217
Supplemental Information	222

DM Yard Services

Dave Michaels started DM Yard Services, a sole proprietorship, in January 2016. The business will provide lawn and landscaping services and products to residential and commercial customers. You have been hired as the accountant for DM Yard Services. You are responsible for completing all aspects of the 2016 financial accounting cycle for DM Yard Services including year-end analysis using accounting software and the preparation of the owner's personal income tax return using tax preparation software.

PROJECT OBJECTIVE:

The objective of this project is to serve as a capstone assessment of the following accounting program outcomes:
- ✓ Process financial transactions through the accounting cycle
- ✓ Analyze financial and business information to support decision-making and planning
- ✓ Process, report, and analyze payroll
- ✓ Perform individual and business income tax preparation
- ✓ Identify internal controls

PROJECT HIGHLIGHT FEATURES:

- ✓ Students complete the entire accounting cycle with year-end account analysis and preparation of business/personal income tax return (this is the only project with all parts coordinated to one business).
- ✓ Students not only use software default forms but also customize forms specific to business.
- ✓ Students account for a wide variety of transactions including recurring transactions, invoicing, payroll, complaint adjustments, and petty cash disbursements.
- ✓ Students account for the use of a business credit card.
- ✓ Students complete payroll tax forms.
- ✓ Students answer monthly questions on internal controls, ethics, and financial decision-making.
- ✓ Students complete the "Monthly Task" list and "To Do" lists.
- ✓ Students prepare an income tax return using source documents.

COMPANY INFORMATION:

Install Intuit QuickBooks Accountant 2015 using the license and product number on program CD.

You may be prompted to register your software, set up a new account, and enter any answers to the questions to complete the registration, noting you must use a real address (suggestion: your school's address). Call the registration number, 1-888-250-7279, to get the validation code.

NOTE 1: If you are a first-time user to QuickBooks, you will find assistance under the Help menu at QuickBooks Help as well as the Learning Center Tutorials.

NOTE 2: Depending on the version of QB (QuickBooks) you are using, not all prompts and screen shots will be exact, but you should be able to easily follow along.

NOTE 3: If you do not have a CD drive to install software, you may go to https://contactus.intuit.com/qbdt_retail_pages/windows and use the license and product number on CD to download. (There is an underscore between qbdt and retail, and retail and pages.)

Create a new company using EXPRESS START: Create a sole proprietor for the calendar year 2016; use YOUR NAME Yard Services, for example, Jones Yard Services, to create a company unique to you.

Use the following company information:

- Industry: Lawn Care or Landscaping

- Federal Employer Identification Number (EIN): 39-1212121

- Business Address: 800 Main St.

    Landscape, WI 53022

    262-356-2141

- Other company set-up, such as customers and vendors, will be completed when needed.

- Compare to the screen shot on the next page.

This should be YOUR last name

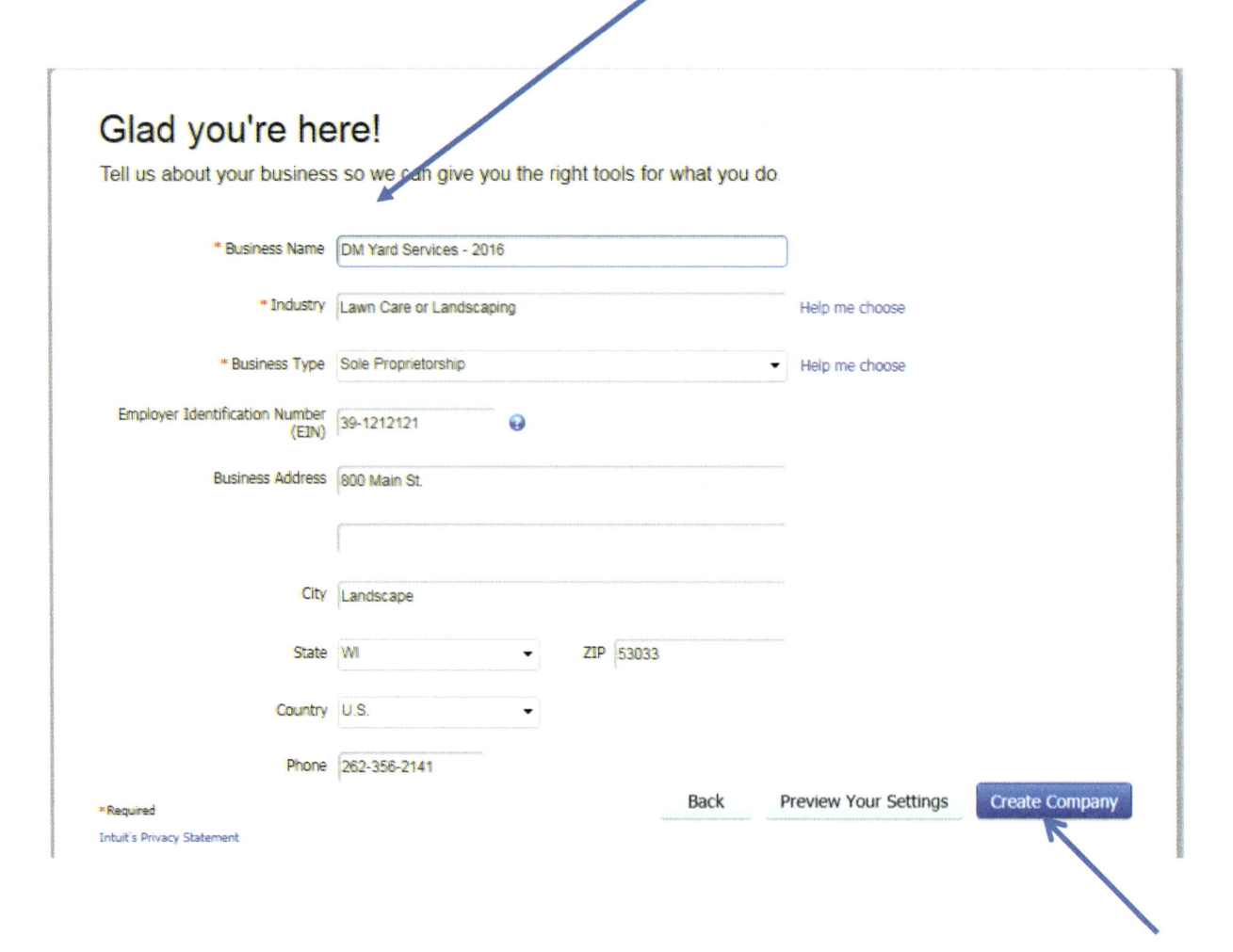

Glad you're here!
Tell us about your business so we can give you the right tools for what you do.

* Business Name: DM Yard Services - 2016
* Industry: Lawn Care or Landscaping
* Business Type: Sole Proprietorship
Employer Identification Number (EIN): 39-1212121
Business Address: 800 Main St.
City: Landscape
State: WI   ZIP: 53033
Country: U.S.
Phone: 262-356-2141

*Required
Intuit's Privacy Statement

Back   Preview Your Settings   **Create Company**

➢ At this time, we will *only* add the bank account information:

  ✓ YOUR NAME — Checking (edit as necessary for the field width)

  ✓ #745-1332 (this is the account number)

  ✓ There is no opening balance

  ✓ Opening balance date: 1/1/2016

  ✓ We will not need the QuickBooks checks.

  ✓ Continue/Start Working

➢ (Continue: At the QB Usage and Analytics Study)

- Close "Ready to Start Working" screen to go to Home Page as shown below:

  (Note: As mentioned, not all prompts and screen shots will apply depending on your QB version if not using the 2015 CD/download version.)

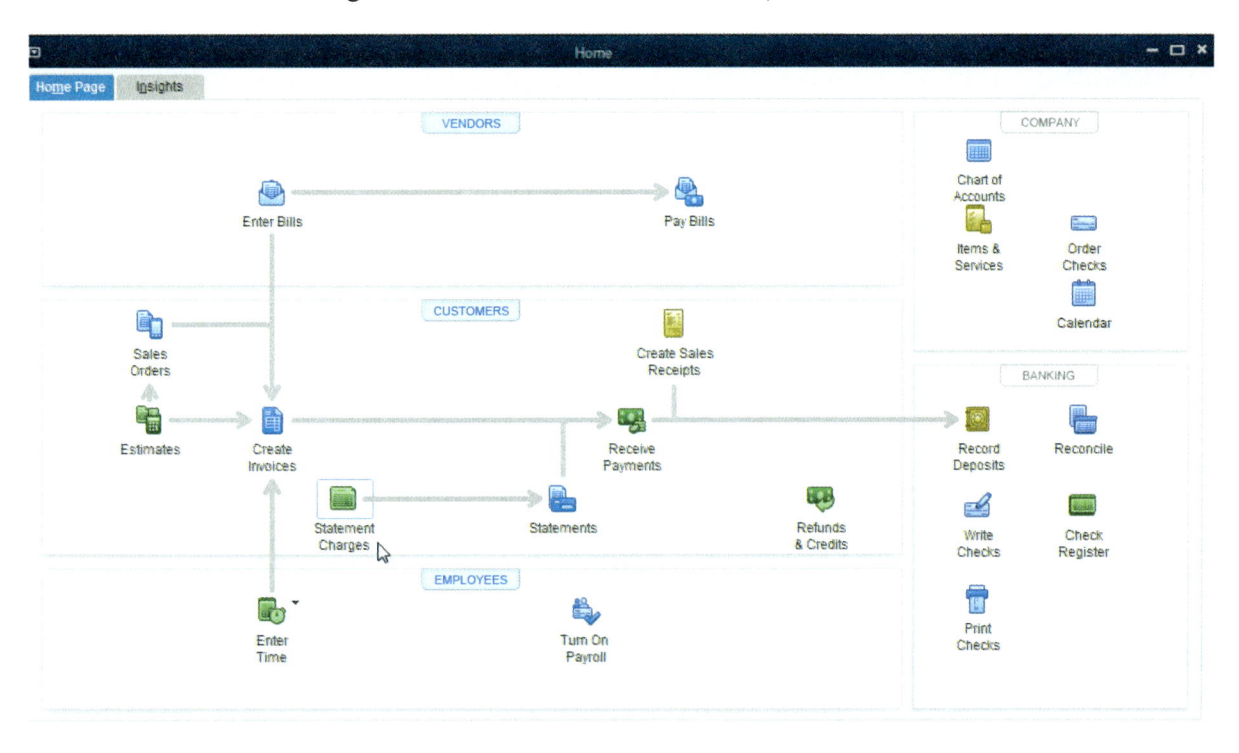

- Next review Company Preferences, found under the pull-down menu: **Edit**/Preferences.

- Under the **Accounting**/Company tab, uncheck the box, "Warn if transactions are 90 days in the past":

DATE WARNINGS

☐ Warn if transactions are 90 day(s) in the past

We will be accounting for transactions for the accounting year 1/1/2016 to 12/31/2016; since our current date (today's date) is greater than the 90 days, we are disabling this warning.

- Also set the closing date: 12/31/2015. This indicates that the books have been closed as of that date and we will be accounting for 2016 transactions.

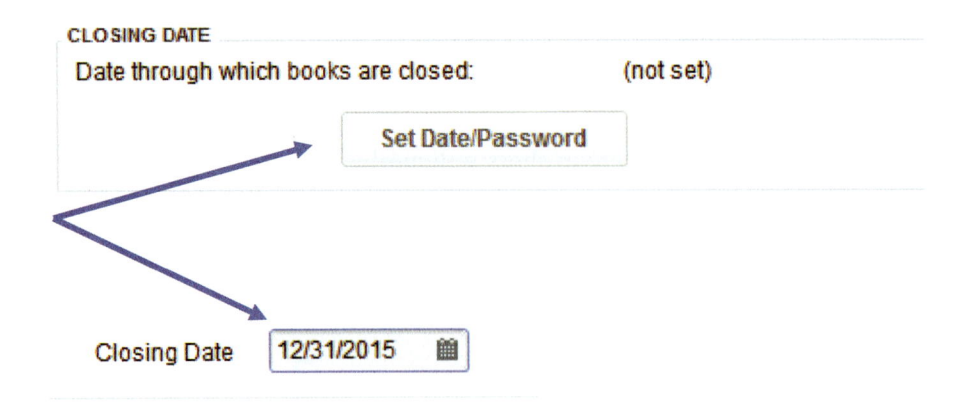

CLOSING DATE
Date through which books are closed: (not set)

Set Date/Password

Closing Date 12/31/2015

> Click OK.

> We will *not* use passwords for this project.

Continuing in Preferences:

> Under Items & Inventory/Company Preferences, check the box "Inventory and purchase orders are active."

Preferences

PURCHASE ORDERS AND INVENTORY
- ✓ Inventory and purchase orders are active.
- ✓ Warn about duplicate purchase order numbers.

When calculating Quantity Available for my inventory, deduct:
- ✓ Quantity reserved for Pending Builds
- ✓ Quantity on Sales Orders

✓ Warn if not enough inventory to sell.
- ○ When the quantity I want to sell exceeds Quantity On Hand
- ● When the quantity I want to sell exceeds Quantity Available

Advanced Inventory Settings — Learn about serial #/lots, FIFO and multi-location inventory

UNIT OF MEASURE
Single U/M Per Item

Also See:
General
Sales and Customers

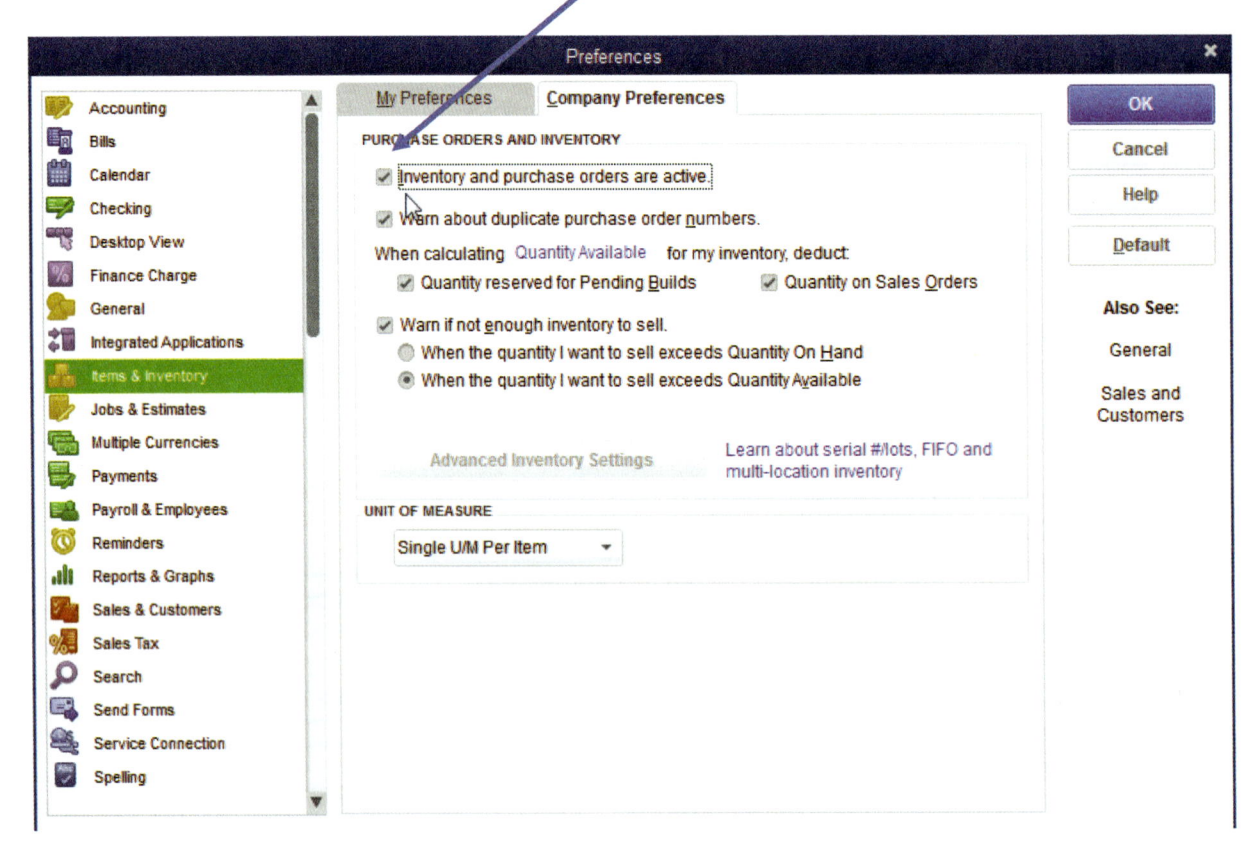

> Click OK for "QB must close all its open windows to change this preference."

> In Edit/Preferences under Sales & Customers/Company, enter "add new" usual shipping method: Hand Deliver.

SALES FORMS

Usual Shipping Method: Hand Deliver

Click OK.

Other General Information to Note

- Dave is the owner; he will handle general management duties, establish company policies, and oversee employees and their duties.

- Maintain customers and vendors as needed, entering only basic information as indicated. Residential customers will have credit terms of n/10 from **statement date** and commercial customers credit terms of 2/10, n/30 from **statement date**. Use invoice numbering as assigned: Invoice #1, 2, 3…. Customer statements will be prepared at the end of each month. Dave (owner) will review, approve, and initial all customer credit memos.

- We will use the state of Wisconsin throughout the project to be able to account for sales and payroll taxes at the state level.

- Vendors are corporations (non-1099) unless otherwise noted.

- Cash related: Make deposits as checks are received each month. Take advantage of cash discounts whenever possible. Dave Michaels must also sign any checks over $1,000. *Dave will review the check register each quarter for reasonableness of payee and amounts and initial*.

- Maintain inventory items as needed; use perpetual inventory system using average costing. Account for discounts through separate purchase discount account.

- Use the expense method to account for supplies.

January 2016 Transactions/Activities

#1: Using the general journal, T-accounts, and two-column form found on the pages following the January To Do/Follow-up/Question List, *manually* journalize the five January transactions (1/6 – 1/24), post to the T-accounts (create account titles and account numbers as needed), and prepare a trial balance.

#2: Account for the following transactions using QuickBooks. Note: We will *add* accounts as needed here for each transaction. At this time, edit the following accounts. At the Home Page, select the Chart of Accounts icon, select each account as noted below, then go to Account at the bottom left, and edit Account. (Note: This is one way to edit an account; you may use the pull-down menus or right click. There is usually more than one way to do a task in QuickBooks!)

> ➤ Change Owner's Draw and Owner's Equity to YOUR NAME, Draw and YOUR NAME, and Capital; save; and close.
> (Note: Make sure to use upper and lower case letters; the account name is used on the financial statements.)

> ➤ Change Furniture and Equipment to Office Equipment, save, and close.

> ➤ Change Landscaping Equipment to Lawn and Landscaping Equipment, save, and close.

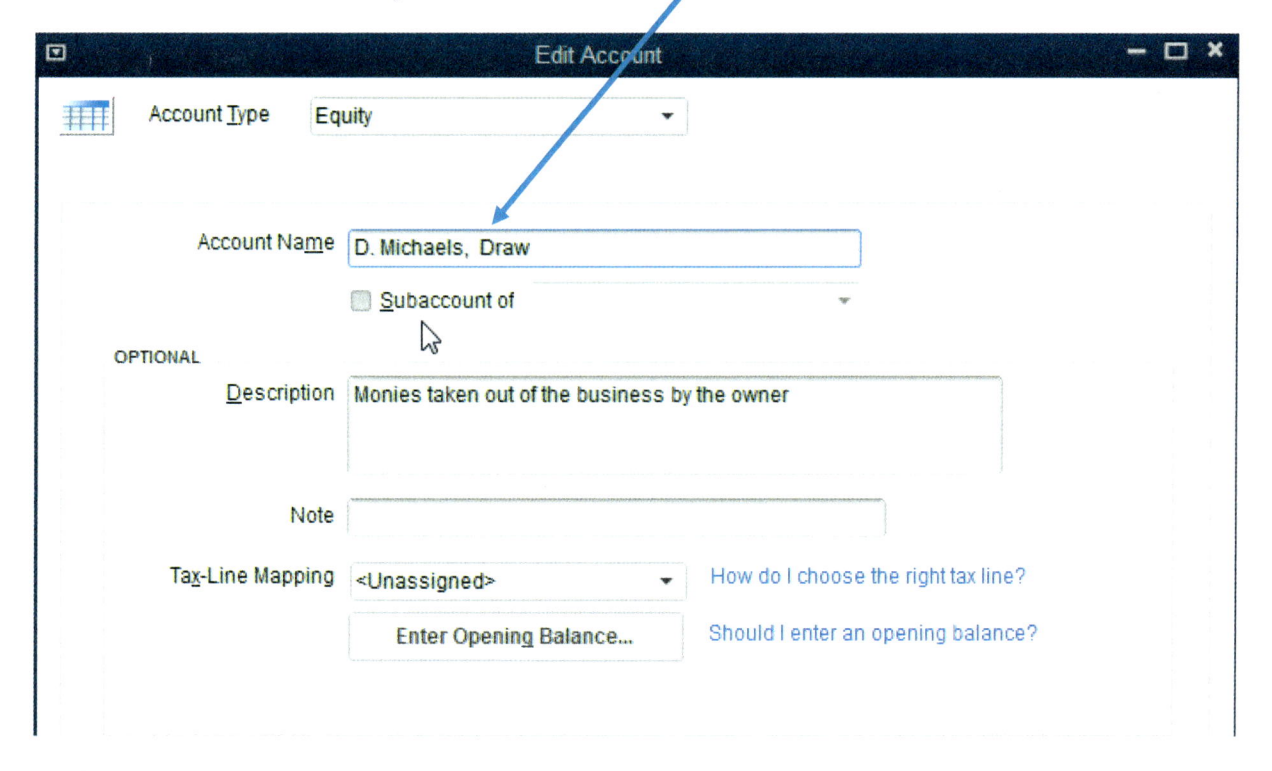

1/6   Record initial investment by Dave (owner) of $30,000; record as a general journal entry.

Pull-down menu item: Accountant/Make General Journal Entries. Click OK to assign entry numbers:

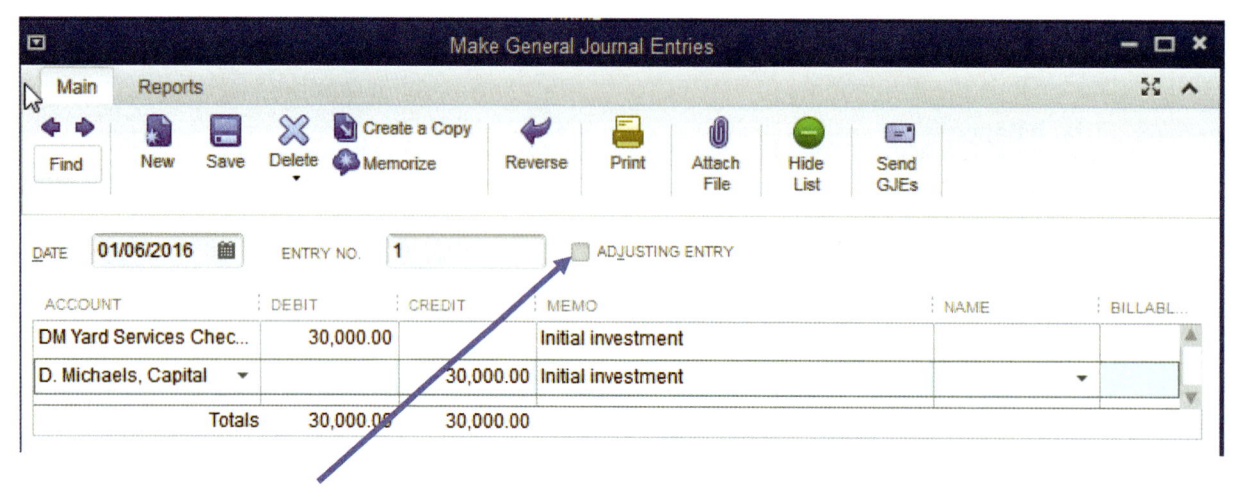

![Make General Journal Entries screenshot showing DATE 01/06/2016, ENTRY NO. 1, with DM Yard Services Checking debited 30,000.00 and D. Michaels, Capital credited 30,000.00, Memo "Initial investment"]

- Uncheck the Adjusting Entry box.

- Save and close.

- Enter "OK" to post the entry to Retained Earnings. Note: Because this general journal entry is being made directly to the DM Yard Services checking account, no further deposit is necessary.

(Note: The Memo field is used in the general ledger as a description of a journal entry.)

1/10   Issued check #1001 to purchase $43 office supplies, $750 computer, and $200 printer at Office City; $1,042.65 total includes sales tax (5%).

- Use a $500 capitalization amount for asset purchases.

- For this transaction only, allocate sales tax to each item; there should not be a sales tax expense. This is to illustrate that sales tax becomes part of the cost of the item.

- Use Write Check from Home Page. At Pay to the Order, add a new vendor. To save data entry time, enter only the vendor name and company name (Office City) and Office Supplies. Expense the account under Account Settings.

- For this and all checks: Uncheck the Print Later box and enter the check number; then the check does not have to be printed to be recorded in the check register.

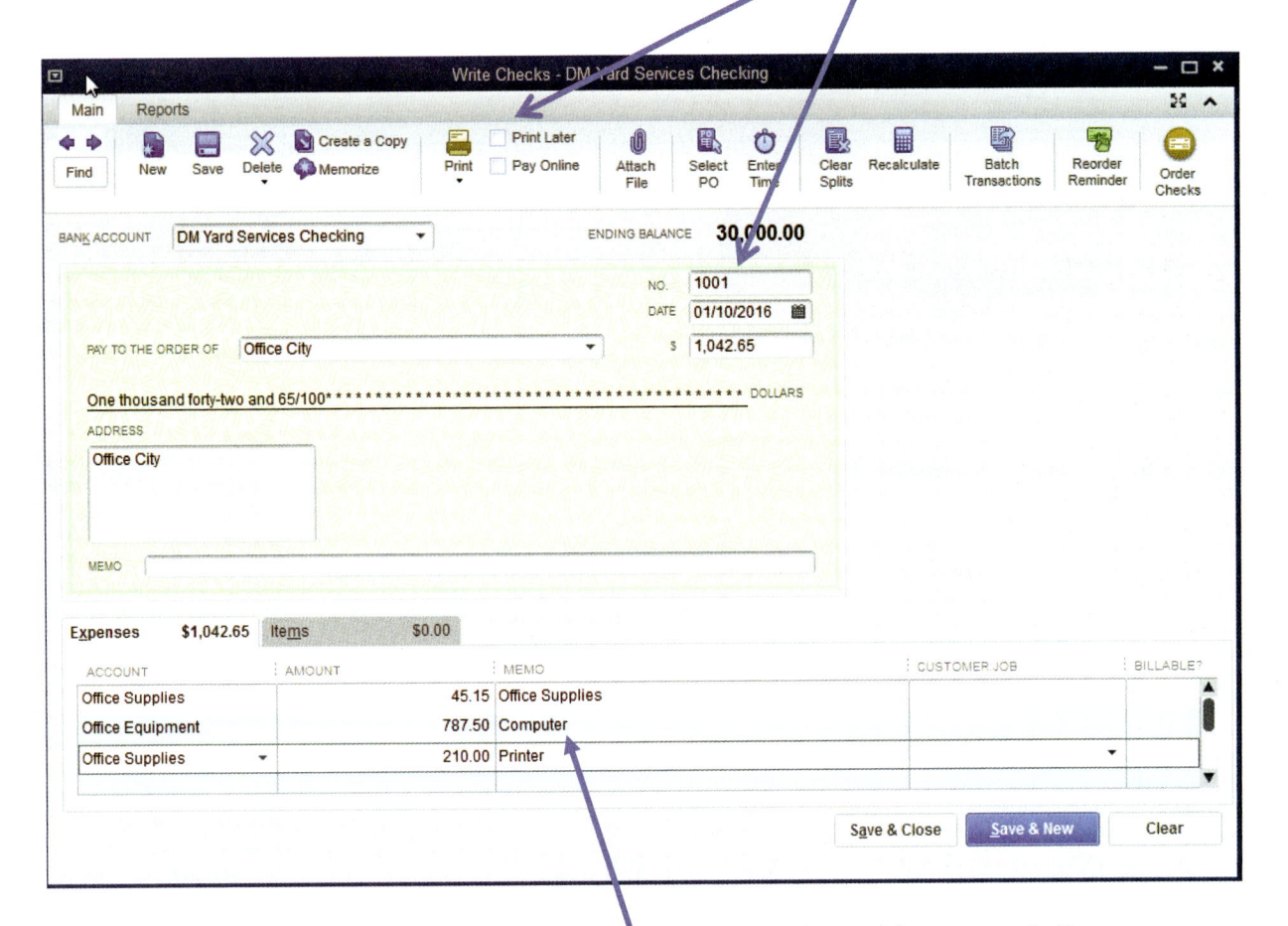

[Screenshot of QuickBooks "Write Checks - DM Yard Services Checking" window showing check #1001 dated 01/10/2016, payable to Office City for $1,042.65, with expenses split: Office Supplies $45.15, Office Equipment $787.50 (Computer), Office Supplies $210.00 (Printer).]

- Note that on the above screen shot the "Expense" tab is used for *any and all non-inventory* transactions, whether they debit an asset or expense account!

- Use of the memo field is optional; as mentioned, it adds detailed information to your general ledger transactions as shown in the image below:

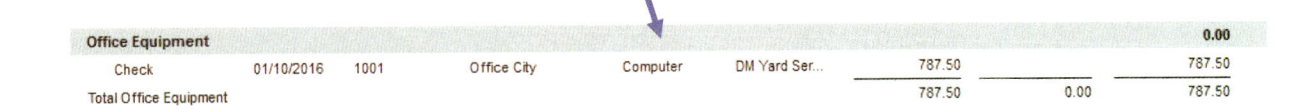

[General ledger excerpt showing Office Equipment, Check 01/10/2016 1001 Office City Computer DM Yard Ser... 787.50 787.50; Total Office Equipment 787.50 0.00 787.50]

- Save and close.

- See the next steps to see the journal entry of this transaction. Note this for future reference! It will be invaluable to you as you go through transactions in this project; it will show you the debit(s) and credit(s) of a particular transaction.

- Re-open Write Checks:

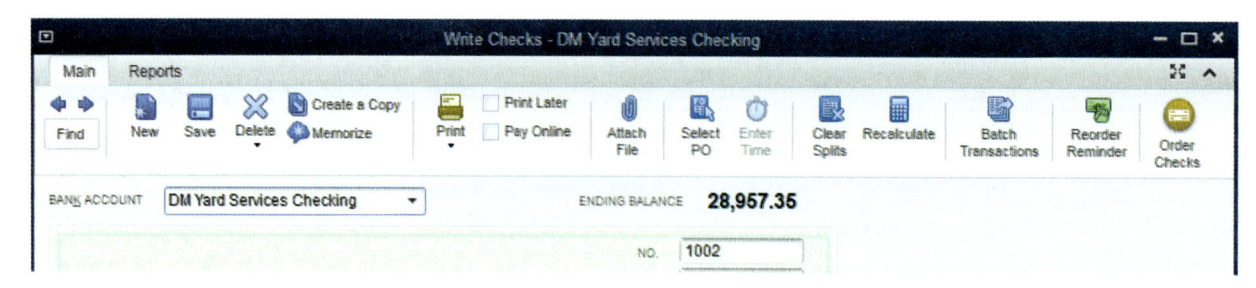

- Using the arrows under the Main tab, arrow back to check #1001.

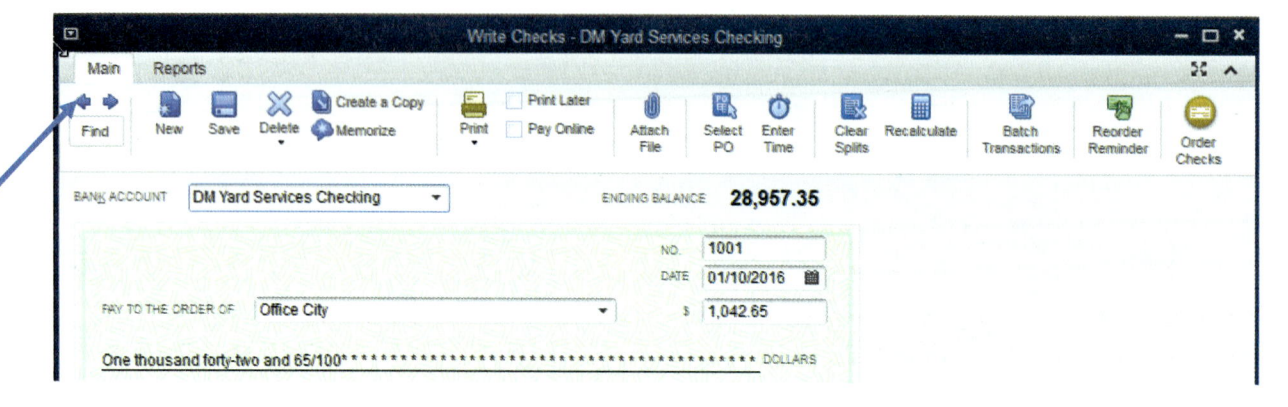

- Go to the Reports tab (next to Main, above icons).

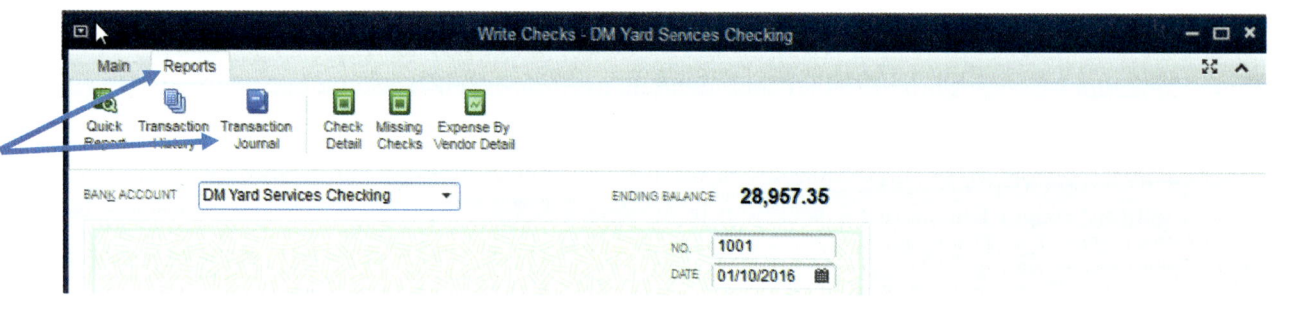

- Go to Transaction Journal to see the journal entry. Remember you can change column widths if necessary (note: the Memo field).

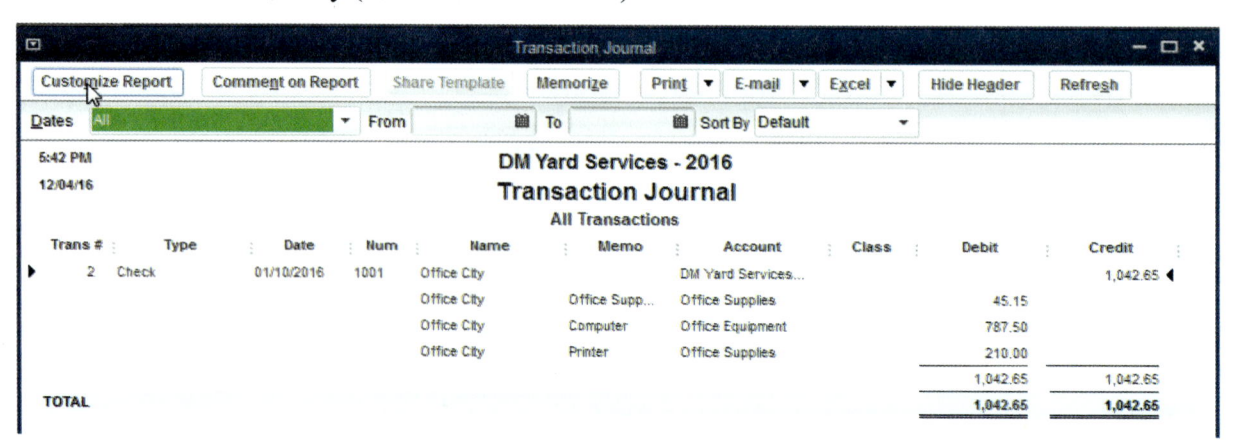

> Next, we will enter the computer into the QuickBooks Fixed Asset Manager. (Note: The Fixed Asset Manager is *not* the same as the fixed item list; we will not maintain a fixed item list in QuickBooks.) At this time, we will only enter the asset information and will complete the calculation of depreciation at year-end.

- ✓ Go to Accountant (pull-down menu)/Manage Fixed Assets:
    - o Create a new Fixed Asset Manager client; click OK.
    - o Click "Next" to use the wizard.
    - o Click "Next" on "The values for…."
    - o Click "Next" on current year (1/1/2016 to 12/31/2016).
    - o "Check" *only* Book basis (unselect others; Federal is automatically selected), and click "Next."
    - o Click "Next" on "Select the default depreciation…." (We will address the deprecation method at year-end.)
    - o For "How would you like the fixed asset items to be brought in from QuickBooks?" Select "Automatically when QuickBooks Fixed Asset Manager opens" and "Both new and modified fixed asset items"; then click "Next."
        - For "How would you like asset information to be saved into the Fixed Asset Item list in QuickBooks?" select "Automatically when QuickBooks Fixed Asset Manager is closed" and "Both new and modified assets"; then click "Next."
    - o Click "Finish" after "Please take a moment to verify…."

- ✓ Use the "Add" icon to add assets, making sure Book basis is selected. See the following screen shot:

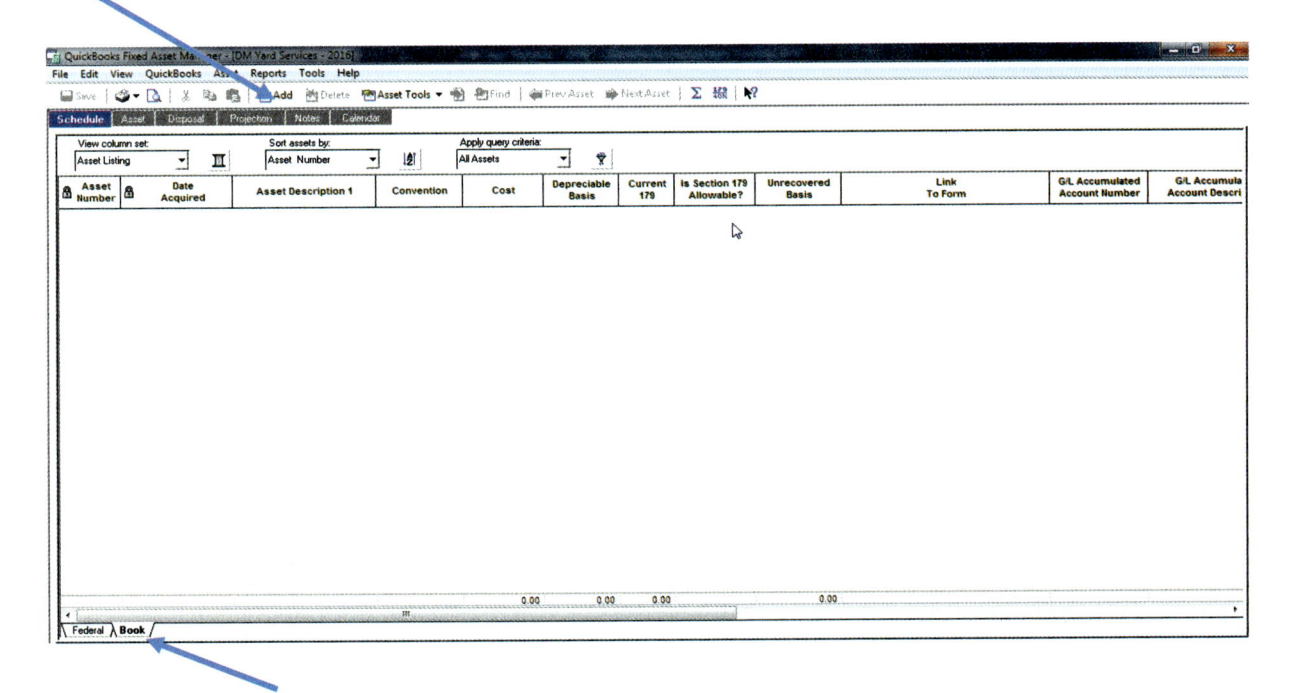

- ✓ Add computer: Asset Number: 1.
  - o Asset Description: Computer
  - o General Ledger Accounts (see the screen shot below)
  - o On the "bottom," we will *only* enter Date Placed in Service and Cost; tax system, depreciation method, and so on will be entered at year-end.

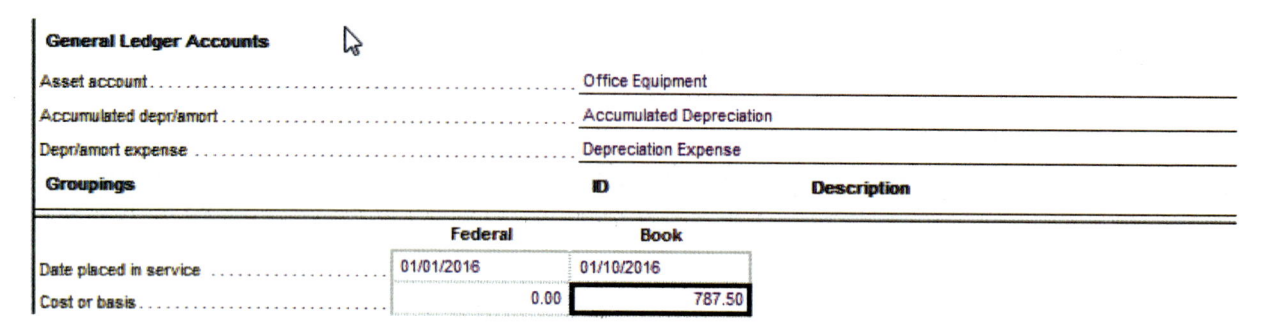

```
General Ledger Accounts
Asset account................................... Office Equipment
Accumulated depr/amort........................ Accumulated Depreciation
Depr/amort expense............................ Depreciation Expense
Groupings                    ID            Description
                   Federal          Book
Date placed in service    01/01/2016    01/10/2016
Cost or basis                  0.00         787.50
```

- ✓ Using the pull-down menu File/Backup, you should see the Asset Synchronization Log:

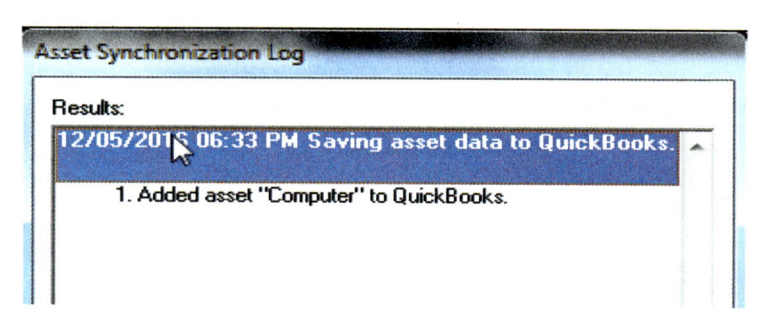

```
Asset Synchronization Log
Results:
12/05/2016 06:33 PM Saving asset data to QuickBooks.
  1. Added asset "Computer" to QuickBooks.
```

- ✓ Click OK and save the file to the same location as QuickBooks backups.

- ✓ Go to File/Exit.

1/15 Bought lawn mower $200, lawn tractor $2,500, and trailer $2,000 from ABC Equipment, invoice #6908, 6 months free financing, 9% interest charged on unpaid balance after 7/15/2016. (Note: These amounts include sales tax.)

  ➢ Use Enter Bill from Home Page, which will account for this invoice in A/P.

  ➢ Add a new vendor (name and company name), using Lawn and Landscaping Equipment as the default account in Account Settings. Add new payment terms for 6 months free financing. (Note: QuickBooks will *not* calculate interest after 7/15/2016.)

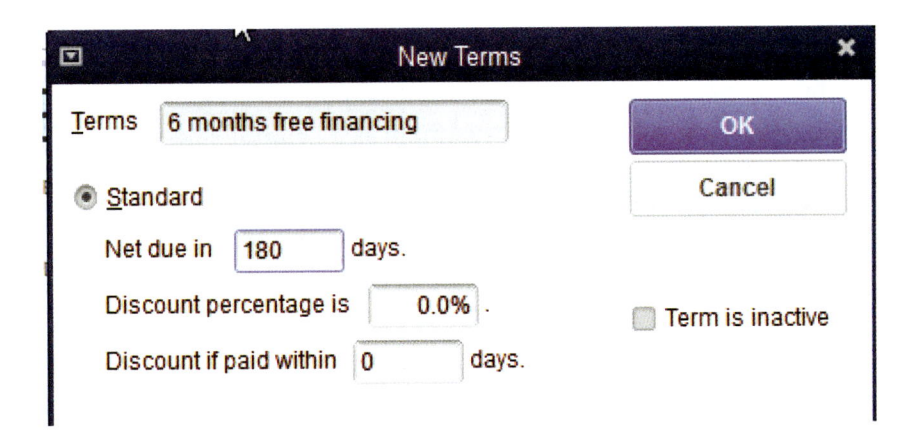

> Add new General Ledger Account for Small Tools and Equipment, an expense account.

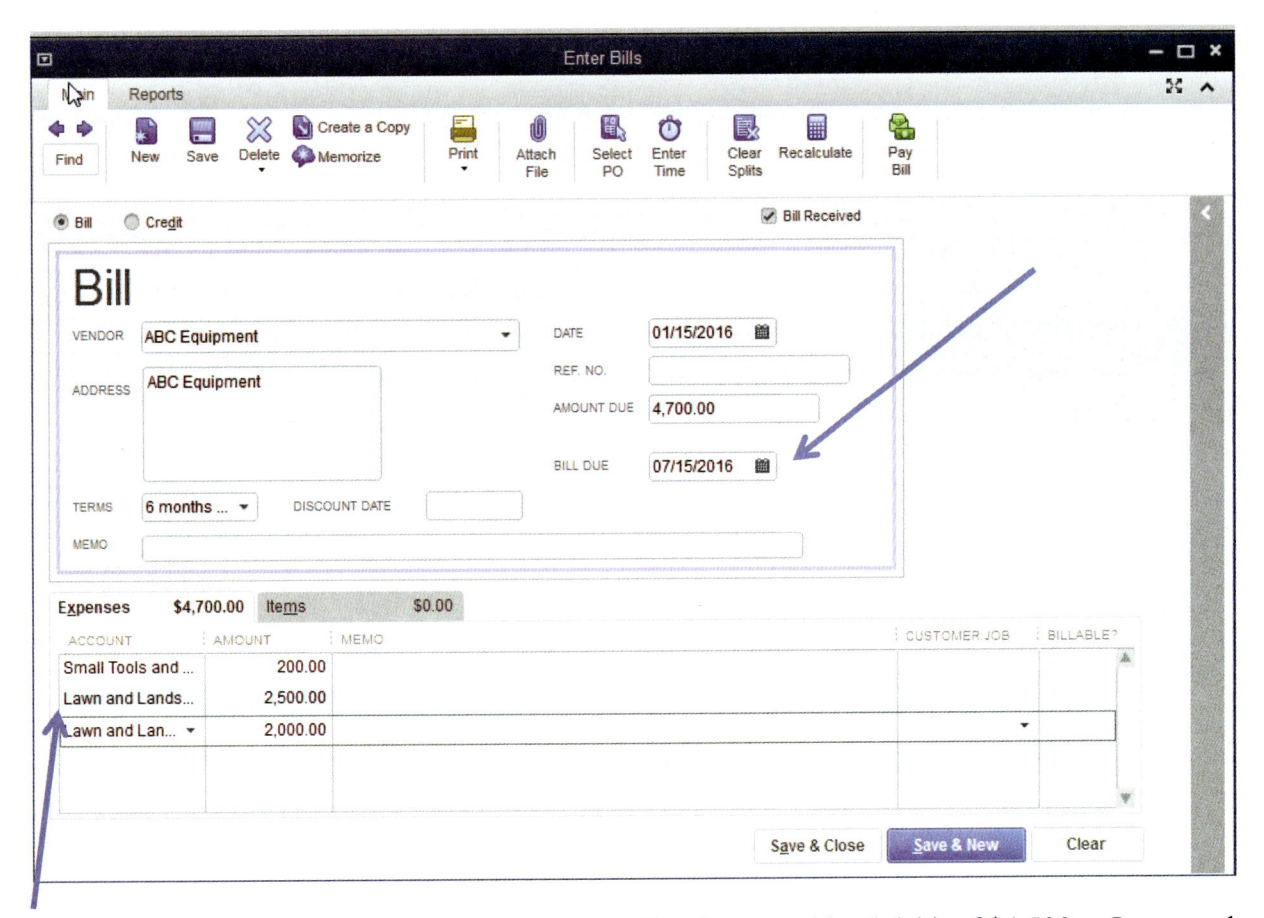

(Note: You may combine the lawn tractor and trailer for a combined debit of $4,500 to Lawn and Landscaping Equipment.)

1/16   Dave invested his 2009 Chevy pick-up truck, with a GVWR (gross vehicle weight rating) of 6250 lbs., into the business. Its cost was $27,500 when purchased new; estimated fair market value (FMV) at the date of investment is $18,200. The truck will be exclusively for business use. *Record at FMV as a general journal entry, and add a new asset account: Truck.*

> Enter the tractor, trailer, and truck in Fixed Asset Manager.

> After entering the truck, your Schedule of Assets in Fixed Asset Manager should show the following:

Asset Number	Date Acquired	Asset Description 1	Convention	Cost
1	01/10/2016	Computer	Act-Days	787.50
2	01/15/2016	Lawn Tractor	Act-Days	2,500.00
3	01/15/2016	Trailer	Act-Days	2,000.00
4	01/16/2016	Truck	Act-Days	18,200.00

✓ Select File/Backup, then File/Exit (in Fixed Asset Manager).

1/24   Bought miscellaneous small tools from PP Equipment. Add a new vendor; use Small Tools and Equipment expense as the default account (account that will normally be debited) under Account Settings. Four shovels, two rakes, four gas cans, one broom total $313.68, including sales tax. Paid with check #1002. *Write Check.*

1/31   Prepare bank reconciliation for January. *Use Reconcile Icon from Home Page.*

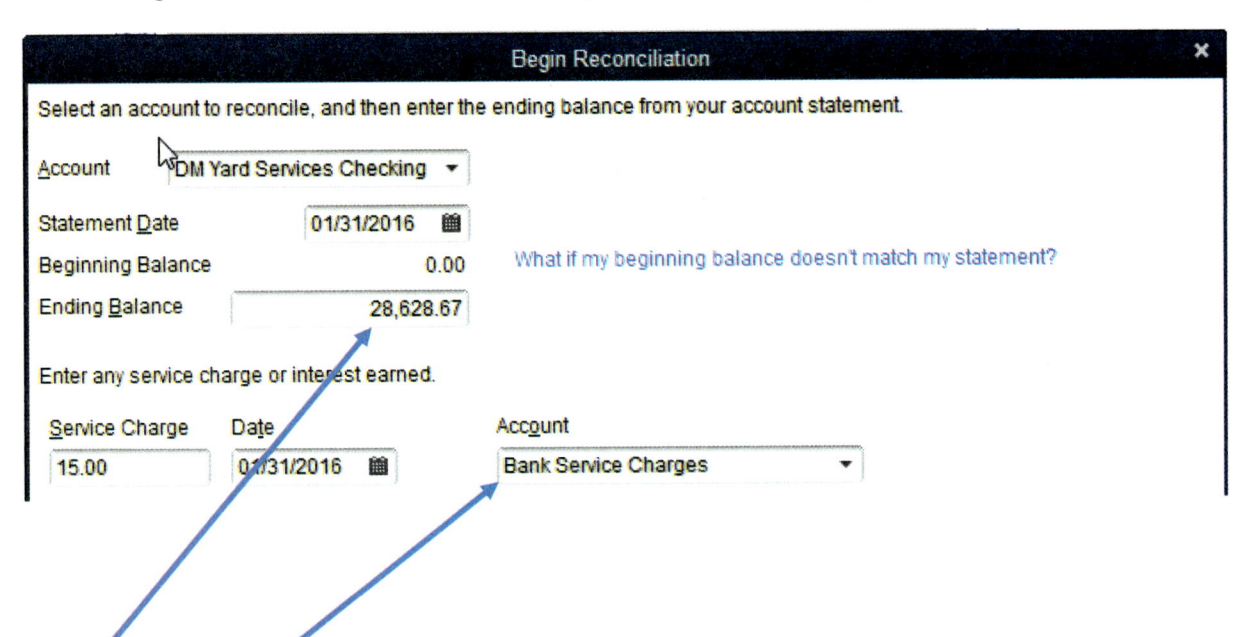

```
╔══════════════════════════ Begin Reconciliation ══════════════════════════ X ╗
  Select an account to reconcile, and then enter the ending balance from your account statement.

  Account          DM Yard Services Checking  ▼

  Statement Date         01/31/2016

  Beginning Balance            0.00          What if my beginning balance doesn't match my statement?

  Ending Balance          28,628.67

  Enter any service charge or interest earned.

  Service Charge    Date                     Account
  15.00             01/31/2016               Bank Service Charges         ▼
```

This amount is from the January bank statement on the following pages. (See statement.)

   ➢ Account for monthly service charge here.

   ➢ On the next screen, check all cleared deposits and checks as noted on the January bank statement.

(Note: Bank statements as well as other supporting information for transactions in future months are found on the pages following the month's transactions.)

For period: 01/31/2016   ☐ Hide transactions after the statement's end date

Checks and Payments   **Deposits and Other Credits**

✓	DATE ▲	CHK #	PAYEE	AMOUNT
✓	01/10/2016	1001	Office City	1,042.65
✓	01/24/2016	1002	PP Equipment	313.68

✓	DATE ▲	CHK #	MEMO	TYPE	AMOUNT
✓	01/06/2016	1	Initial investment	GENJRNL	30,000.00

☑ Highlight Marked   [Mark All] [Unmark All] [Go To]   [Columns to Display...]

Beginning Balance   0.00   [Modify]   Service Charge   -15.00
Items you have marked cleared   Interest Earned   0.00
  1 Deposits and Other Credits   30,000.00   Ending Balance   28,628.67
  2 Checks and Payments   1,356.33   Cleared Balance   28,628.67
                                                                                   Difference   0.00

                                                                                           [Reconcile Now]   [Leave]

> ➤ Your January reconciliation detail report should show the following:

DM Yard Services - 2016
Reconciliation Detail
All Transactions

Type	Date	Num	Name	Clr	Amount	Balance
Beginning Balance						0.00
Cleared Transactions						
Checks and Payments - 3 items						
Check	01/10/2016	1001	Office City	✓	-1,042.65	-1,042.65
Check	01/24/2016	1002	PP Equipment	✓	-313.68	-1,356.33
Check	01/31/2016			✓	-15.00	-1,371.33
Total Checks and Payments					-1,371.33	-1,371.33
Deposits and Credits - 1 item						
General Journal	01/06/2016	1		✓	30,000.00	30,000.00
Total Deposits and Credits					30,000.00	30,000.00
Total Cleared Transactions					28,628.67	28,628.67
Cleared Balance					28,628.67	28,628.67
Register Balance as of 01/31/2016					28,628.67	28,628.67
Ending Balance					**28,628.67**	**28,628.67**

✓ Save the report as a PDF file to submit with the January work.

➢ To complete January, reconcile (review and make corrections if needed) your trial balance found under Reports/Accountant and Taxes/Trial Balance to the trial balance below, making sure the cash balance per bank reconciliation report equals the cash balance on the trial balance.

DM Yard Services - 2016
Trial Balance
As of January 31, 2016

	Jan 31, 16 Debit	Credit
DM Yard Services Checking	28,628.67	
Lawn and Landscaping Equipment	4,500.00	
Office Equipment	787.50	
Truck	18,200.00	
Accounts Payable		4,700.00
D. Michaels, Capital		48,200.00
Bank Service Charges	15.00	
Office Supplies	255.15	
Small Tools and Equipment	513.68	
TOTAL	**52,900.00**	**52,900.00**

January Bank Statement:

XYZ Bank

DM Yard Services

Acct. #745-1332   1/1/2016 thru 1/31/2016

Beginning Balance: $0.00

Deposits & CM

1/6 $30,000

Checks & DM

#1001 $1,042.65

#1002   313.68

1/31   SC   15.00

Ending Balance: $28,628.67

January Questions

SUBMIT YOUR ANSWERS TO THE MONTHLY QUESTIONS IN *ONE* WORD DOCUMENT.

1. What type of company is DM Yard Services? Briefly describe the characteristics of a sole proprietorship, a limited liability company, and a corporation; *specifically* address the equity section of the balance sheet for each.

2. Describe the overall objective of internal controls. Identify three internal control risks of a landscape business (e.g., theft of assets) and a possible solution to mitigate those risks (e.g., locks).

3. Discuss the financial statement impact of *capitalizing* versus *expensing* costs.

4. On the 1/16 transaction, the FMV was used as the basis to record the transaction. Support this with an *excerpt* from an IRS publication citing this reasoning. (Hint: Search on the topic *property changed from personal use.* Copy the excerpt into a Word document and highlight the answer.)

5. Integrity and ethics are key characteristics of a good accountant; briefly explain how you will address those as you complete this project.

6. Complete a) the Monthly Task List (check off and initial tasks as completed) and b) your To Do/Follow-up Question List with at least two items to be addressed by your "manager"/teacher (see next page.) You will complete and submit these two items every month.

CHAPTER PRINT/SUBMISSION SUMMARY

Note: Your instructor will indicate how to submit monthly work, through paper reports and/or electronic files.

1. _____ Manual general journal, T-accounts, and trial balance.

2. _____ January bank reconciliation detail report from QuickBooks (save report as a PDF to submit electronically).

3. _____ January trial balance (Reports/Accountant and Taxes/Trial Balance); note you can save most QB reports as a PDF or export them into Excel and save to submit.

4. _____ Word document with answers to questions 1 – 5.

5. _____ Task List/To Do/Question List (question 6); submit page from text.

JANUARY TASK LIST

Check here if completed	Task	Initials
	Review trial balance for completeness and accuracy	
	Back up your monthly transactions to an external destination (e.g., flash drive), changing the file name to the month (e.g., January) Go to File/Backup Company/Create Local Backup/Local Backup… *Backup Options dialog: Use this window to set default options for your manual and automatic backups. LOCAL BACKUP ONLY. Tell us where to save your backup copies (required): W:\Capstone\January\ [Browse…] ☑ Add the date and time of the backup to the file name (recommended) ☐ Limit the number of backup copies in this folder to ___*	_____

To Do/Follow-up/Question List

Example: "Reminder to always compare reconciled cash balance per the bank reconciliation report to the checking account balance per the trial balance" OR "I do not understand the capitalization amount of $500 in the 1/10 transaction."

General Journal

Page:

	Date	Description	Posting Ref.	Debit	Credit	
1						1
2						2
3						3
4						4
5						5
6						6
7						7
8						8
9						9
10						10
11						11
12						12
13						13
14						14
15						15
16						16
17						17
18						18
19						19
20						20
21						21
22						22
23						23
24						24
25						25
26						26
27						27
28						28
29						29
30						30

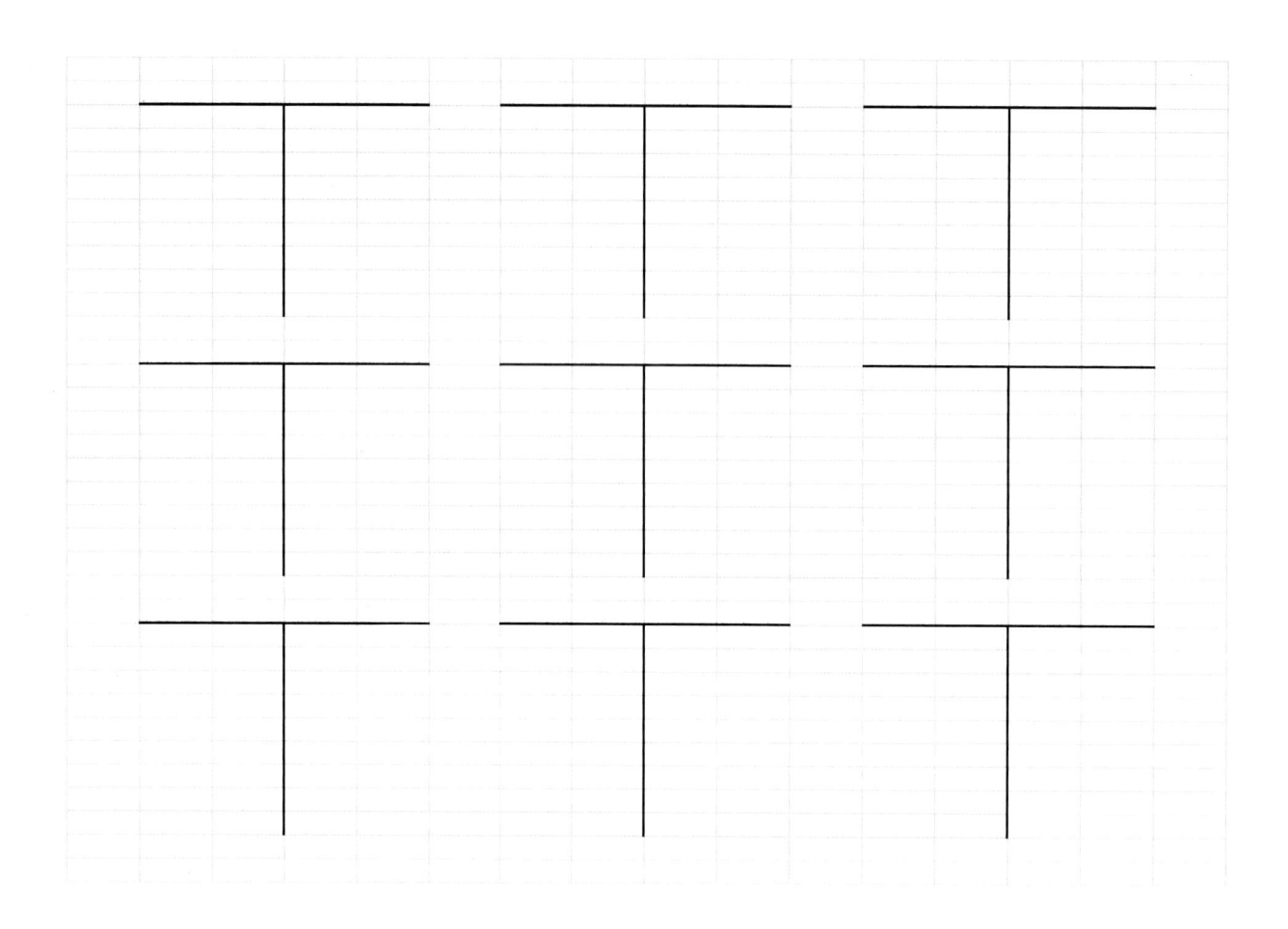

Reminder: Create account numbers for the posting process from the general journal to T-accounts.

February Transactions/Activities

Note: If you are moving between computers, for example, school and home, you will "Open or Restore an Existing Company" from your backup made at the end of January.

2/1 Dave wants to stuff mailboxes with a flyer advertising his services. Prepare a Word document identifying his services:

- Sell, deliver, lay mulch
- Sell, deliver, lay top soil
- Sell and plant small evergreens
- Full lawn maintenance including cutting and trimming

Use different fonts, WordArt, or other tools to enhance the advertisement.

2/5 Applied for a seller's permit to collect Wisconsin sales tax from customers:

➢ Print the Business Tax Registration (BTR-101, using any year available) application found on the Wisconsin Department of Revenue website. Note: If you save the BTR-101 as a PDF file, then open the saved file; you will get the option to Fill & Sign to complete the form and save.

➢ Complete parts A thru D, then F (projecting $901 – $7200 of monthly sales).

➢ You can use your name or Dave's to complete and sign these forms; his social security number is 388-22-6666. The permit number assigned upon submission of the BTR-101 is #789078-5. The objective is to introduce you to these forms; we will *not* pay the associated fee.

Rate = 5%, no county sales tax (Winnebago County).

Set up sales tax in QuickBooks: Edit/Preferences/Sales Tax/Company Preferences.

➢ Add a Sales Tax Item. See the screen shot. Add a new vendor, WI Dept. of Revenue. No specific account under vendor account settings is necessary; we will use this vendor for *all* payments to the Wisconsin Department of Revenue.

➢ QuickBooks will set up a "Tax" item and "Non" taxable item. We will owe sales tax as of the invoice date and will pay sales tax *quarterly* (when do we pay sales tax?).

> We will make all existing customers, non-inventory, and inventory items taxable *at this time*. (Note: We will have non-taxable customers and will indicate their sales tax setting when we enter their customer information.)

> Upon completion of the sales tax preference, review your chart of accounts, noting QuickBooks added a current liability, Sales Tax Payable.

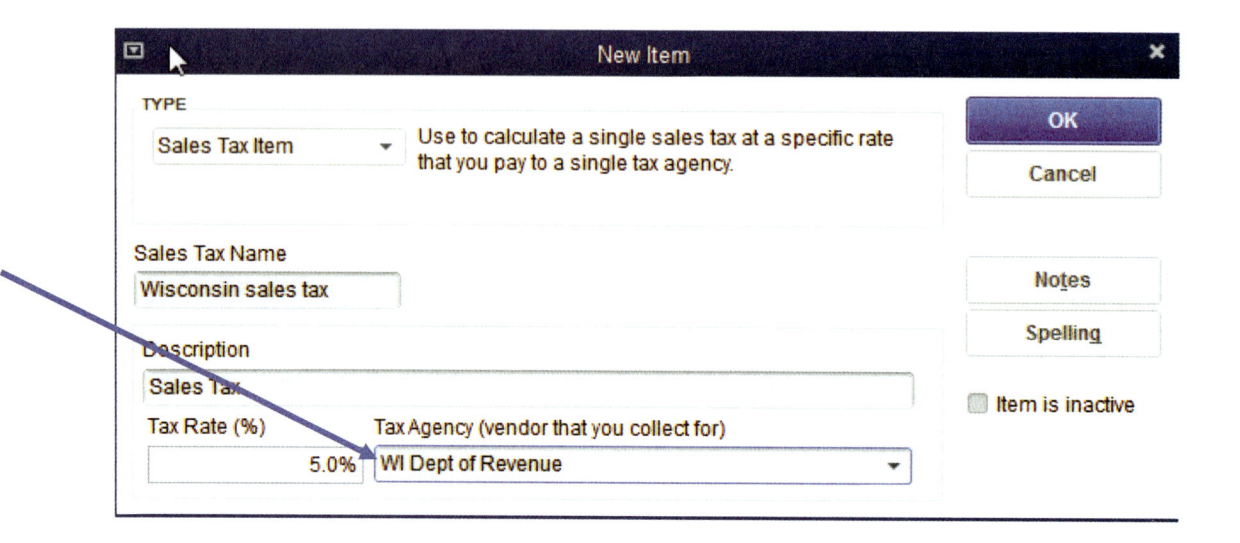

2/15   Purchased a string trimmer for $262.50 and a blower for $147 from PP Equipment on the business credit card, a total of $409.50. Enter as a credit card charge: Banking/Enter Credit Card Charges. Add a new account: Type: Credit Card. Account Name: Credit Card Payable.

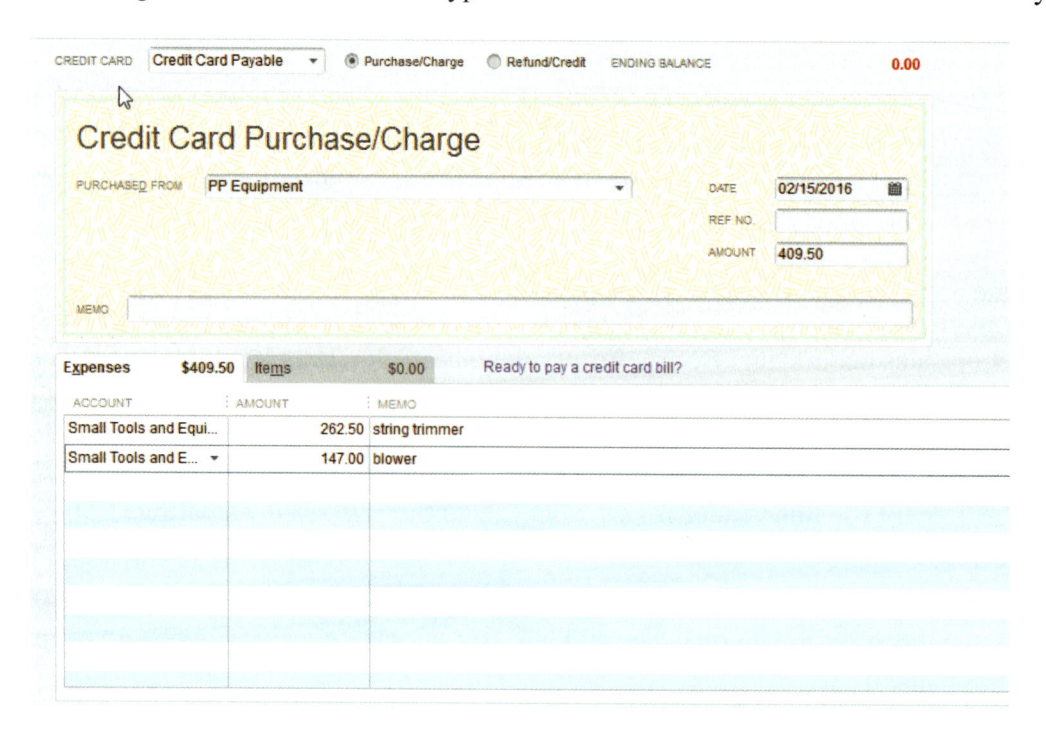

2/17   Signed a 1-year service contract with Cell World. Terms of the contract include a $100 set-up fee for two phones, one for Dave (262-555-3535) for business and one for his wife, Sue, for personal use. Total cost for both phones will be $60 per month.

> All charges will be automatically billed to credit card and will be recorded upon receipt of the credit card statement each month. *Nothing* is to be recorded at this time.

2/20   Dave ordered the following from JS Garden Supply (new vendor; name and company name only at this time) on purchase order #1; enter P.O. from the Home Page:

- 100 cubic yards of screened topsoil
- 100 cubic yards of mulch
- 10 bags of grass seed
- 10 bags of fertilizer
- 10 bales of straw
- 12 36" pine trees
- 5 5' pine trees
- 10 boxwood bushes

✓ Add new Inventory Items for the above items as you complete the purchase order; use Costs and create new Cost of Goods Sold Accounts, Retail Prices, and new Income Accounts as shown in the chart below. All items are taxable.

Inventory Items	Cost ($)	Cost of Goods Sold Account (COGS)	Retail ($)	Income Account
Screened Topsoil	17.50/cu. yd.	Topsoil Costs	21.00/cu. yd.	Topsoil Sales
Mulch	38.50/cu. yd.	Mulch Costs	46.00/cu. yd.	Mulch Sales
Grass Seed	48.13/bag	Seeding Costs	55.00/bag	Seeding Income
Fertilizer	14.95/bag	Fertilizing Costs	18.00/bag	Fertilizing Income
Straw	6.00/bale	Seeding Costs	8.00/bale	Seeding Income
Pine Tree 36"	12.00/each	Nursery Stock Costs	17.95/each	Nursery Stock Income
Pine Tree 5'	25.00/each	Nursery Stock Costs	30.00/each	Nursery Stock Income
Boxwood Bushes	12.95/each	Nursery Stock Costs	24.95/each	Nursery Stock Income
Service Items				
Lawn Cutting and Trimming			$35/hour	Lawn Cutting and Trimming
Landscaping Services			$35/hour	Landscaping Services
Snowplowing			$45/hour	Snowplowing

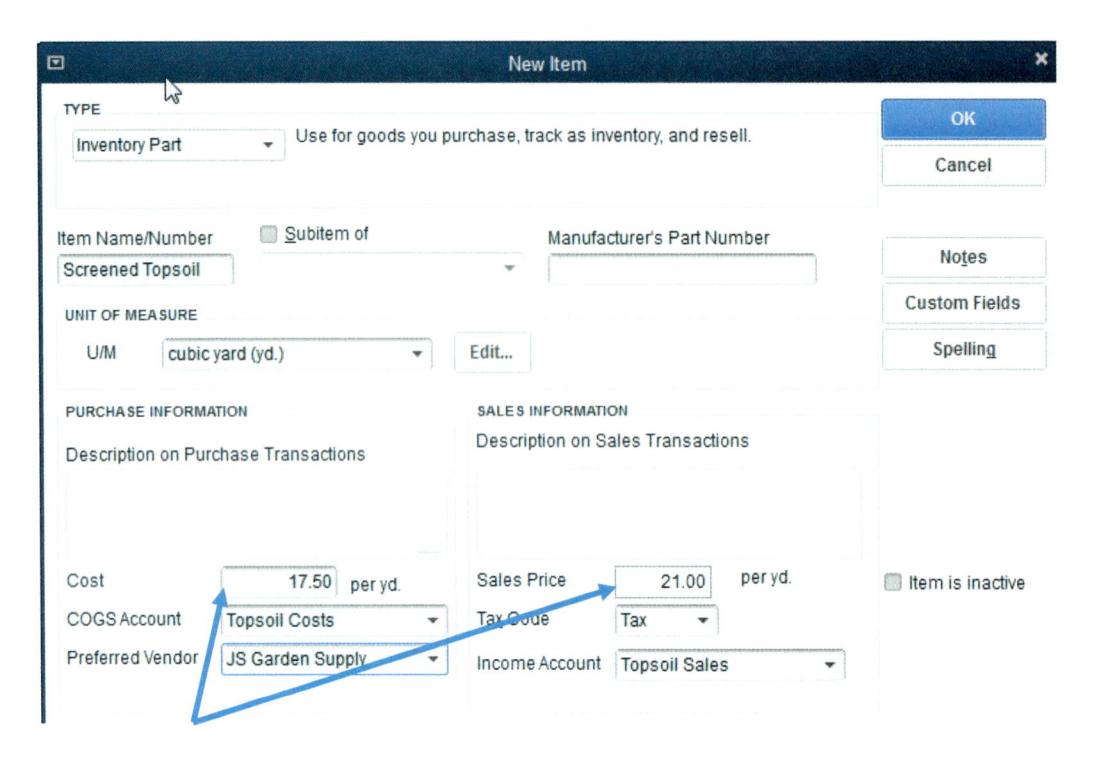

[New Item dialog screenshot: Type: Inventory Part; Item Name/Number: Screened Topsoil; U/M: cubic yard (yd.); Cost: 17.50 per yd.; COGS Account: Topsoil Costs; Preferred Vendor: JS Garden Supply; Sales Price: 21.00 per yd.; Tax Code: Tax; Income Account: Topsoil Sales]

➢ Note: New accounts added: Topsoil Costs and Topsoil Sales.

➢ Enter Cost and Sales Price per chart.

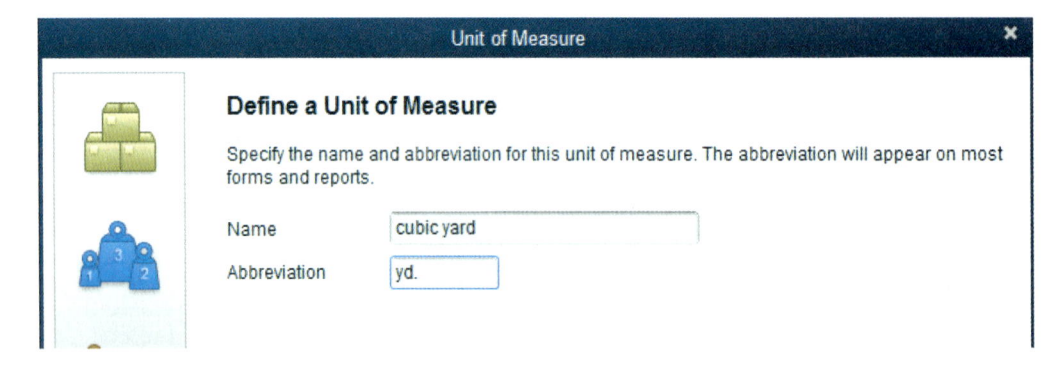

[Unit of Measure dialog: Define a Unit of Measure — Name: cubic yard; Abbreviation: yd.]

➢ Create other units of measures as needed.

Should be unchecked

Purchase Order

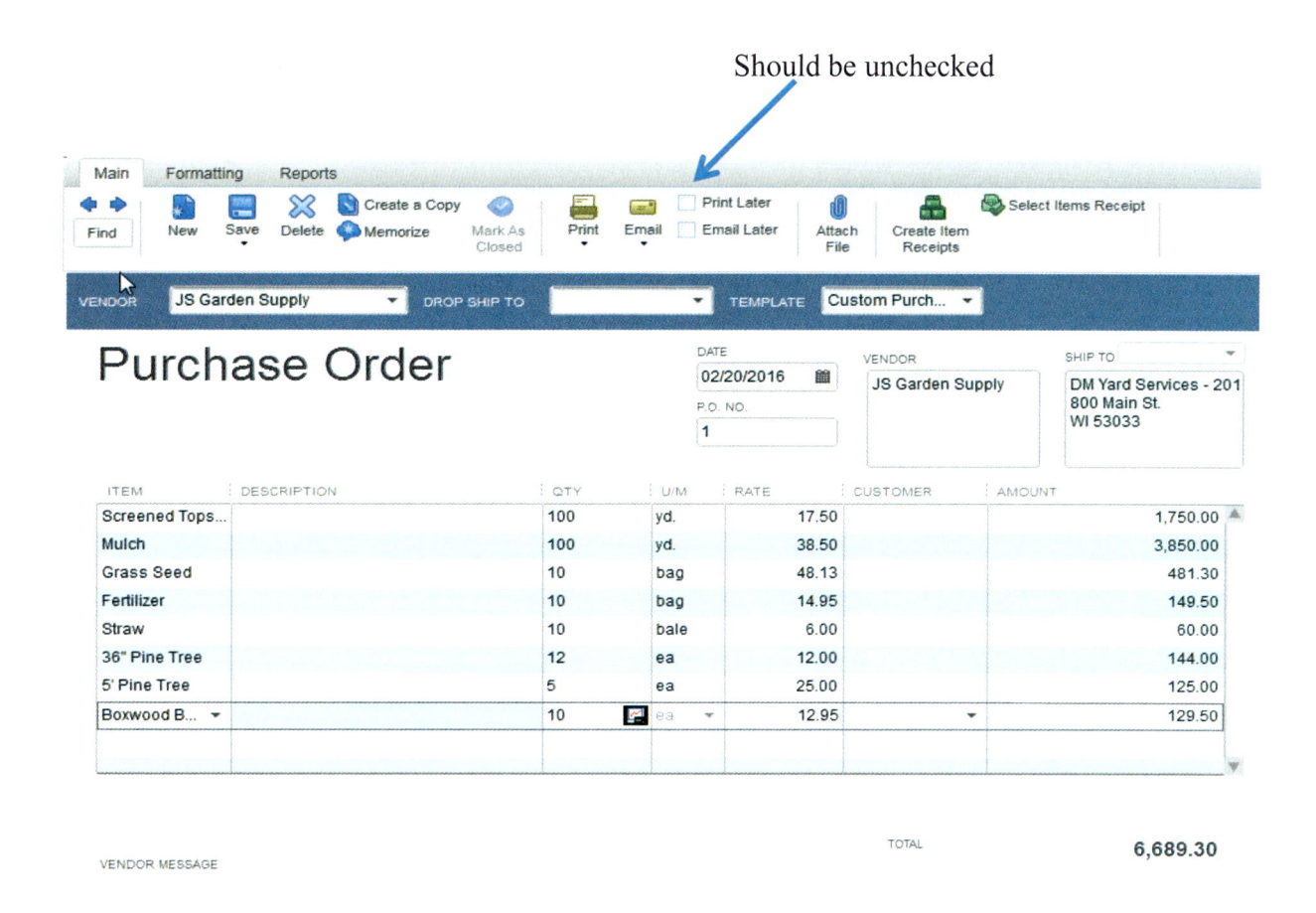

VENDOR: JS Garden Supply
TEMPLATE: Custom Purch...
DATE: 02/20/2016
P.O. NO.: 1
VENDOR: JS Garden Supply
SHIP TO: DM Yard Services - 201 800 Main St. WI 53033

ITEM	DESCRIPTION	QTY	U/M	RATE	CUSTOMER	AMOUNT
Screened Tops...		100	yd.	17.50		1,750.00
Mulch		100	yd.	38.50		3,850.00
Grass Seed		10	bag	48.13		481.30
Fertilizer		10	bag	14.95		149.50
Straw		10	bale	6.00		60.00
36" Pine Tree		12	ea	12.00		144.00
5' Pine Tree		5	ea	25.00		125.00
Boxwood B...		10	ea	12.95		129.50

TOTAL 6,689.30

VENDOR MESSAGE

2/22 Filled gas cans, charged $75 on business credit card. Enter as a credit card charge, adding a new vendor: Gas to Go and charging to Auto and Truck Expenses. All future gas charges are business related.

2/25 Purchased Microsoft Office and other miscellaneous office supplies at Office City, $387.45; issued check #1003. *Use Write Check*. (Reminder: As outlined in the 1/10 entry, go to the Transaction Journal found under the Reports tab to review the journal entry for a transaction.)

2/27 Establish a petty cash fund of $200, check #1004. Use Write Check, add "Cash" as a new vendor, and create a petty cash account. (Note: Since Petty Cash is considered a cash equivalent, it should be accounted for as a "bank" type account.)

2/28 Dave took a draw of $1,000, check #1005. Use Write Check, add "Your Name" as a new vendor, and edit the drawing account with your name if not previously done. Use the draw account as the default account (account settings).

2/28   Reconcile cash account for February. See the bank statement on the following pages.

Begin Reconciliation

Select an account to reconcile, and then enter the ending balance from your account statement.

Account: DM Yard Services Checking — last reconciled on 01/31/2016.

Statement Date: 02/29/2016
Beginning Balance: 28,628.67   What if my beginning balance doesn't match my statement?
Ending Balance: 27,413.67

Enter any service charge or interest earned.

Service Charge: 15.00   Date: 02/29/2016   Account: Bank Service Charges
Interest Earned: 0.00   Date: 02/28/2017   Account:

[Locate Discrepancies] [Undo Last Reconciliation] [Continue] [Cancel] [Help]

Note 1: Beginning Balance should agree with beginning balance on the February bank statement.

Note 2: Ending Balance should be the ending balance from your February bank statement.

> Enter the service charge and click "Continue."

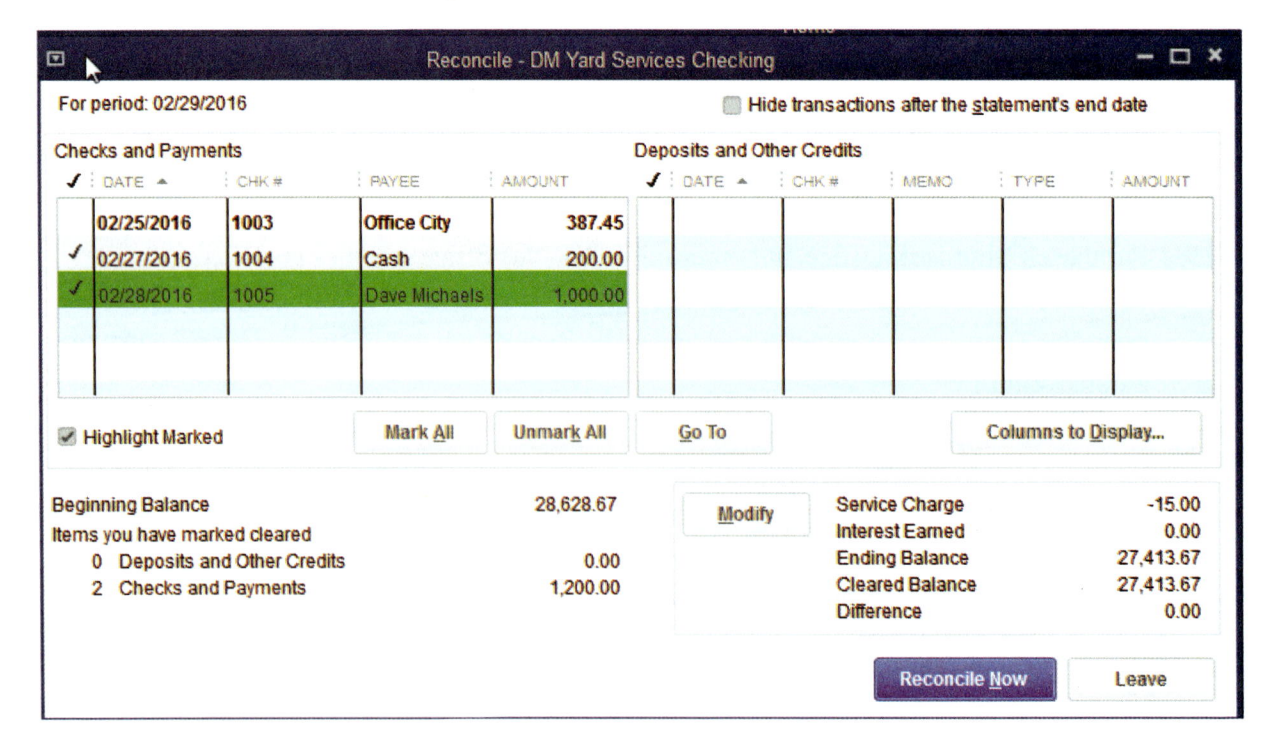

Reconcile - DM Yard Services Checking

For period: 02/29/2016   ☐ Hide transactions after the statement's end date

Checks and Payments

✓	DATE	CHK #	PAYEE	AMOUNT
	02/25/2016	1003	Office City	387.45
✓	02/27/2016	1004	Cash	200.00
✓	02/28/2016	1005	Dave Michaels	1,000.00

Deposits and Other Credits

✓	DATE	CHK #	MEMO	TYPE	AMOUNT

☑ Highlight Marked   [Mark All] [Unmark All] [Go To]   [Columns to Display...]

Beginning Balance   28,628.67   [Modify]   Service Charge   -15.00
Items you have marked cleared   Interest Earned   0.00
    0 Deposits and Other Credits   0.00   Ending Balance   27,413.67
    2 Checks and Payments   1,200.00   Cleared Balance 27,413.67
                                                                       Difference   0.00

                                                                       [Reconcile Now] [Leave]

> Your February reconciliation detail report should show the following:

DM Yard Services - 2016
Reconciliation Detail
All Transactions

Type	Date	Num	Name	Clr	Amount	Balance
Beginning Balance						28,628.67
Cleared Transactions						
Checks and Payments - 3 items						
Check	02/27/2016	1004	Cash	✓	-200.00	-200.00
Check	02/28/2016	1005	D. Michaels	✓	-1,000.00	-1,200.00
Check	02/29/2016			✓	-15.00	-1,215.00
Total Checks and Payments					-1,215.00	-1,215.00
Total Cleared Transactions					-1,215.00	-1,215.00
Cleared Balance					-1,215.00	27,413.67
Uncleared Transactions						
Checks and Payments - 1 item						
Check	02/25/2016	1003	Office City		-387.45	-387.45
Total Checks and Payments					-387.45	-387.45
Total Uncleared Transactions					-387.45	-387.45
Register Balance as of 02/29/2016					-1,602.45	27,026.22
Ending Balance					-1,602.45	27,026.22

Note: The reconciled ending balance should *always* agree with your checking account balance on the trial balance!

To complete February:

> Review and compare the chart of accounts on the following page, editing as necessary. Note the separate income and cost of goods sold accounts to facilitate profit analysis of each area of this new business.
> Accounts deleted: Installation Services
>   Maintenance Services
>   Cost of Goods Sold
>   Material Costs
>   Worker's Compensation Insurance
>   Computer & Internet Expense
>   Ask My Accountant (this account is used when your client does not know where to record a part of an entry)

Account	Type
DM Yard Services Checking	Bank
Petty Cash	Bank
Inventory Asset	Other Current Asset
Accumulated Depreciation	Fixed Asset
Lawn and Landscaping Equipment	Fixed Asset
Office Equipment	Fixed Asset
Truck	Fixed Asset
Accounts Payable	Accounts Payable
Credit Card Payable	Credit Card
Payroll Liabilities	Other Current Liability
Sales Tax Payable	Other Current Liability
D. Michaels, Draw	Equity
D. Michaels, Capital	Equity
Opening Balance Equity	Equity
Fertilizing Income	Income
Landscaping Services	Income
Lawn Cutting and Trimming	Income
Mulch Sales	Income
Nursery Stock Income	Income
Seeding Income	Income
Snow plowing	Income
Topsoil Sales	Income
Fertilizing Costs	Cost of Goods Sold
Mulch Costs	Cost of Goods Sold
Nursery Stock Costs	Cost of Goods Sold
Seeding Costs	Cost of Goods Sold
Topsoil Costs	Cost of Goods Sold
Advertising and Promotion	Expense
Auto and Truck Expenses	Expense
Bank Service Charges	Expense
Depreciation Expense	Expense
Insurance Expense	Expense
Interest Expense	Expense
Meals and Entertainment	Expense
Office Supplies	Expense
Payroll Expenses	Expense
Postage and Delivery	Expense
Professional Fees	Expense
Rent Expense	Expense
Repairs and Maintenance	Expense
Small Tools and Equipment	Expense
Telephone Expense	Expense
Travel Expense	Expense
Utilities	Expense
Purchase Orders	Non-Posting

> Reconcile (review and make corrections if needed) your trial balance found under Reports/Accountant and Taxes/Trial Balance to the trial balance below, noting the cash balance agrees with the bank reconciliation report.

DM Yard Services - 2016
Trial Balance
As of February 29, 2016

	Debit (Feb 29, 16)	Credit (Feb 29, 16)
DM Yard Services Checking	27,026.22	
Petty Cash	200.00	
Lawn and Landscaping Equipment	4,500.00	
Office Equipment	787.50	
Truck	18,200.00	
Accounts Payable		4,700.00
Credit Card Payable		484.50
D. Michaels, Draw	1,000.00	
D. Michaels, Capital		48,200.00
Auto and Truck Expenses	75.00	
Bank Service Charges	30.00	
Office Supplies	642.60	
Small Tools and Equipment	923.18	
TOTAL	**53,384.50**	**53,384.50**

XYZ Bank

DM Yard Services

Acct. #745-1332   2/1/2016 thru 2/29/2016

Beg. Balance: $28,628.67

Deposits & CM

Checks & DM

#1004	$200.00
#1005	1,000.00
2/28 SC	15.00

Ending Balance: $27,413.67

February Questions

1. Sales tax related:
    a. Determine which services or items of DM Yard Services are subject to Wisconsin sales tax, support by the Wisconsin sales tax publication specific to landscaping services; copy and paste only the pertinent area into your Word document for February questions.
    b. List three county or additional sales tax rates.
    c. List one type of organization exempt from sales tax.
    d. Print (screen shot/snip*) the QuickBooks Help screen on how to set up sales tax.

    *Use Microsoft snipping tool or other snipping product.

2. Explain the use of purchase orders as a measure of internal control.

3. Set up an Excel or Word petty cash sheet to account for fund activity throughout the year. The account will be replenished at year-end. This task is noted in your February task list.

4. Complete a) the Monthly Task List and b) your To Do/Follow-up Question List with at least two items to be addressed by your "manager"/teacher (see next page).

CHAPTER PRINT/SUBMISSION SUMMARY

1. _____ Advertising flyer

2. _____ Seller's permit application (BTR-101)

3. _____ February bank reconciliation detail report

4. _____ February trial balance

5. _____ Questions 1 – 2

6. _____ Question 3: Excel or Word file

7. _____ Task List/To Do/Question List

FEBRUARY TASK LIST

Check here if completed	Task	Initials
	Set up sales tax	
	Set up inventory items	
	Set up a petty cash sheet (may use Excel or Word)	
	Review and edit chart of accounts	
	Verify cash balance on trial balance equals cash balance on bank reconciliation	
	Review trial balance for completeness and accuracy	
	Back up monthly transactions to an external destination (e.g., flash drive), changing file name to the month	

To Do/Follow-up/Question List

March Transactions/Activities

3/2 Received three calls from our advertising flyers for mulching jobs. Visited jobs and prepared estimates. (Note: Estimates do not create a journal entry; the invoice will!)

> Walter Brown: 5 yards, delivered and spread, estimated 2 hours of landscaping services.

- Note: Add new customers as entering estimates:

<u>Address Info</u>: Enter customer name and company name (same)

<u>Payment Settings/Payment Terms</u>: Residential will have terms of n/10, statement date (add new terms) and commercial 2/10, n/30 from statement date (add new).

- Note: Our terms are tailored to our company because in the upcoming months, there will be several times during the month services will be rendered to our customers; they would not be expected to pay each invoice but rather a single amount from their monthly statement. QuickBooks does *not* calculate discounts based on these terms. You will have to calculate discounts.

<u>Sales Tax</u>: All customers are taxable unless otherwise noted.

<u>Additional Info</u>: Add new customer type: residential or commercial; Walter Brown is residential.

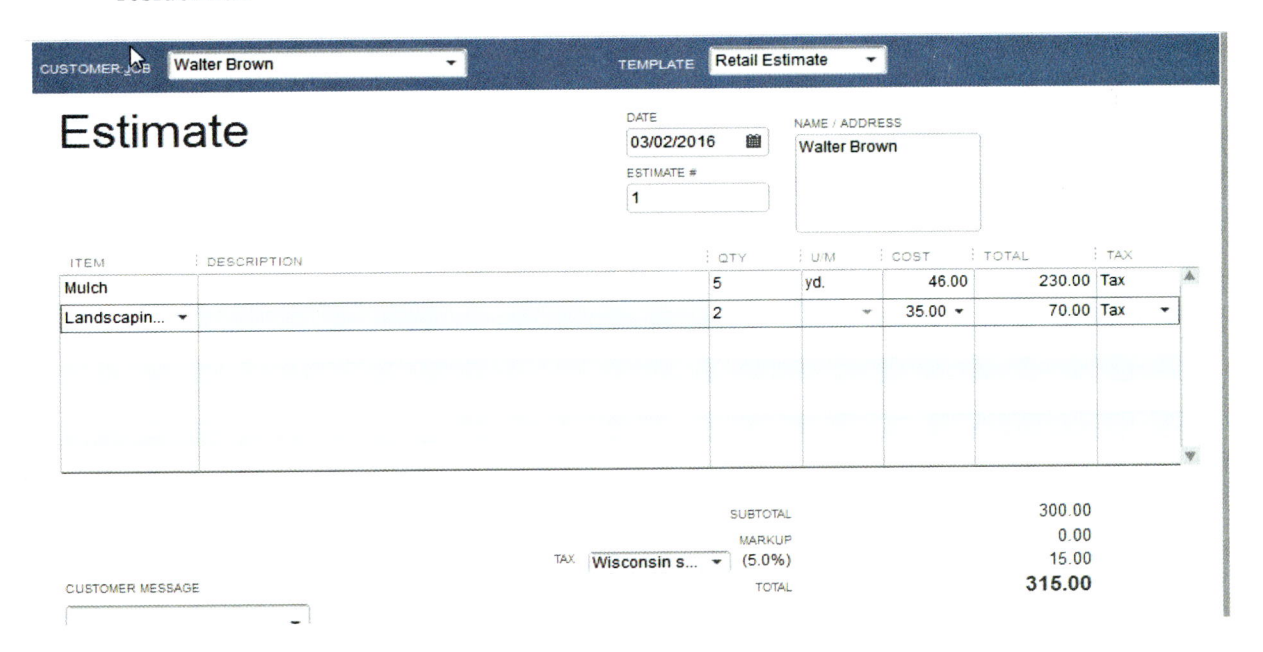

Estimate

CUSTOMER:JOB: Walter Brown
TEMPLATE: Retail Estimate
DATE: 03/02/2016
ESTIMATE #: 1
NAME / ADDRESS: Walter Brown

ITEM	DESCRIPTION	QTY	U/M	COST	TOTAL	TAX
Mulch		5	yd.	46.00	230.00	Tax
Landscapin...		2		35.00	70.00	Tax

SUBTOTAL: 300.00
MARKUP: 0.00
TAX: Wisconsin s... (5.0%) 15.00
TOTAL: 315.00

> Print to PDF Walter Brown's estimate. (Note: It may not show the item (i.e., Mulch) description.)

- Davidson Foods (commercial customer): 12 yards of mulch, delivered and spread, 6 hours of landscaping services estimated.

- Forest Hill School (*commercial, non-profit — exempt from sales tax*): 20 yards of mulch delivered and spread, 16 hours estimated.

3/3 Signed a 5-year lease to rent 2 acres with garage and heated office space at 900 Main Street for $750 per month from John Smith.

- Pay security deposit of $1,000 *and* March rent, check #1006. Write check.

- Add a new vendor, and check the box on tax settings for a vendor eligible for 1099 with vendor tax ID 777-77-7777; account settings: Rent Expense.

    ✓ Add a new account: Other Asset: Security Deposit.
    ✓ Update company address information (My Company).

3/4 Had shelves and counters installed in office and garage. Received invoice from Tom George, carpenter. See INVOICE from Tom George on the following pages.

- Note: Remember capitalization limit — *total* invoice amount considered for capitalization.

- Enter bill; add the vendor account and general ledger account as needed.

- Add the asset to QuickBooks Fixed Asset Manager (FAM) (see January transactions for help).
  Note: When exiting FAM, Go to File/Backup. You should see the following screen to integrate assets between the FAM add-on and QuickBooks; then follow backup instructions.

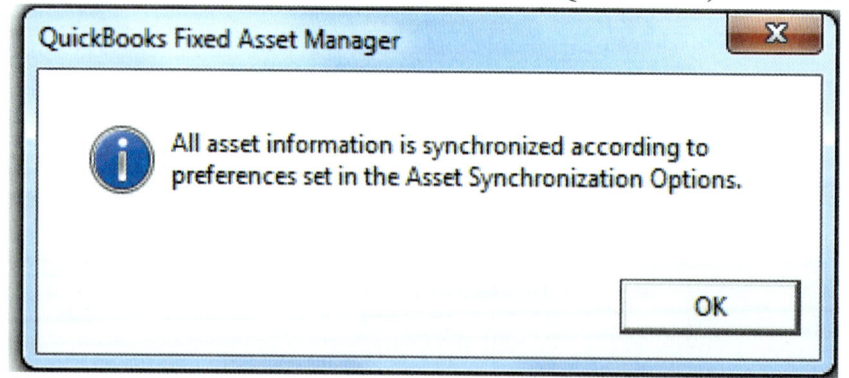

QuickBooks Fixed Asset Manager

All asset information is synchronized according to preferences set in the Asset Synchronization Options.

OK

Reminder: The integration between the Fixed Asset Manager add-on and QuickBooks has not always been successful; if this is the case, you will simply enter the assets during the year-end account analysis work.

3/5 Hired Mary Martin and Max Smith.

> Note: The monthly payroll will be paid by check on the last day of each month, starting on 4/30/2016.
>
> ✓ Due to the cost of the QuickBooks Payroll Tax Service, for this project we will process our payroll manually, calculating/inputting the employee withholdings and employer payroll taxes. In QuickBooks Help/Search, type "process payroll manually" and follow the procedure below:

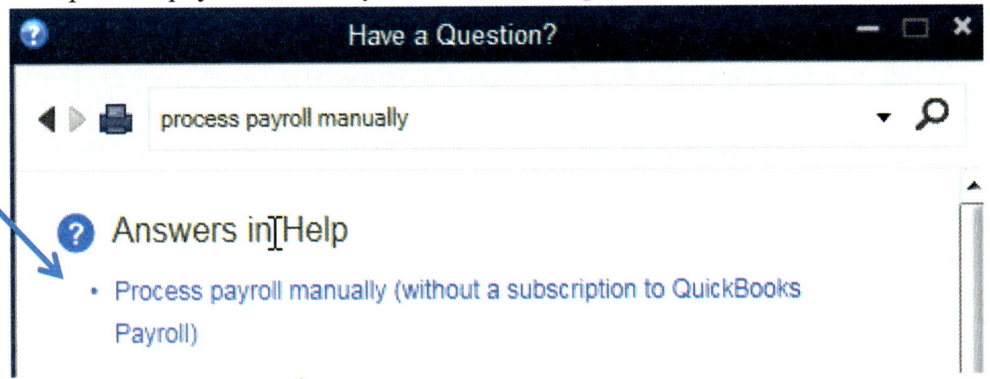

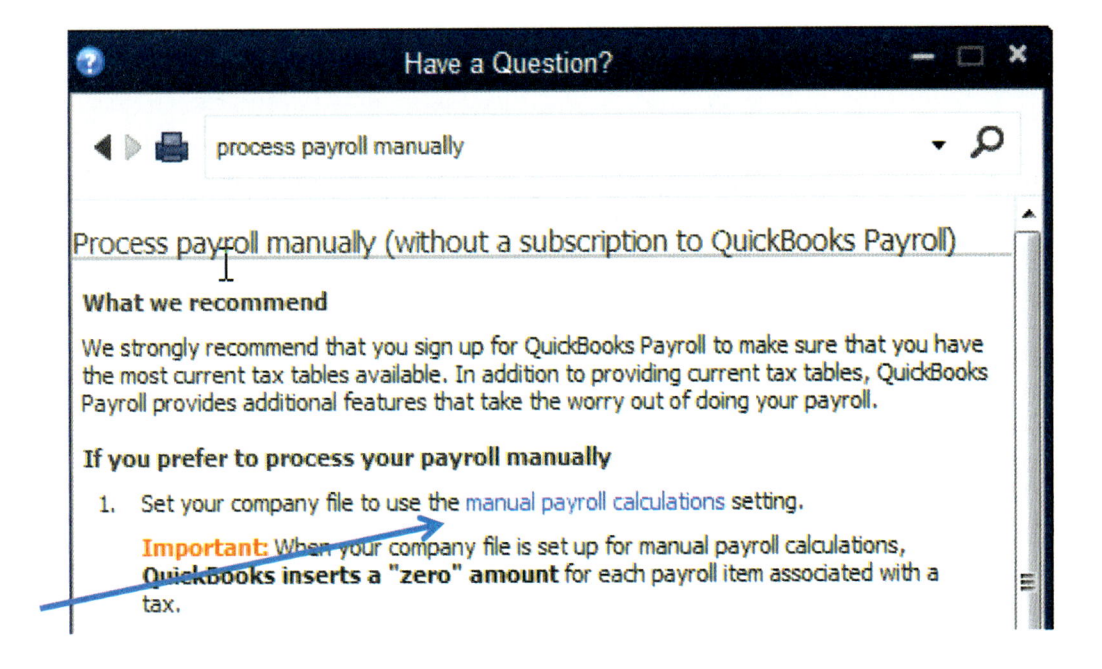

Have a Question?

process payroll manually

Answers in Help
- Process payroll manually (without a subscription to QuickBooks Payroll)

Have a Question?

process payroll manually

Process payroll manually (without a subscription to QuickBooks Payroll)

What we recommend

We strongly recommend that you sign up for QuickBooks Payroll to make sure that you have the most current tax tables available. In addition to providing current tax tables, QuickBooks Payroll provides additional features that take the worry out of doing your payroll.

If you prefer to process your payroll manually

1. Set your company file to use the manual payroll calculations setting.

   Important: When your company file is set up for manual payroll calculations, QuickBooks inserts a "zero" amount for each payroll item associated with a tax.

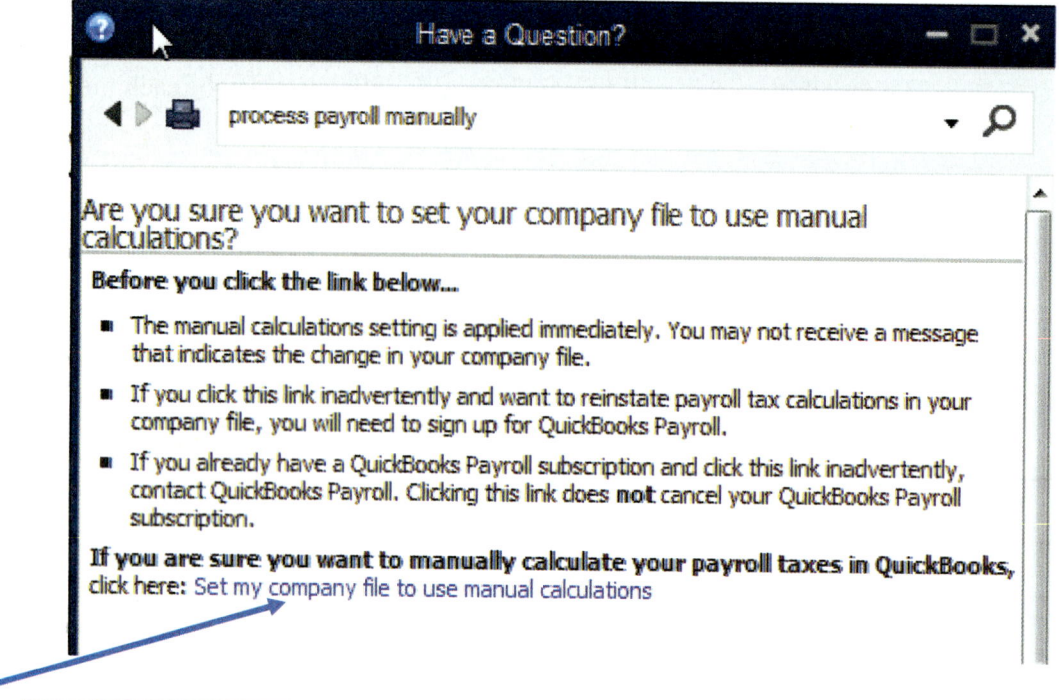

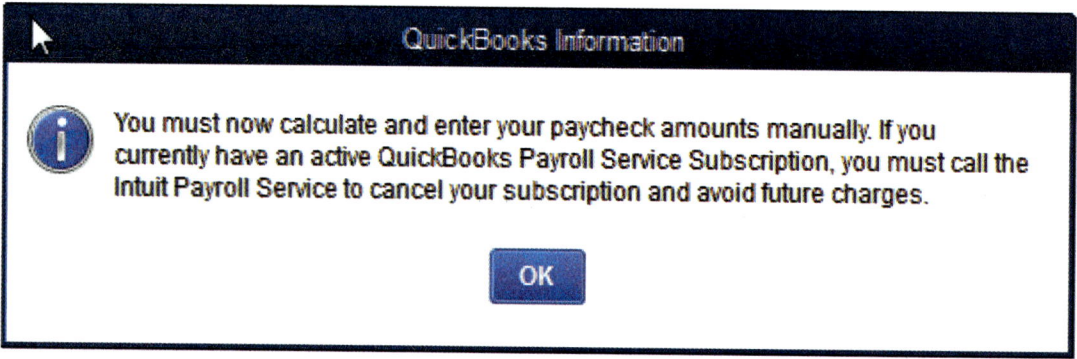

Have a Question?
process payroll manually
Are you sure you want to set your company file to use manual calculations?
Before you click the link below...
The manual calculations setting is applied immediately. You may not receive a message that indicates the change in your company file.
If you click this link inadvertently and want to reinstate payroll tax calculations in your company file, you will need to sign up for QuickBooks Payroll.
If you already have a QuickBooks Payroll subscription and click this link inadvertently, contact QuickBooks Payroll. Clicking this link does not cancel your QuickBooks Payroll subscription.
If you are sure you want to manually calculate your payroll taxes in QuickBooks, click here: Set my company file to use manual calculations
QuickBooks Information
You must now calculate and enter your paycheck amounts manually. If you currently have an active QuickBooks Payroll Service Subscription, you must call the Intuit Payroll Service to cancel your subscription and avoid future charges.
OK

➢ Click OK.

The Home Page should now show the following:

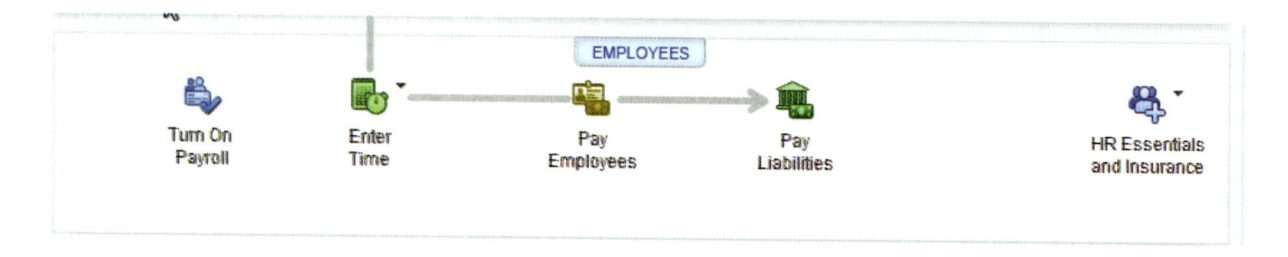

EMPLOYEES
Turn On Payroll
Enter Time
Pay Employees
Pay Liabilities
HR Essentials and Insurance

> Next, go to the Employees drop-down menu/Payroll Setup.

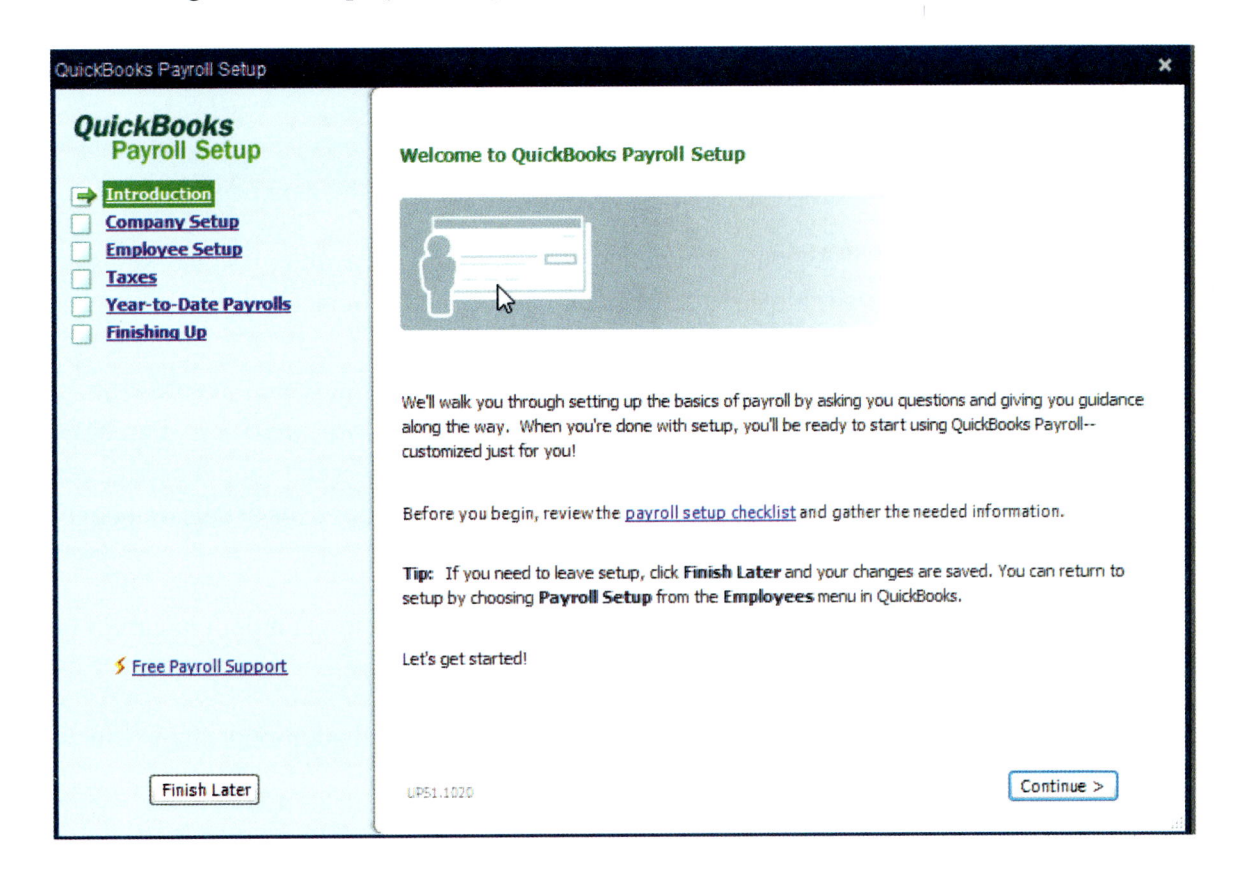

Company Setup: Compensation:
> Check *only* Salary and Hourly wage and overtime. Click "Finish."
> Delete Double-time hourly; click "Continue."

(We will set up employee benefits in July.)

We will set up employees next month.

Taxes/Set up your payroll taxes: There is nothing to edit for federal and state taxes at this time; continue using the following information:

> Schedule Payments:

Form	Payee	Frequency
940	US Treasury	Quarterly
941	US Treasury	Quarterly
WI Unemployment	Division of Unemployment Insurance	Quarterly Rate: 4.1% #876543-211-1
WI Withholding	WI Dept. of Revenue*	Quarterly #036-3456789012-04

*Review vendor list; we will use **WI** Dept. of Revenue for all WI payments, delete Wisconsin Dept. of Revenue vendor, if one was created.

There are no *YTD Payroll* amounts to enter.

Finishing Up: Payroll setup is complete. Click "Finish."

3/5   Received monthly credit card statement (see the statement on the next pages).

> ➢ In the Chart of Accounts, right click on Credit Card Payable; Use the Register to compare charges already recorded to the March statement charges.

> ➢ Using the Enter Credit Card Charges icon on the Home screen, record any *additional* charges not previously recorded *using the statement date*. Purchases from any food store or drug store are personal expenses and should be charged to the drawing account. (Reminder: See 2/17 transactions for details on phone charges. See the screen shot of additional charges.)

Note 1: As we go through the months, the charges may not be in the month incurred; but all charges will be accounted for in the year 2016.

> ✓ Use Credit Card Services as a generic vendor for all additional charges, new terms n/10:

Credit Card Purchase/Charge

| CREDIT CARD | Credit Card Payable | ● Purchase/Charge ○ Refund/Credit | ENDING BALANCE | 484.50 |

PURCHASED FROM: Credit Card Services
DATE: 03/05/2016
REF NO.:
AMOUNT: 228.01

MEMO:

Expenses $228.01 | Items $0.00 | Ready to pay a credit card bill?

ACCOUNT	AMOUNT	MEMO
D. Michaels, Draw	52.87	personal expense
D. Michaels, Draw	15.14	personal expense
D. Michaels, Draw	80.00	personal expense
Telephone Expense	80.00	business expense

➢ After saving and starting a new entry, note the updated ending balance, which agrees with the credit card statement and balance of Credit Card Payable per the general ledger; then close:

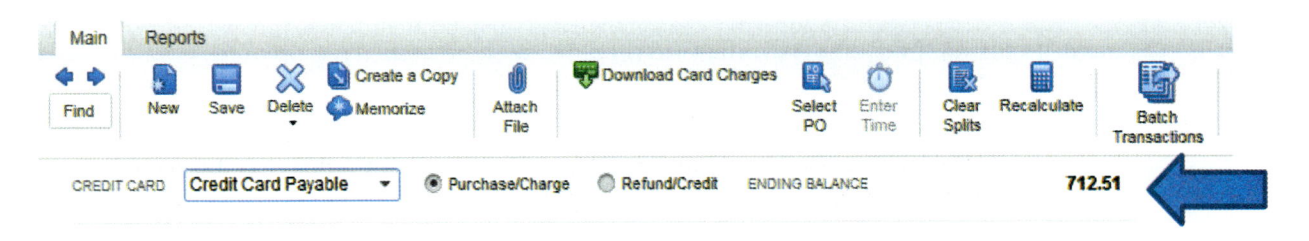

Credit Card Services, Inc.

DM Yard Services

Statement Date: 3/5/2016

Use month as invoice number

Amount Due: $712.51

Due Date: 3/15/2016

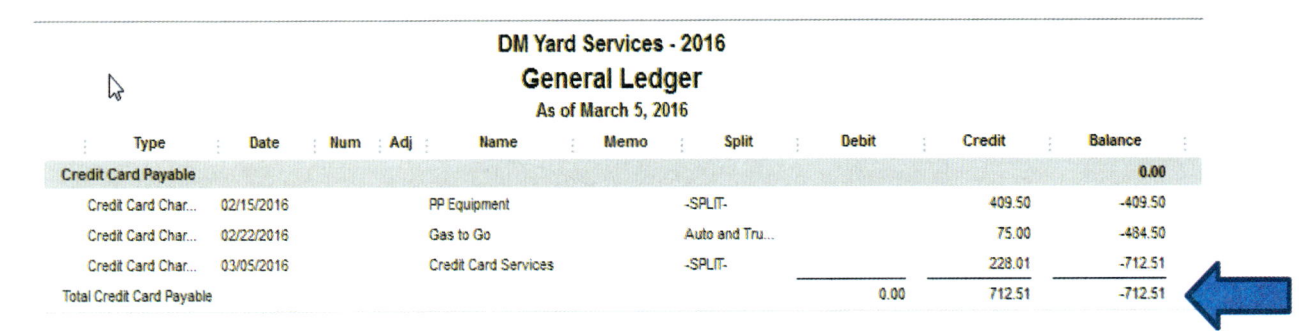

Note: When reconciling or comparing an account balance, the General Ledger (found under Reports/Accountant & Taxes) or a Trial Balance (Reports/Accountant & Taxes) may be used, remembering the general ledger is the source for trial balance amounts!

3/7 Received items ordered from JS Garden Supply. There were no boxwood bushes available. JS Garden Supply invoice #475 received with terms 2/10, n/30; set terms on bill. Verify that total amount due does not include amounts for boxwood bushes. ($6,559.80)
Click "Yes" to change terms for JS Garden Supply.

(Reminder: After saving and closing, you can go back to the bill and see the debits and credits of the transaction through the Reports tab/Transaction Journal.)

3/12 To edit fields on the Default Product Invoice, we will *customize the invoice.*

> ➢ Create invoices. Use the Formatting tab to customize data layout. Make a copy. Delete fields as shown below. Click OK for the Layout Designer message.

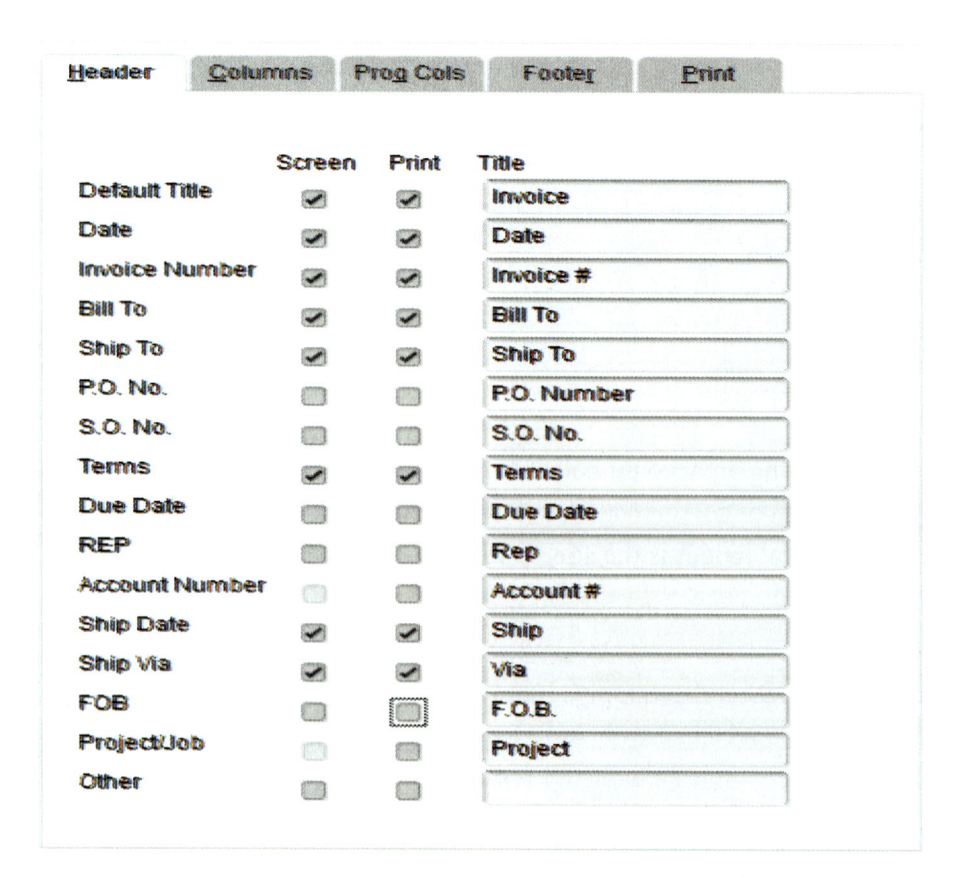

- Use Layout Designer to move "Terms," "Ship," and "Via" boxes over next to the right margin. Click OK.

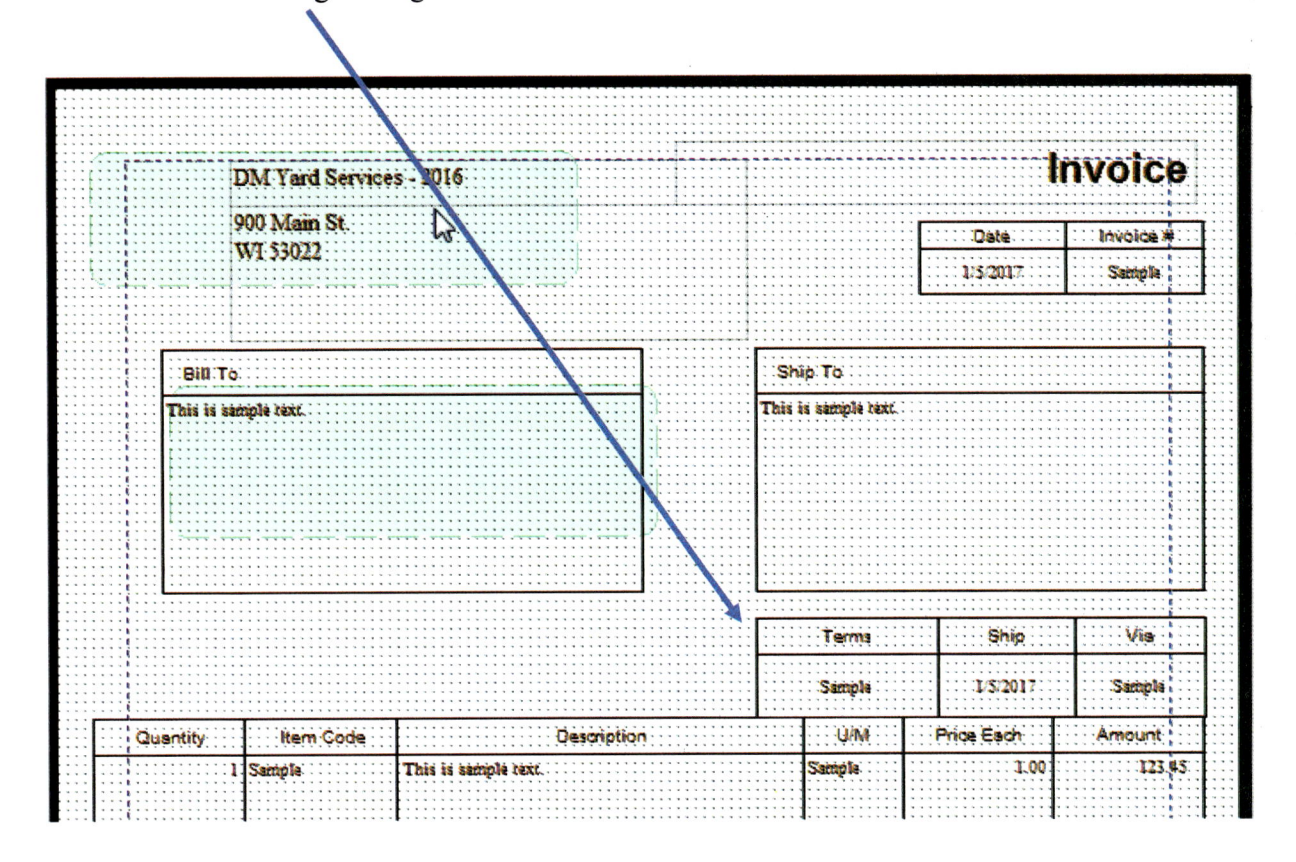

- Manage Templates and change the template name to your company name invoice in the preview window on the right side. Click OK. Click OK again.

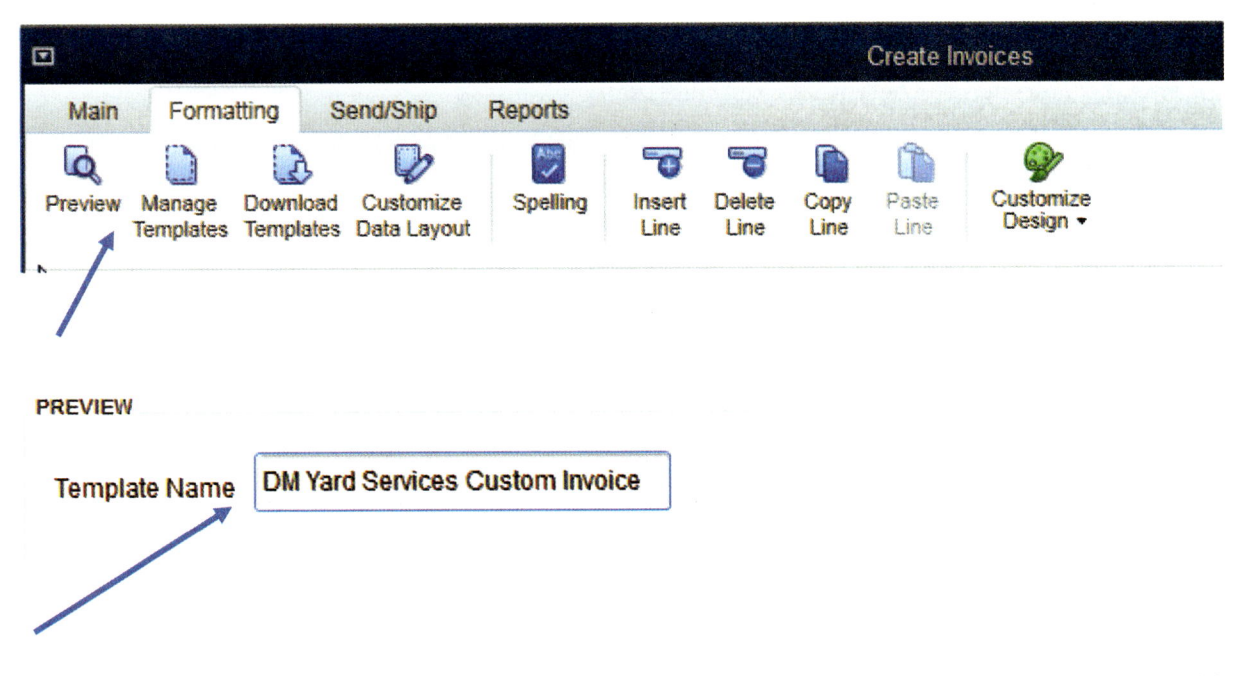

PREVIEW

Template Name: DM Yard Services Custom Invoice

> Prepare an invoice using a customized invoice. Delivered and spread mulch at Davidson Foods. Convert the sales estimate to invoice; use the default invoice number.

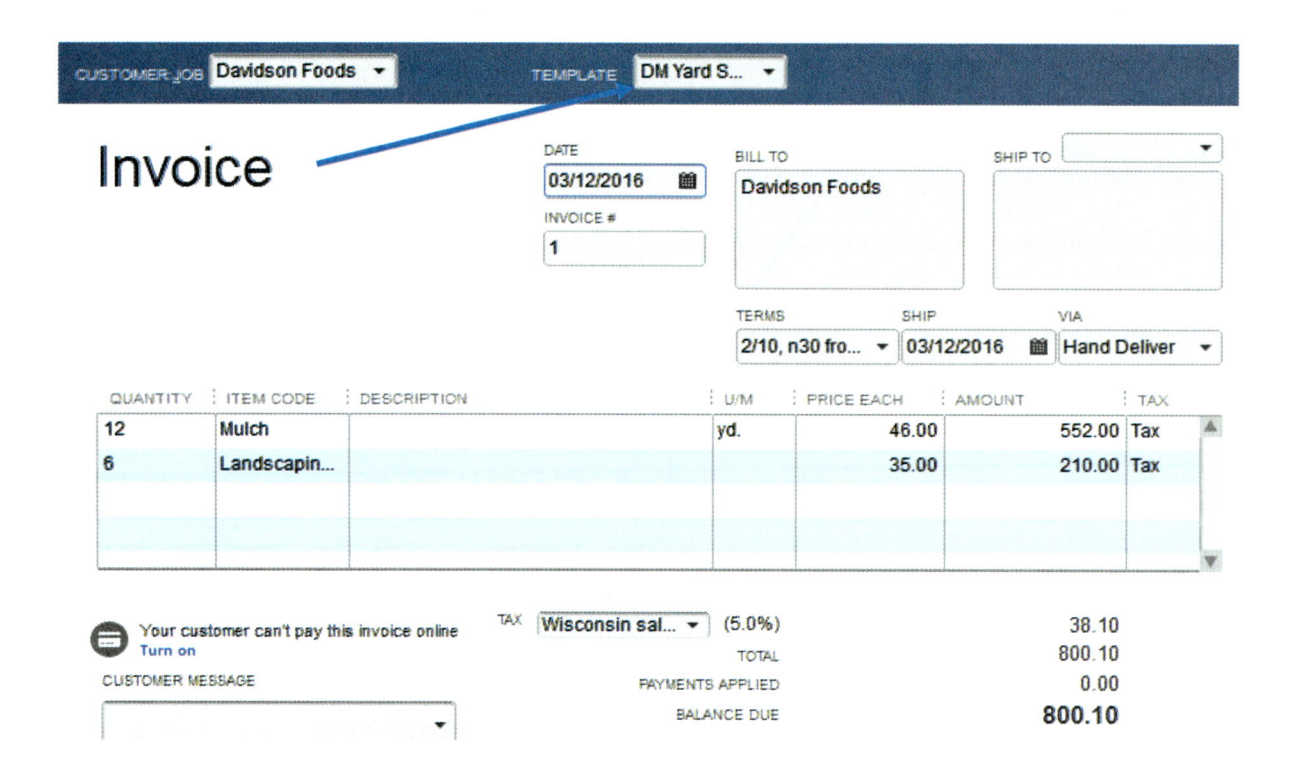

| CUSTOMER:JOB | Davidson Foods | | TEMPLATE | DM Yard S... |

Invoice

DATE: 03/12/2016
INVOICE #: 1
BILL TO: Davidson Foods
TERMS: 2/10, n30 fro...
SHIP: 03/12/2016
VIA: Hand Deliver

QUANTITY	ITEM CODE	DESCRIPTION	U/M	PRICE EACH	AMOUNT	TAX
12	Mulch		yd.	46.00	552.00	Tax
6	Landscapin...			35.00	210.00	Tax

TAX: Wisconsin sal... (5.0%) — 38.10
TOTAL — 800.10
PAYMENTS APPLIED — 0.00
BALANCE DUE — **800.10**

3/13 Record credit card charge for gas of $52 from Gas to Go. (Although this will be on the April credit card statement, record at this time as a March expense.)

As mentioned, credit card charges may not always be in the month incurred, but more importantly will be in 2016.

3/15 Dave approved payment of the March credit card statement; on the *enter credit card charges* screen, select **Ready to pay a credit card bill?**

> Follow help instructions to reconcile Credit Card Payable to the March statement (see the screen shot on the following page).

> After Reconcile Now, select Make Payment and Write a Check for Payment Now (#1007), *only* for the amount owed on the March statement.

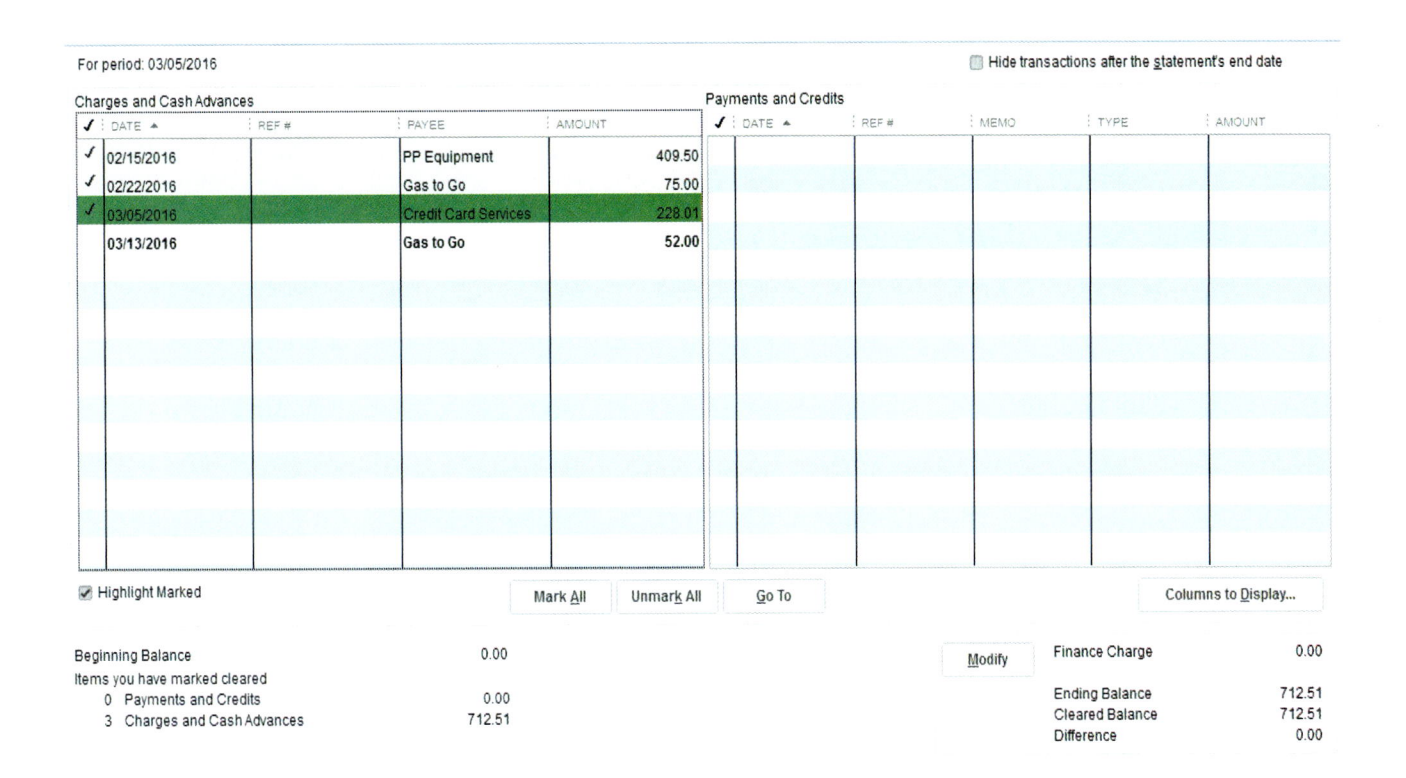

	For period: 03/05/2016								Hide transactions after the statement's end date	
Charges and Cash Advances					Payments and Credits					
✓	DATE ▲	REF #	PAYEE	AMOUNT	✓	DATE ▲	REF #	MEMO	TYPE	AMOUNT
✓	02/15/2016		PP Equipment	409.50						
✓	02/22/2016		Gas to Go	75.00						
✓	03/05/2016		Credit Card Services	228.01						
	03/13/2016		Gas to Go	52.00						

☑ Highlight Marked   Mark All   Unmark All   Go To   Columns to Display...

Beginning Balance   0.00   Modify   Finance Charge   0.00
Items you have marked cleared
  0 Payments and Credits   0.00   Ending Balance   712.51
  3 Charges and Cash Advances   712.51   Cleared Balance   712.51
                                                              Difference   0.00

> Dave also reviewed A/P Aging Detail as of 3/15/2016, paying open invoices for JS Garden Supply (set discount, charging to new account: Purchase Discounts, type: Cost of Goods Sold) and Tom George and assigning checks #1008 – 1009.

3/17   Contracted with the following customers for seasonal lawn care, which includes cutting and trimming (income account).

> Create sales orders for these customers for this day's service *only*. (We will not prepare a sales order for every service). Add new customers as needed (see March 2 for detailed instructions for adding customers).

-Walter Brown	2 hours
-Joe Calhoun	3 hours
-Forest Hill School	4 hours
-Jacksonville Industrial Park (commercial customer)	6 hours
-Larry Laxson	2 hours
-Paul Garrett	3 hours
-Nottingham Condominium Complex (commercial customer)	8 hours

3/20   Record charged gas of $68.

3/22   Completed *estimated* mulch work at Forest Hill School. Create invoice.

3/26   Arranged for the utility budget billing of $150 per month for office gas and electric with Utility Service Corp., charged to business credit card. Record the transaction and add a vendor.

3/31   Dave reviewed the Unpaid Bills Detail report (Vendors & Payables), authorizing payments for any invoices due (not ABC Equipment until indicated).

3/31   Dave withdrew $500, check #1010.

3/31   Prepare *customized customer statements* for March.

- ➤ Go to Lists/Templates and select Intuit Standard Statement. Click "Manage Template." Copy it, then change the template name to "Your Name" Yard Services Statement. Click OK.

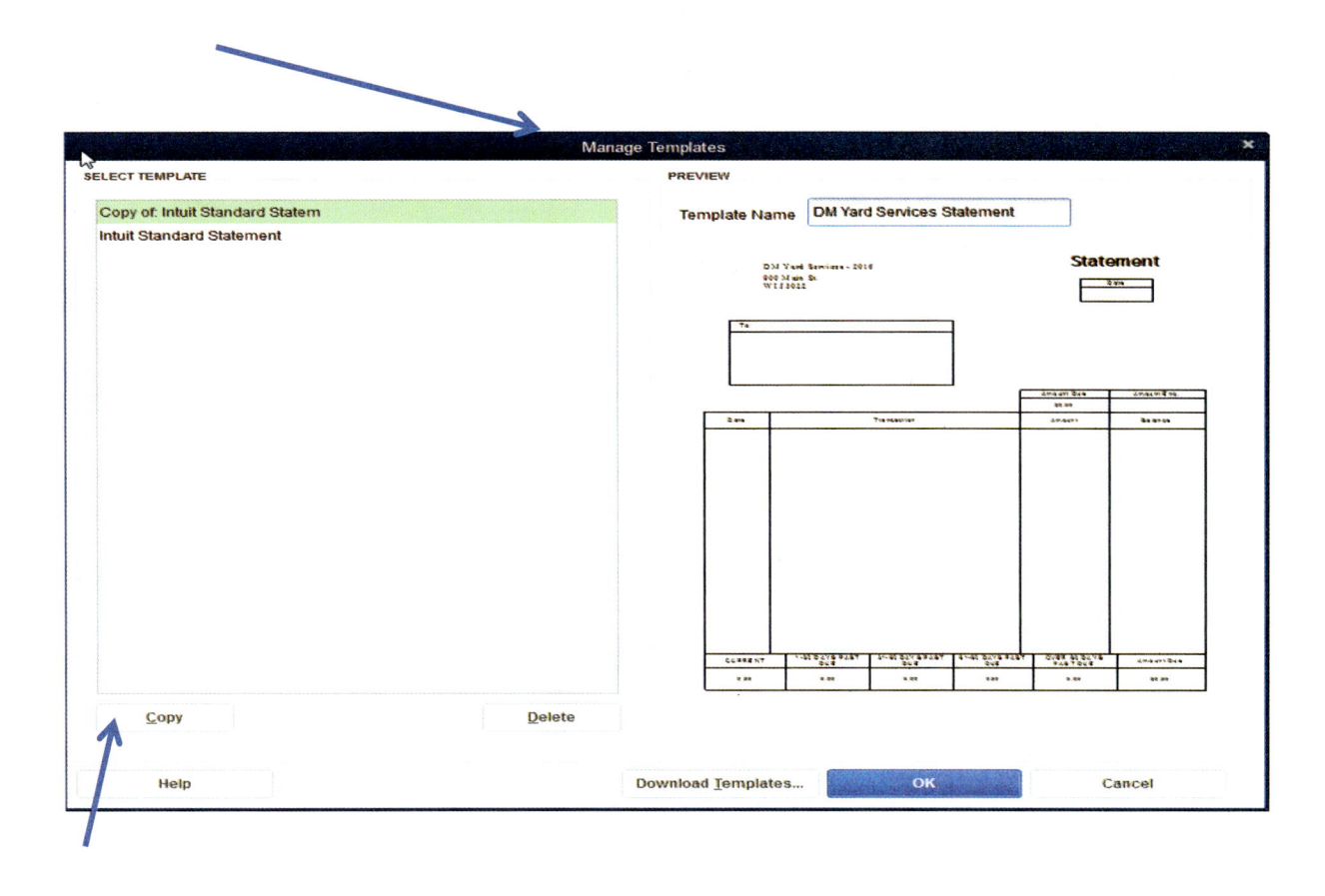

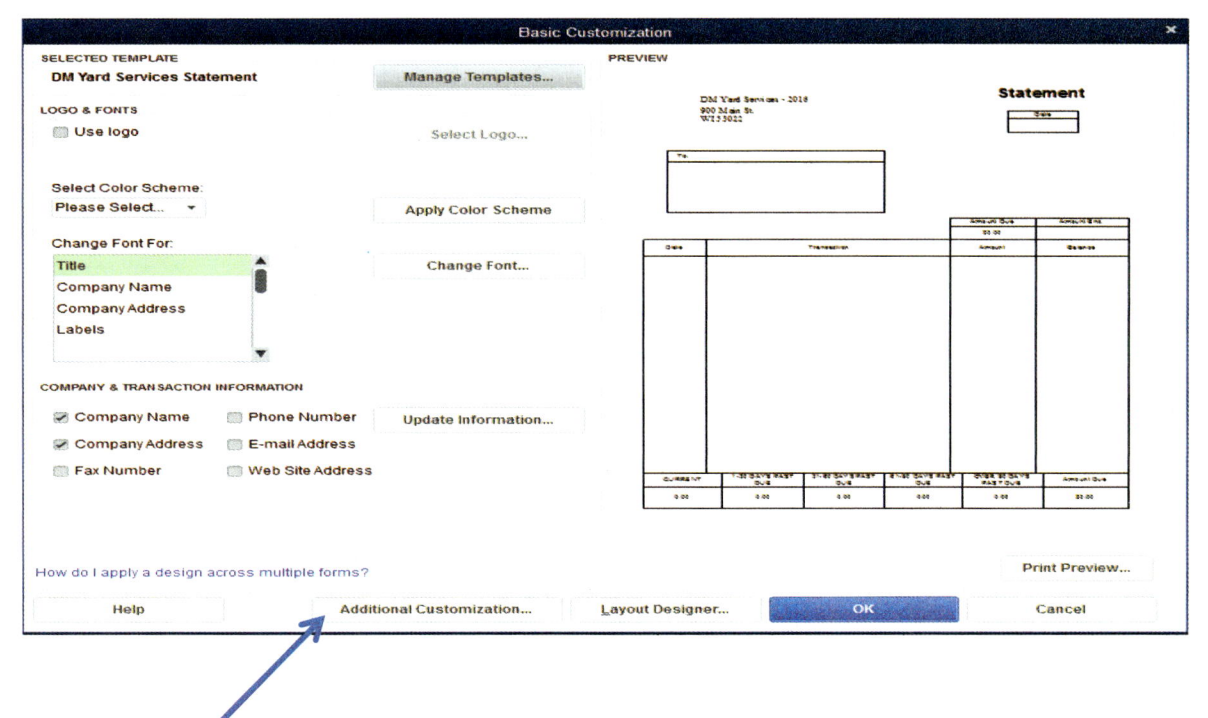

- Select Additional Customization on the bottom of the screen.

- Select Footer and check the box for long text. Click OK at the Layout Designer prompts and then click "Continue." Enter text as seen in the third screen shot below. Click OK to Layout Designer and continue. Click OK. Click OK again.

[Screenshot of QuickBooks "Selected Template: DM Yard Services Statement" dialog, Footer tab, showing Print/Title settings for Amount Due, Show Aging, and Long text (disclaimer) containing: "Residential Customers: Terms n/10 from statement date / Commerical Customers: Terms 2/10 n30 from statement date / Thank you for your business". Preview pane on the right shows the statement template.]

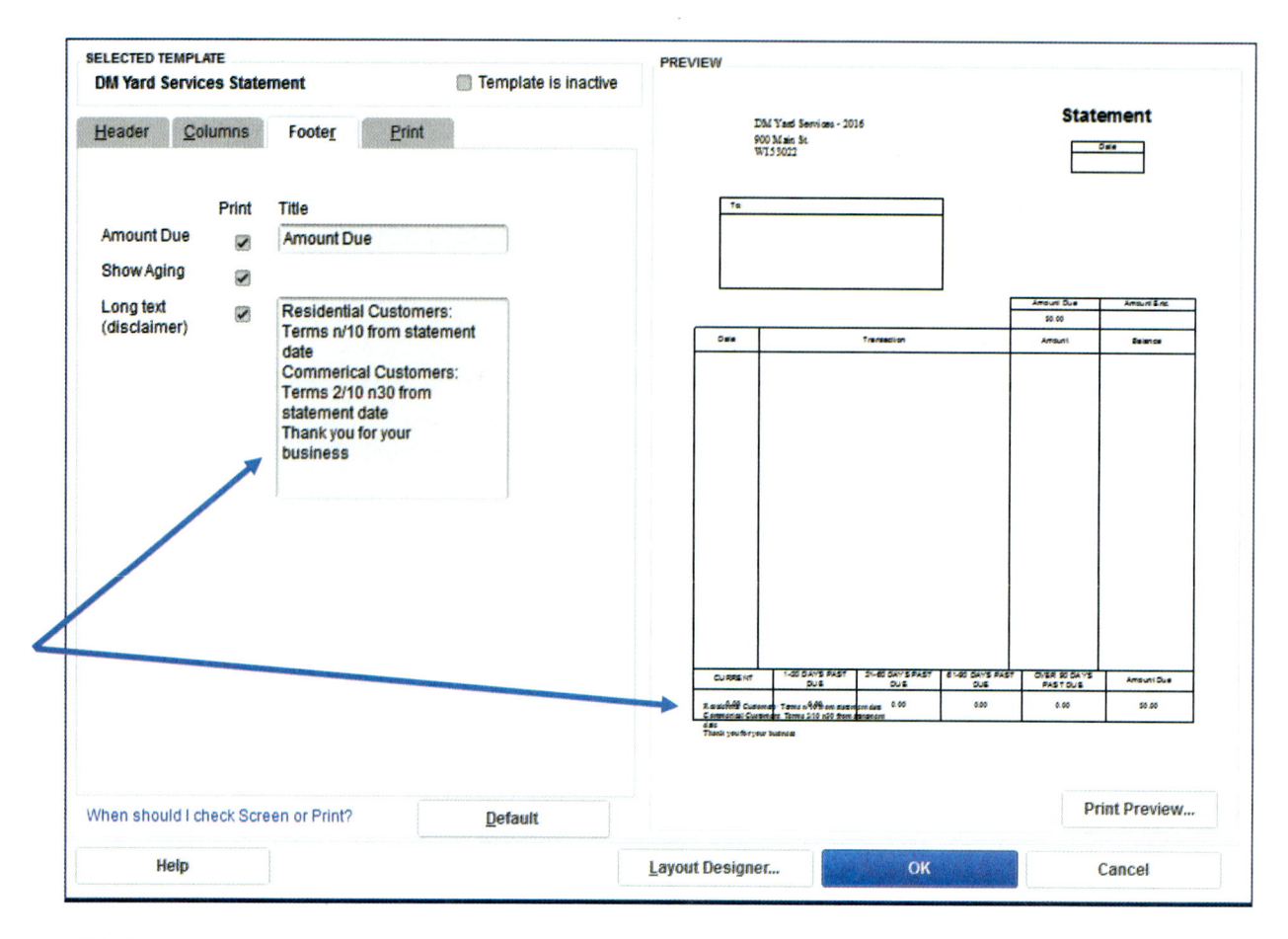

This is referred to as a dunning message, which means "demanding payment on a debt."

> Note 1: This footer is just an example; you would customize your footer for residential versus commercial customers.

> Note 2: The objective is to introduce you to customizing the customer statement with a dunning message; at this point, it is not necessary to further edit for the overlap of text in the Layout Designer.

In your template list (Lists/Templates), you should now see a DM Yard Services Statement template as seen below:

DM Yard Services Statement	Statement

3/31 Create statements for Davidson Foods and Forest Hill School using your *customized* statement for the period 1/1/2016 to 3/31/2016; print to PDF file for submission (all open transactions as of statement date). Customer statements will be prepared (not necessarily submitted) each month.

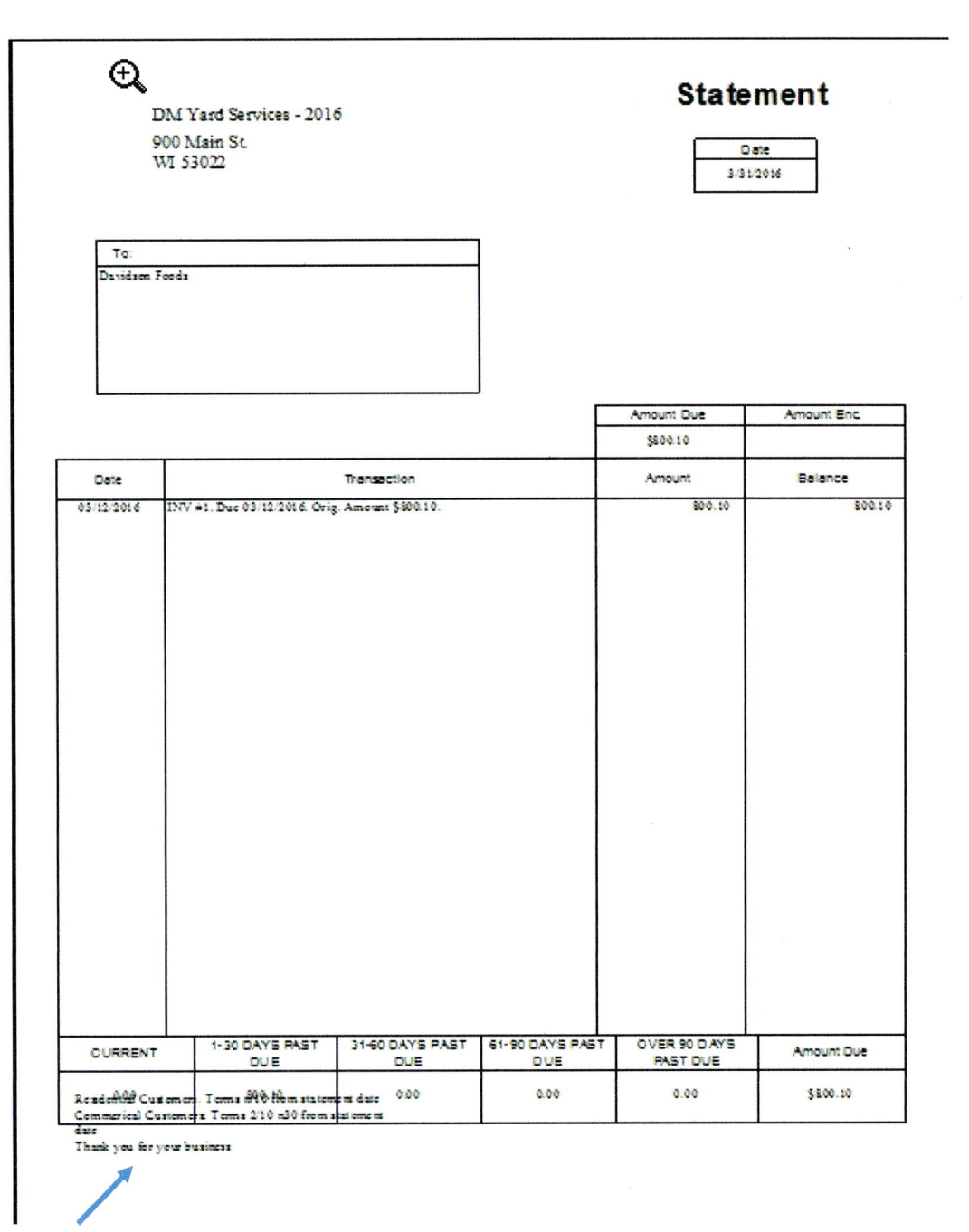

Statement

DM Yard Services - 2016
900 Main St.
WI 53022

Date: 3/31/2016

To:
Davidson Foods

Amount Due	Amount Enc.
$800.10	

Date	Transaction	Amount	Balance
03/12/2016	INV #1. Due 03/12/2016. Orig. Amount $800.10.	800.10	800.10

CURRENT	1-30 DAYS PAST DUE	31-60 DAYS PAST DUE	61-90 DAYS PAST DUE	OVER 90 DAYS PAST DUE	Amount Due
800.10	0.00	0.00	0.00	0.00	$800.10

Residential Customers: Terms n/10 from statement date
Commercial Customers: Terms 2/10 n30 from statement date
Thank you for your business

Note: As mentioned above, it is not necessary to adjust for this overlap.

3/31   Reconcile the cash account for March, using the bank statement on the following pages. (Note: You would inquire on old outstanding checks.)

- Use *only* the Reconciliation Detail Report shown below; if necessary, review screen shots of each step in January and February.

DM Yard Services - 2016
Reconciliation Detail
All Transactions

Type	Date	Num	Name	Clr	Amount	Balance
Beginning Balance						**27,413.67**
Cleared Transactions						
Checks and Payments - 4 items						
Check	03/03/2016	1006	John Smith	✓	-1,750.00	-1,750.00
Bill Pmt -Check	03/15/2016	1008	JS Garden Supply	✓	-6,428.60	-8,178.60
Check	03/15/2016	1007	Credit Card Services	✓	-712.51	-8,891.11
Check	03/31/2016			✓	-15.00	-8,906.11
Total Checks and Payments					-8,906.11	-8,906.11
Total Cleared Transactions					-8,906.11	-8,906.11
Cleared Balance					-8,906.11	18,507.56
Uncleared Transactions						
Checks and Payments - 3 items						
Check	02/25/2016	1003	Office City		-387.45	-387.45
Bill Pmt -Check	03/15/2016	1009	Tom George		-850.00	-1,237.45
Check	03/31/2016	1010	D. Michaels		-500.00	-1,737.45
Total Checks and Payments					-1,737.45	-1,737.45
Total Uncleared Transactions					-1,737.45	-1,737.45
Register Balance as of 03/31/2016					-10,643.56	16,770.11
Ending Balance					**-10,643.56**	**16,770.11**

Note: Make sure your reconciled cash balance agrees with the checking account balance on trial balance.

> Compare/reconcile (review and make corrections if needed) your trial balance found under Reports/Accountant & Taxes/Trial Balance to the following report.

DM Yard Services – 2016

Trial Balance
As of March 31, 2016

	Mar 31, 16 Debit	Credit
DM Yard Services Checking	16,770.11	
Petty Cash	200.00	
Accounts Receivable	2,280.10	
Inventory Asset	5,327.80	
Lawn and Landscaping Equipment	4,500.00	
Leasehold Improvements	850.00	
Office Equipment	787.50	
Truck	18,200.00	
Security Deposit	1,000.00	
Accounts Payable		4,700.00
Credit Card Payable		270.00
Sales Tax Payable		38.10
D. Michaels, Capital		48,200.00
D. Michaels, Draw	1,648.01	
Landscaping Services		770.00
Mulch Sales		1,472.00
Mulch Costs	1,232.00	
Purchase Discounts		131.20
Auto and Truck Expenses	195.00	
Bank Service Charges	45.00	
Office Supplies	642.60	
Rent Expense	750.00	
Small Tools and Equipment	923.18	
Telephone Expense	80.00	
Utilities	150.00	
TOTAL	**55,581.30**	**55,581.30**

Note: This trial balance was exported to Excel to fit to this page; to have the complete heading on the Excel worksheet, go to Advanced/Printing Options/Show Report Header: on printed report and screen.

Tom George Carpenter			**INVOICE**

Address City, State, ZIP	500 Main St. Pewaukee, WI 53072 Tax ID: 39-4568791 (sole-proprietor)		
Sold To:			
Name	DM Yard Services	Invoice Number	536524
Address City, State, ZIP	900 Main St. Landscape, WI 53022	Invoice Date	March 4, 2016
		Terms	Net 15

	DESCRIPTION	AMOUNT
	Installed shelves and counter in office and garage	$650.00
	Materials	200.00
		$850.00 Pay This Amount

THANK YOU FOR YOUR BUSINESS!

Credit Card Services, Inc.

DM Yard Services

Statement Date: 3/5/2016

Use month as invoice number

Amount Due: $712.51

Due Date: 3/15/2016

Charge Summary:

- ABC Food Store   52.87
- PP Equipment   409.50
- Max's Drug Store   15.14
- Cell World   160.00
- Gas to Go   75.00

XYZ Bank

DM Yard Services

Acct. #745-1332 3/1/2016 thru 3/31/2016

Beg. Balance: $2,7413.67

Deposits & CM

Checks & DM

#1006	$1,750.00
#1007	712.51
#1008	6,428.60
3/31 SC	15.00

Ending Balance: $1,8507.56

March Questions

1. The business credit card is being used for business and personal expenses; list the business and then the personal expenses from the March credit card statement. Address the *accounting* and *ethical* reasons for this separation of expenses.

2. Dave Michaels takes advantage of cash discounts from vendors whenever possible. Address the business reason for this decision. Then, address the *ethical* ramifications if Dave would take the discount when paying outside the discount period.

3. Support the accounting for the installation of shelves and counters as a leasehold improvement (no specific source). Copy and paste the support into your Word document.

4. For new employees, a W-4 and I-9 must be completed. Prepare them for Mary only.

    Mary A. Martin
    Birth date: 12/7/1962
    Passport Issued by U.S. government: #000056789 (date of expiration: 10/01/2023)

    Paste snips in your Word document or submit the W-4 and I-9 with your March submissions. (No signatures required.)

5. **QUARTERLY TASKS**

    ➤ Verify the A/R, Inventory, and A/P subsidiary ledger balances agree with the trial balance; document this in your Word document of March questions.

    Example: Show the comparison by using snips of the reports**; this will prepare you for more detail comparisons with payroll reports in July.

    **QuickBooks has many reports; review the variety of reports in the different areas, for example, Company & Financial, Customers & Receivables.

DM Yard Services - 2016
Customer Balance Detail
All Transactions

Type	Date	Num	Account	Amount	Balance
Davidson Foods					
Invoice	03/12/2016	1	Accounts Receiva...	800.10	800.10
Total Davidson Foods				800.10	800.10
Forest Hill School					
Invoice	03/22/2016	2	Accounts Receiva...	1,480.00	1,480.00
Total Forest Hill School				1,480.00	1,480.00
TOTAL				2,280.10	2,280.10

DM Yard Services - 2016
Trial Balance
As of March 31, 2016

	Mar 31, 16 Debit	Credit
DM Yard Services Checking	16,770.11	
Petty Cash	200.00	
Accounts Receivable	2,280.10	

> As measures of internal control (continued Quarterly Tasks):

a) Print (create PDF or Excel) a report of *quarterly* numerically sorted invoices from the Customer Center/Transactions/Invoice/Run Report to ensure all invoices accounted for.

b) Print a quarterly check detail report for Dave's review for reasonableness of payees and amounts; Dave initials report. (Hint: Export to Excel to enter initials, or to PDF and enter text.)

c) Review the general ledger on screen *only* — no printing. The general ledger will be used extensively to reconcile differences in your accounts compared to "check figure" trial balances. Review the general ledger for information presented and note the review in your Word document for monthly questions.

6. Identify and list two managerial/business-related (e.g., address controls to safeguard inventory) and three financial-related (e.g., current ratio is…) observations through March for your landscaping business.

7. Complete a) the Monthly Task List and b) your To Do/Follow-up Question List with at least two items to be addressed by your "manager"/teacher.

CHAPTER PRINT/SUBMISSION SUMMARY

Note: As we did "new" transactions this month, submissions include various reports as examples of reports in these areas, that is, sales/customers, vendors/payables, etc. These will *not* all be printed each month! Also, note all reports can be converted into Excel or PDF files (via print) on the report window.

1. _____ Walter Brown's estimate

2. _____ Davidson Foods invoice (using customized invoice template)

3. _____ Davidson Foods and Forest Hill School customized customer statements

4. _____ W-4 and I-9 for Mary Martin (if you did not include snips in question 4)

5. _____ QuickBooks report to support A/R subsidiary ledger balance. (Note: Ask your instructor if it is necessary to submit reports here if the reports are shown as snips as in the example for question 5.)

6. _____ QuickBooks report to support A/P subsidiary ledger balance (if you did not include snips)

7. _____ QuickBooks report to support Inventory subsidiary ledger balance (if you did not include snips)

8. _____ Report of numerically sorted invoices for quarter (question 5)

9. _____ Check Detail for quarter (initialed by "Dave" to indicate review for the quarter, question 5)

10. _____ Bank Account Detail Reconciliation Report

11. _____ Trial Balance

12. _____ Questions 1 – 6

13. _____ Task List/To Do/Question List

MARCH TASK LIST

Check here if completed	Task	Initials
	Review of Unpaid Bills Detail Report on March 15th and 31st	
	Compare A/R control account balance (A/R on trial balance) to a detail report of the A/R subsidiary ledger	
	Compare A/P control account balance (A/P on trial balance) to a detail report of the A/P subsidiary ledger	
	Compare Inventory control account balance (Inventory on trial balance) to a detail report of the Inventory subsidiary ledger	
	Prepare report of numerically sorted invoices from the Customer Center/Transactions/Invoice	
	Review check detail for quarter; Dave indicates review with his initials on report (see cash-related information at the beginning of project). Export report into Excel to note initials.	
	Review general ledger for January – March (Note: on screen *only* — no printing)	
	Verify cash balance on trial balance equals cash balance on bank reconciliation	
	Review trial balance for completeness and accuracy	
	Back up your monthly transactions to an external destination (e.g., flash drive), changing file name to the month	

To Do/Follow-up/Question List

April Transactions/Activities

Note 1: Enter check numbers when preparing checks to avoid printing checks; remember to uncheck the "print later" box.

Note 2: Since you have now completed the 1st quarter of transactions, fewer instructions will be provided. Add customers, vendors, and accounts as needed. Use QuickBooks Help when needed.

4/1   Paid monthly rent, check #1011; *memorize* this transaction. We will "Add to my Reminders List" versus automating the entry, so the check number can be entered each month.

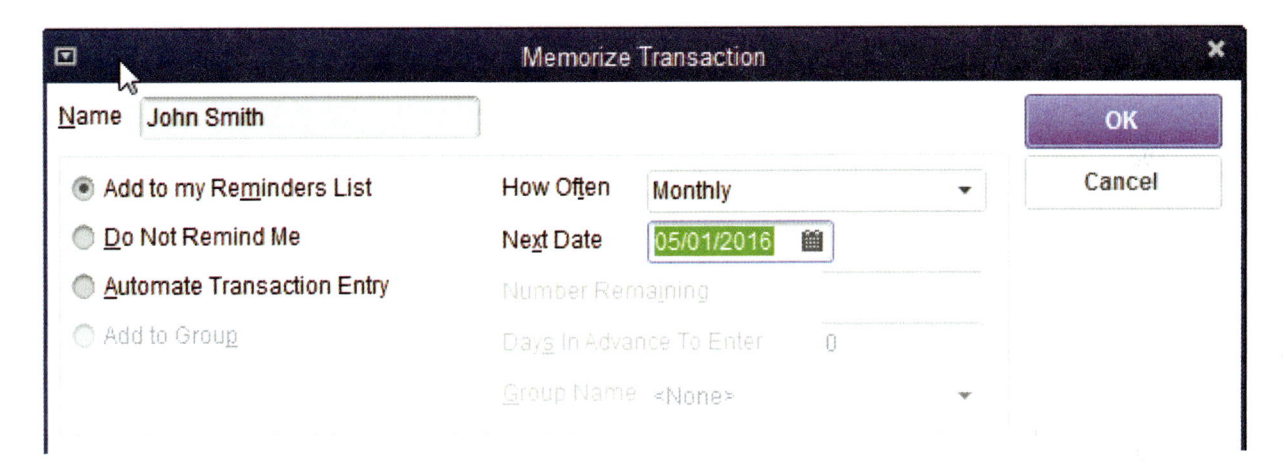

[Screenshot: Memorize Transaction dialog box — Name: John Smith; Add to my Reminders List selected; How Often: Monthly; Next Date: 05/01/2016]

4/2   Mary and Max started today; employee data will be entered as well as payroll being paid at the end of the month. (No transaction at this time.)

4/2   Bought a small refrigerator for the office for $30.45 on the credit card. Record the purchase. A vendor is not required; however, as mentioned before, you could use Credit Card Services as a generic vendor.

4/2   Completed Brown's mulch job. Create an invoice from the estimate.

4/3   Used $7.86 of petty cash to buy water and soda for office. Update your petty cash sheet.

4/3   Received payments in full from Davidson Foods and Forest Hill School March statements. *Watch discounts — you will have to calculate them based on each invoice (when there is more than one)*.

> ➢ *Enter using discounts and credits icon!*
> ➢ Create a new Sales Discounts account.
> ➢ Also record the deposit as of date received.

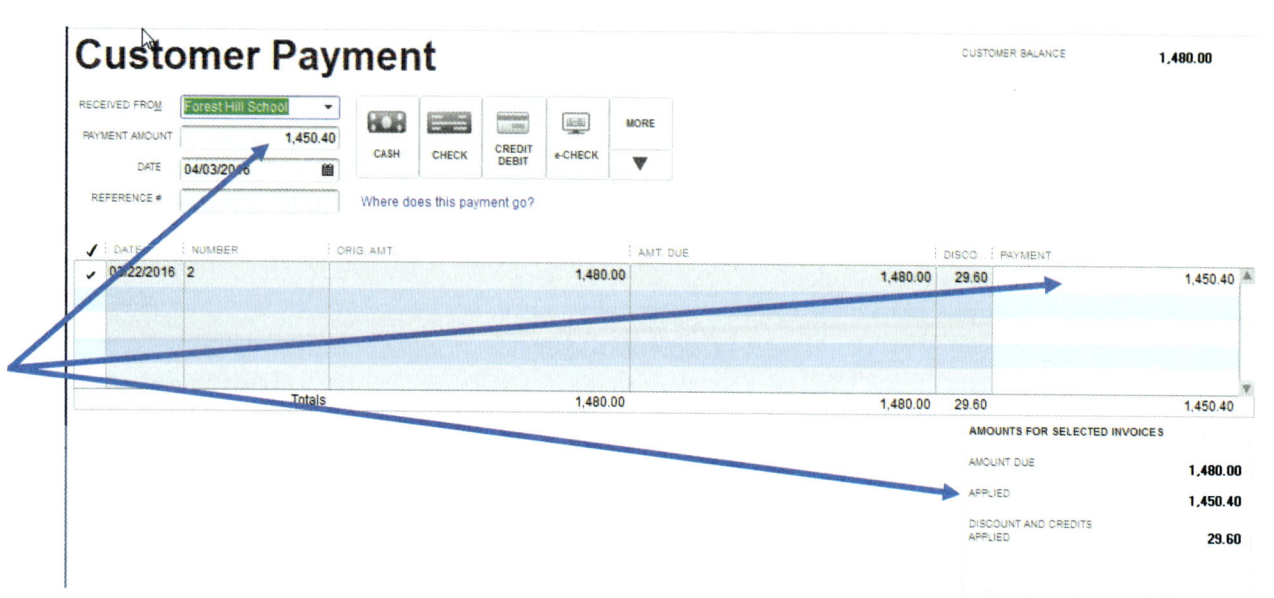

Customer Payment

	DATE	NUMBER	ORIG. AMT.	AMT. DUE	DISC.	PAYMENT
✓	03/22/2016	2		1,480.00	1,480.00	29.60	1,450.40
	Totals			1,480.00	1,480.00	29.60	1,450.40

RECEIVED FROM: Forest Hill School
PAYMENT AMOUNT: 1,450.40
DATE: 04/03/2016
CUSTOMER BALANCE: 1,480.00

AMOUNTS FOR SELECTED INVOICES
AMOUNT DUE: 1,480.00
APPLIED: 1,450.40
DISCOUNT AND CREDITS APPLIED: 29.60

Note: Your payment amount in the upper left should agree with the Payment and Applied amounts, *and* you should *always* have an *applied* discount or credit. At no point will you have a customer with an overpayment.

4/5   Bought office paper and printer ink from Office City, charged credit card $36.42; record.

4/5   Received credit card statement. As in March (*refer back to the 3/5 transaction for more detailed steps*), use the register to compare charges already recorded and enter any additional amounts using the statement date and Credit Card Services as the vendor. We will pay the statement amount on the 15th.

Reminders:

> ➢ All gas charges on the credit card are for the business only.
> ➢ The Cell World bill is for Dave's business phone and his wife's personal phone.
> ➢ ABC Food Store, Deli Stop, etc. are personal charges.
> ➢ Utility Service Corp. is a business charge.
> ➢ April charges for office supplies (4/2 and 4/5 entries) will appear on the next month's statement; as mentioned, charges incurred may not be in the month incurred but will be reconciled at year-end.

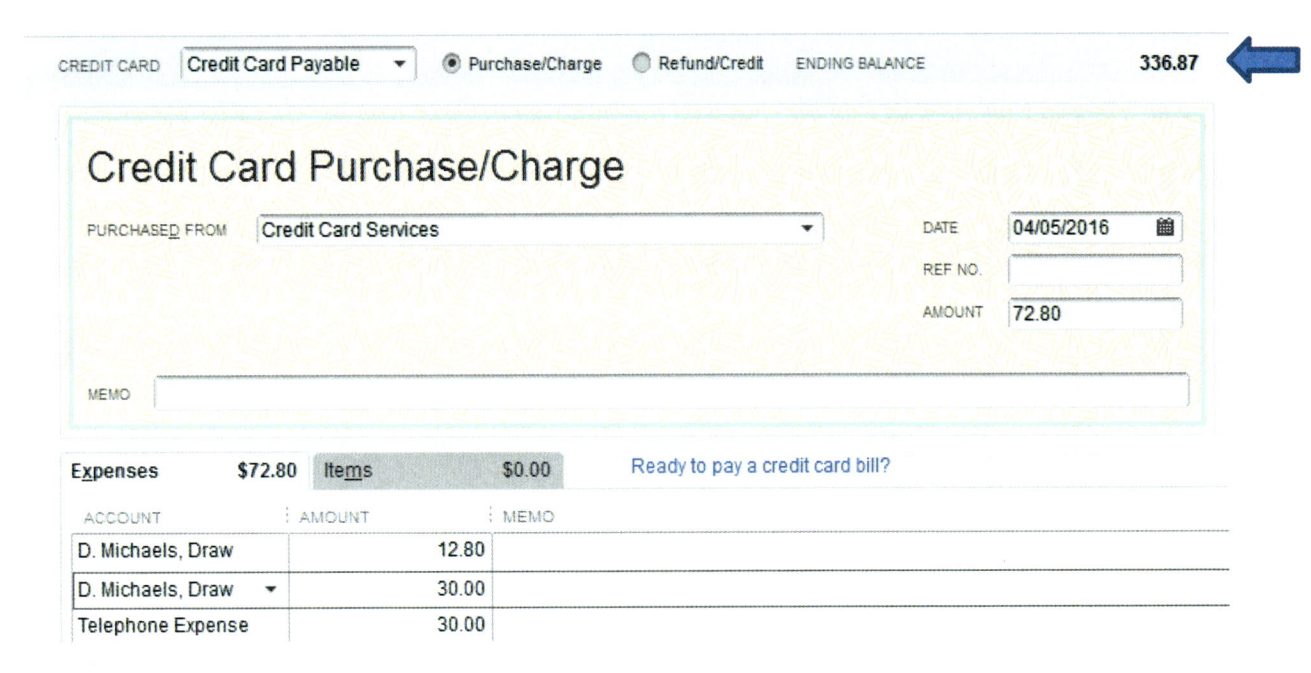

| CREDIT CARD | Credit Card Payable ▼ | ● Purchase/Charge ○ Refund/Credit | ENDING BALANCE | 336.87 |

Credit Card Purchase/Charge

PURCHASED FROM	Credit Card Services ▼	DATE	04/05/2016
		REF NO.	
		AMOUNT	72.80

MEMO

| Expenses | $72.80 | Items | $0.00 | Ready to pay a credit card bill? |

ACCOUNT	AMOUNT	MEMO
D. Michaels, Draw	12.80	
D. Michaels, Draw ▼	30.00	
Telephone Expense	30.00	

Note: The Ending balance will not recalculate (see above screen shot) until the transaction is saved.

After these charges are recorded, the balance in Credit Card Payable is as follows:

ENDING BALANCE   **409.67**   (336.87 + 12.80 + 30.00 + 30.00 = 409.67)

	Less:	30.45	(4/2 charge; which will appear on **May** statement and be paid with **May** statement
	Less:	36.42	(4/5 charge; same as above)
4/5 Statement Balance:		342.80	balance will be paid on 4/15

4/7   Paid $960 and $450 to American Insurance for 6 months, April – September, for workers compensation (comp) and business owner's insurance, respectively; check #1012. Charge the entire amount to prepaid insurance.

> ➢ Next, make a general journal entry as of 4/30/2016 to record the expiration of April insurance, and then memorize the transaction and Automate Transaction Entry to recur for the next 5 months; both types of insurance may be charged to Insurance Expense. (See the following screen shot.)

Memorize Transaction

Name: Insurance Adjustment

- Add to my Reminders List
- Do Not Remind Me
- ● Automate Transaction Entry
- Add to Group

How Often: Monthly
Next Date: 05/31/2016
Number Remaining: 5
Days In Advance To Enter: 0
Group Name: <None>

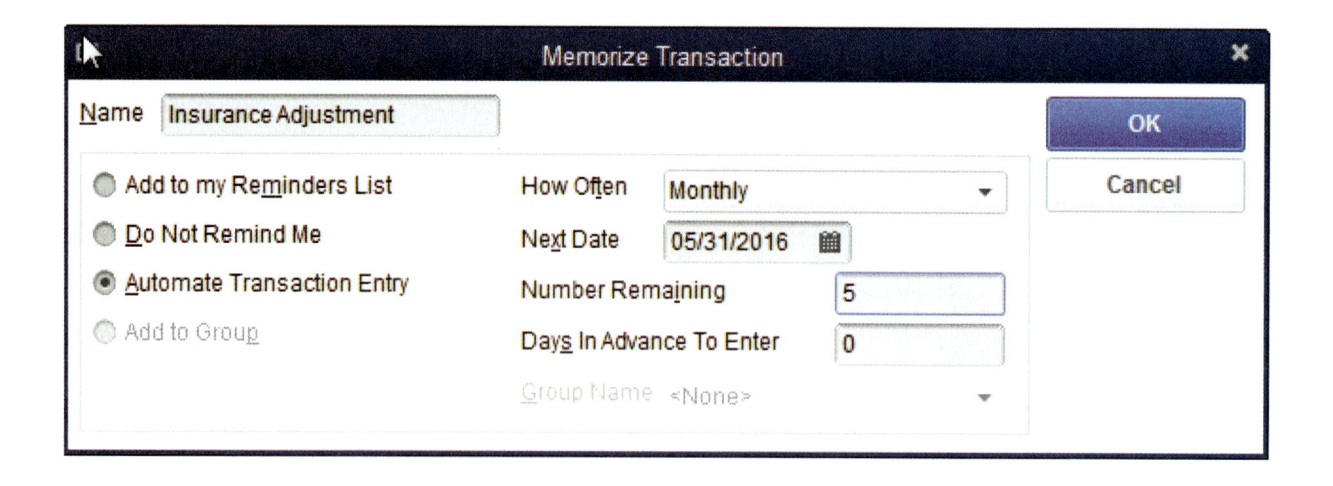

4/8   Ten boxwood bushes from JS Garden Supply were delivered with invoice #782, terms from the original order still apply. Enter the bill.

4/10   Applied spring fertilizer for customers; credit all labor to Landscaping Services:

Brown: 1 bag/1 hour

Calhoun: 1 bag/1 hour

Forest Hill School: 4 bags/2 hours

Jacksonville Industrial Park: 4 bags/2 hours

Create *new* invoices (these are *not* from estimates or sales orders), noting customers will receive statements at month-end and pay from statements.

4/15   Dave reviewed A/P Aging Detail and approved payment to JS Garden Supply, as well as payment due to Credit Card Services (*see March 15th transaction to reconcile and pay a credit card bill*), checks #1013 and 1014. Watch the discount. Assign check numbers.

4/15   Picked up 10 bags of fertilizer from JS Garden Supply, invoice #841. No discount was given on small orders, terms n/15. (Do not change terms for JS Garden Supply.)

4/15 Paid quarterly income tax estimates, $500 federal, $150 Wisconsin.

> - Set up a vendor account to IRS; Wisconsin Department of Revenue has already been added from sales tax. We will use that vendor account for all state-related checks.
>
> - Print/PDF forms for estimates (IRS 1040-ES and WI 1-ES) and write checks #1015 and 1016, respectively. The Social Security number for Dave is 388-22-6666, and that for Dave's wife, Sue, is 360-24-9781.
>
> - Note: DM Yard Services is a sole proprietorship for which the income will be reported on Dave's and Sue's federal and state income tax returns; these deposits should be properly charged to drawing. A sole proprietorship does *not* have Income Tax Expense. Save forms for future estimates.

Note 1: You can download the WI 1-ES, save, and then open with Adobe for a fill-in form. (See instructions when saving/completing the Business Tax Registration on 2/5.)

Note 2: You can use Dave's and Sue's names here because we are using their social security numbers.

Form 1040-ES — Department of the Treasury, Internal Revenue Service — **2016 Estimated Tax** — Payment Voucher 1 — OMB No. 1545-0074

File only if you are making a payment of estimated tax by check or money order. Mail this voucher with your check or money order payable to "**United States Treasury**." Write your social security number and "2016 Form 1040-ES" on your check or money order. Do not send cash. Enclose, but do not staple or attach, your payment with this voucher.

Calendar year — Due April 18, 2016
Amount of estimated tax you are paying by check or money order: Dollars 500 Cents 00

Your first name and initial	Your last name	Your social security number
Dave A	Michaels	388-22-6666

If joint payment, complete for spouse

Spouse's first name and initial	Spouse's last name	Spouse's social security number
Sue G.	Michaels	360-24-9781

Address (number, street, and apt. no.): 800 Main St.
City, state, and ZIP code: Landscape, WI 53022

For Privacy Act and Paperwork Reduction Act Notice, see instructions. Form 1040-ES (2016)
-11-

2016 WISCONSIN ESTIMATED INCOME TAX VOUCHER — Form **1-ES**

File only if submitting payment. Make your check payable to and mail your voucher to: Wisconsin Department of Revenue, PO Box 930208, Milwaukee WI 53293-0208

Calendar year due dates: Apr 18, 2016 / Sep 15, 2016 / Jun 15, 2016 / Jan 17, 2017
Fiscal year filers: Enter year ending (month and year)

Check box if address is corrected and new address was not provided on a prior payment voucher.

Check the box below which applies to you:
☐ Trust (Enter FEIN as "your social security number")
☐ Estate (Enter decedent's social security number)
☐ Individual
☒ Joint

Your legal last name	Your legal first name and initial	Your social security number
Michaels	David A	388-22-6666
Spouse's legal last name	Spouse's legal first name and initial	Spouse's social security number
Michaels	Sue G	360-24-9781

Home address: 800 Main St.
Telephone number: (262)356-2141
City or post office: Landscape
State: WI   Zip code: 53022

Amount of Payment: $ 150.00

Please do not staple your payment to this voucher.
D-101 (R. 6-15)

2080164013999999999999999902016061619800000000000

4/21 Applied spring fertilizing for customers; all labor credited to Landscaping Services:

Laxson: 1 bag/1 hour

Garrett: 1 bag/1 hour

Nottingham Condos: 6 bags/3 hours; also spread 2 bags of grass seed, using 3 straw bales and an additional 2 hours.

> Create new invoices.

4/26 Completed lawn maintenance for all contracted customers. Create invoices from March 17th sales orders.

> To save *lots* of time invoicing routine lawn maintenance, memorize these invoices.

✓ After completing each invoice, save it using the icon on the top bar of the invoice. Remove the invoice and sales order number (S. O. No.) and memorize the invoice for future use ("Do not remind me"); then click X to exit. Do *not* record invoices with changes of deleted invoice and sales order number. Create the next invoice.

> Next month, to invoice monthly customers, go to Lists, Memorized Transaction List, select the transaction, edit the date, and save! This is a great time saver — watch dates!

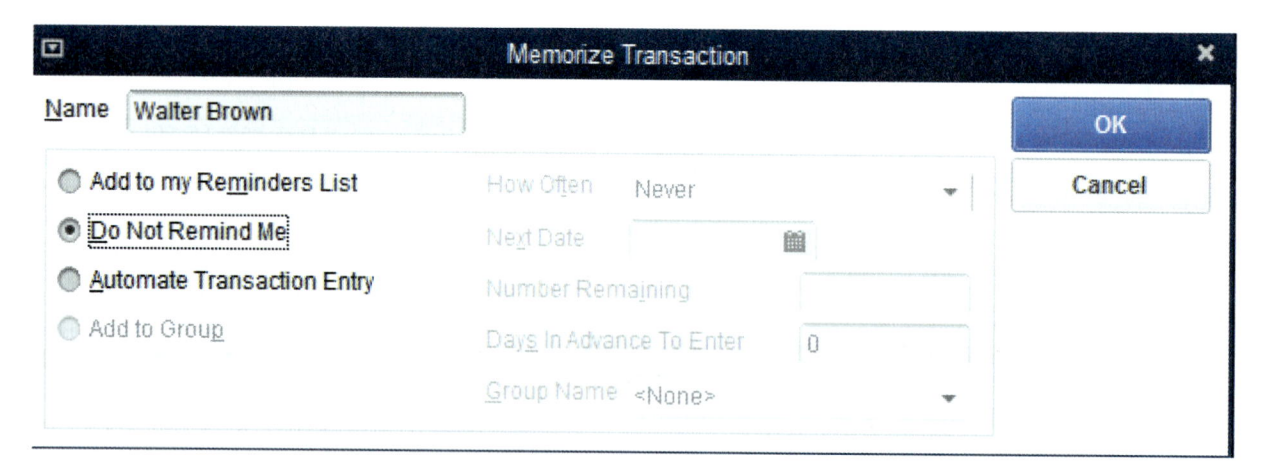

4/30 Set up and prepare monthly payroll:

From the payroll setup information you entered in March, your Employees/Manage Payroll Items/View/Edit Payroll Item List should have the following deductions and employer taxes set up. However, due to the fee, we will not be using a QuickBooks payroll service to calculate payroll withholdings and taxes; therefore, QuickBooks will *not* access these payroll items.

QuickBooks preset items, noting the Social Security wage limit is from 2014:

ITEM NAME	TYPE	AMOUNT	LIMIT	TAX TRACKING	PAYABLE TO	ACCOUNT ID
Salary	Yearly Salary			Compensation		
Hourly	Hourly Wage			Compensation		
Overtime (x1.5) hourly	Hourly Wage			Compensation		
Advance Earned Income Cre...	Federal Tax			Advance EIC Payment	United States Treasury	39-1212121
Federal Unemployment	Federal Tax	0.6%	7,000.00	FUTA	United States Treasury	39-1212121
Federal Withholding	Federal Tax			Federal	United States Treasury	39-1212121
Medicare Company	Federal Tax	1.45%		Comp. Medicare	United States Treasury	39-1212121
Medicare Employee	Federal Tax	1.45%		Medicare	United States Treasury	39-1212121
Social Security Company	Federal Tax	6.2%	117,000.00	Comp. SS Tax	United States Treasury	39-1212121
Social Security Employee	Federal Tax	6.2%	-117,000.00	SS Tax	United States Treasury	39-1212121
WI - Withholding	State Withholding Tax			SWH	Wisconsin Dept. of Revenue	036-3456789012-04
WI - Unemployment	State Unemployment Tax	4.1%	14,000.00	Comp. SUI	Division of Unemployment Insura...	876543-211-1
Medicare Employee Addl Tax	Other Tax	0.9%		Medicare Addl Tax	United States Treasury	39-1212121

- ✓ We will make each payroll item from Advanced Earned Income Credit to Medicare Employee Addl Tax *inactive* and add new deductions and company contributions, being careful not to use the exact same item name as those above.
    - ✓ Right click on each item: Make Payroll Item Inactive; your payroll items will now just show the following:

Salary	Yearly Salary			Compensation
Hourly	Hourly Wage			Compensation
Overtime (x1.5) hourly	Hourly Wage			Compensation

TO SET-UP PAYROLL:

- On the payroll screen shown on previous page, right click, create new entry, and choose Custom Set-up Method; we will create new payroll items for all deductions (employee) and company contributions (employer).

- *Add* new accounts for payables and expenses (QuickBooks records all liabilities to one account, Payroll Liabilities and all expenses to one account, Payroll Expense). See screen shots of the first deduction for Social Security:

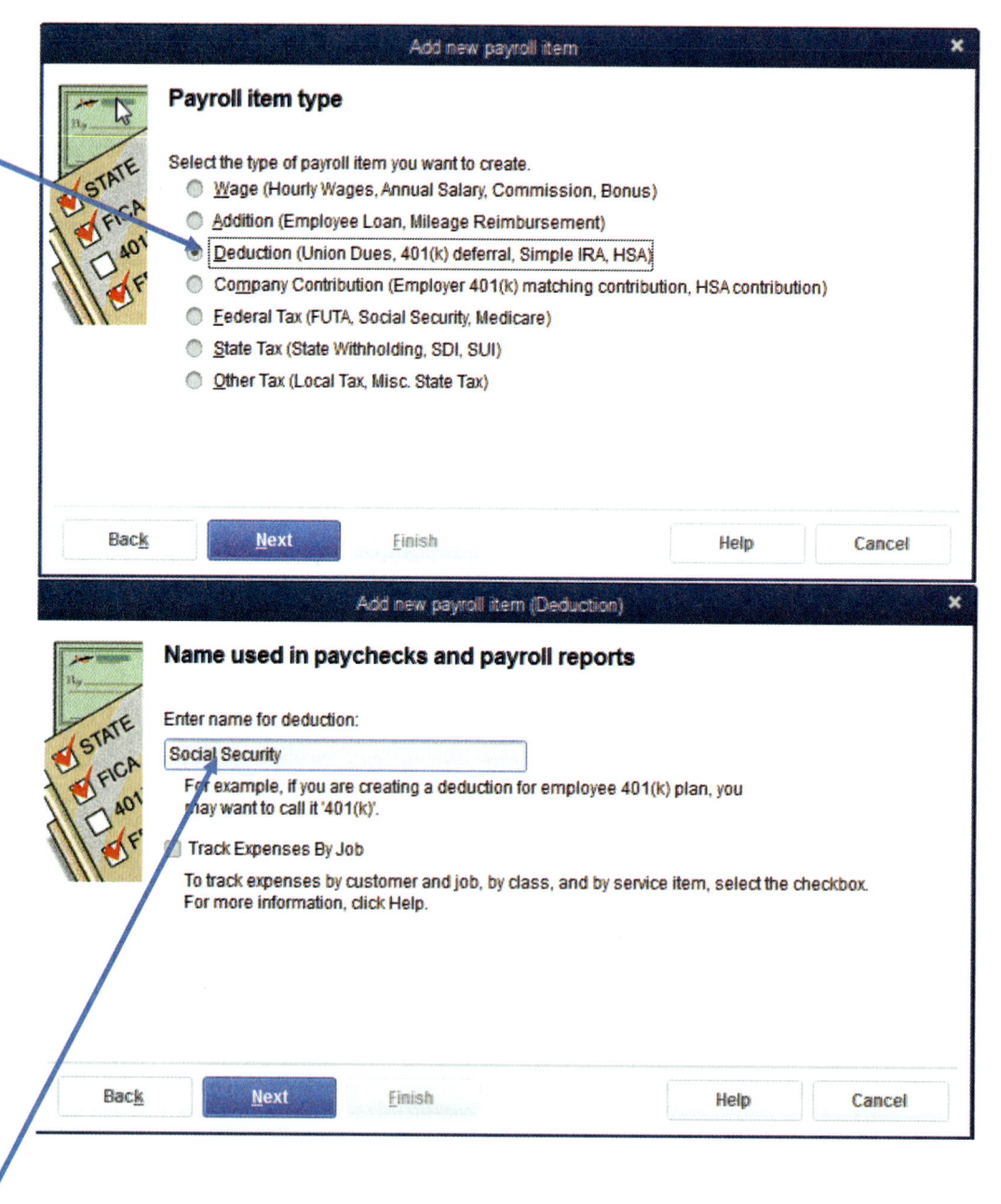

Add new payroll item

Payroll item type

Select the type of payroll item you want to create.
- ○ Wage (Hourly Wages, Annual Salary, Commission, Bonus)
- ○ Addition (Employee Loan, Mileage Reimbursement)
- ● Deduction (Union Dues, 401(k) deferral, Simple IRA, HSA)
- ○ Company Contribution (Employer 401(k) matching contribution, HSA contribution)
- ○ Federal Tax (FUTA, Social Security, Medicare)
- ○ State Tax (State Withholding, SDI, SUI)
- ○ Other Tax (Local Tax, Misc. State Tax)

Add new payroll item (Deduction)

Name used in paychecks and payroll reports

Enter name for deduction:

Social Security

For example, if you are creating a deduction for employee 401(k) plan, you may want to call it '401(k)'.

☐ Track Expenses By Job

To track expenses by customer and job, by class, and by service item, select the checkbox. For more information, click Help.

Note 1: Watch wording; it *must* be different from QuickBooks items.

Note 2: You could add "Employee" after the Social Security name to be consistent with other payroll items that will be added.

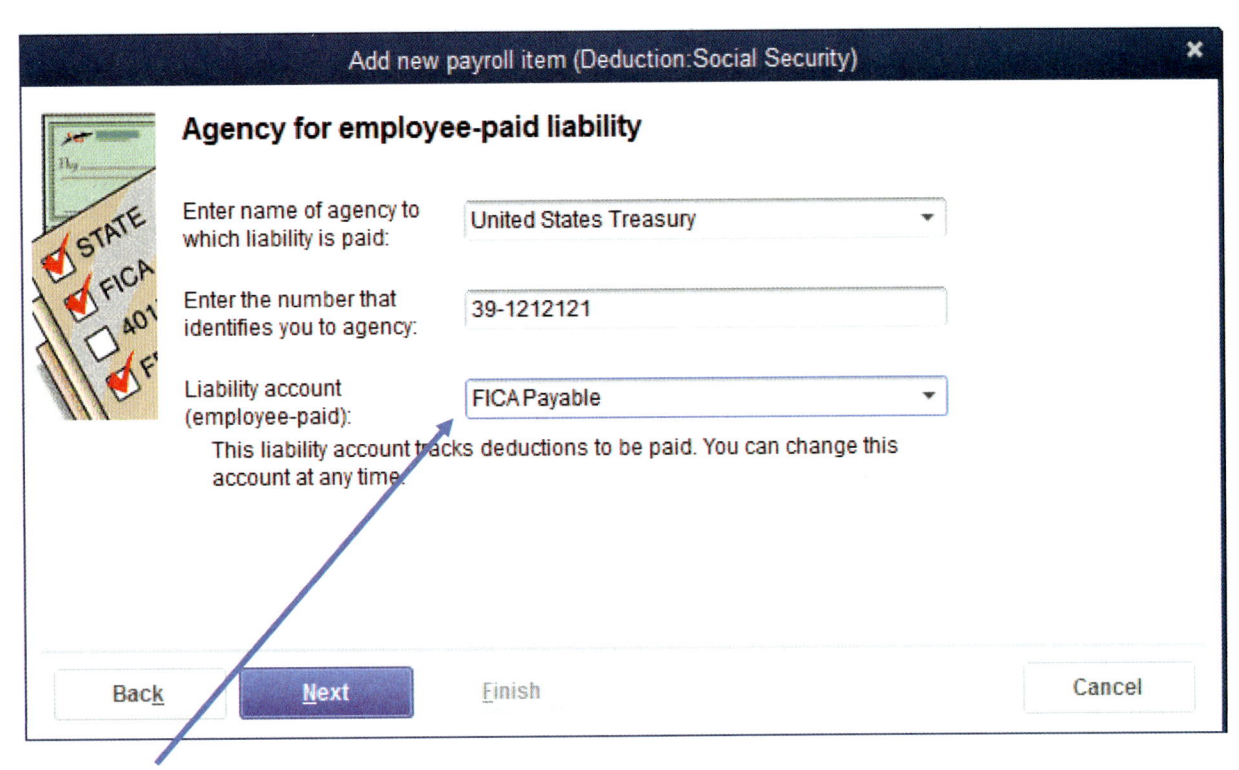

Add new payroll item (Deduction:Social Security)

Agency for employee-paid liability

Enter name of agency to which liability is paid: United States Treasury

Enter the number that identifies you to agency: 39-1212121

Liability account (employee-paid): FICA Payable

This liability account tracks deductions to be paid. You can change this account at any time.

[Back] [Next] [Finish] [Cancel]

Note: *New* account created: A liability account for the Social Security *and* Medicare portions (both employee and employer) of the 941 taxes.

- ✓ Social Security, Medicare, and FWT Withholding are reported on the quarterly form 941.

- ➢ This separates our payroll deductions and taxes into accounts as reported on their respective payroll forms versus an all-in-one liability/expense account as done by QuickBooks.

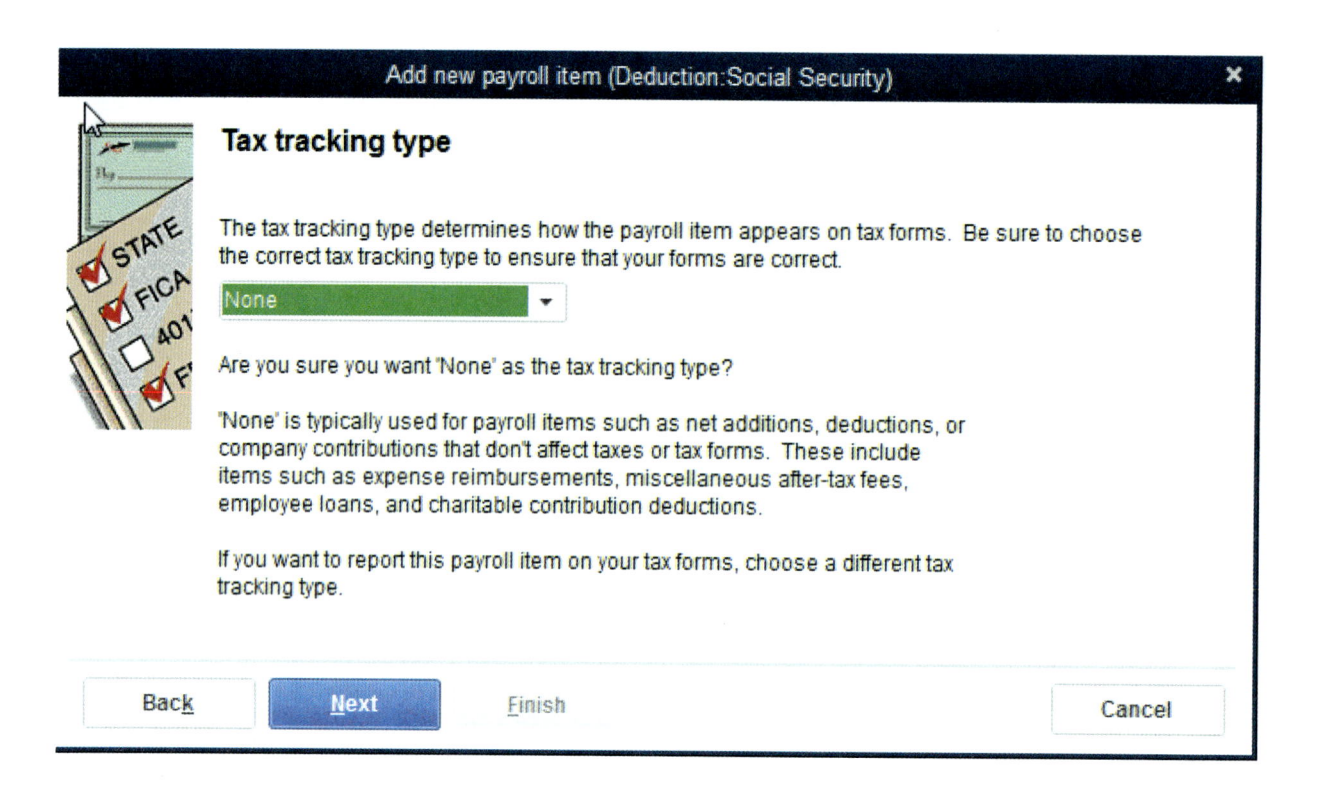

Add new payroll item (Deduction:Social Security)

Tax tracking type

The tax tracking type determines how the payroll item appears on tax forms. Be sure to choose the correct tax tracking type to ensure that your forms are correct.

[None ▼]

Are you sure you want 'None' as the tax tracking type?

'None' is typically used for payroll items such as net additions, deductions, or company contributions that don't affect taxes or tax forms. These include items such as expense reimbursements, miscellaneous after-tax fees, employee loans, and charitable contribution deductions.

If you want to report this payroll item on your tax forms, choose a different tax tracking type.

[Back] [Next] [Finish] [Cancel]

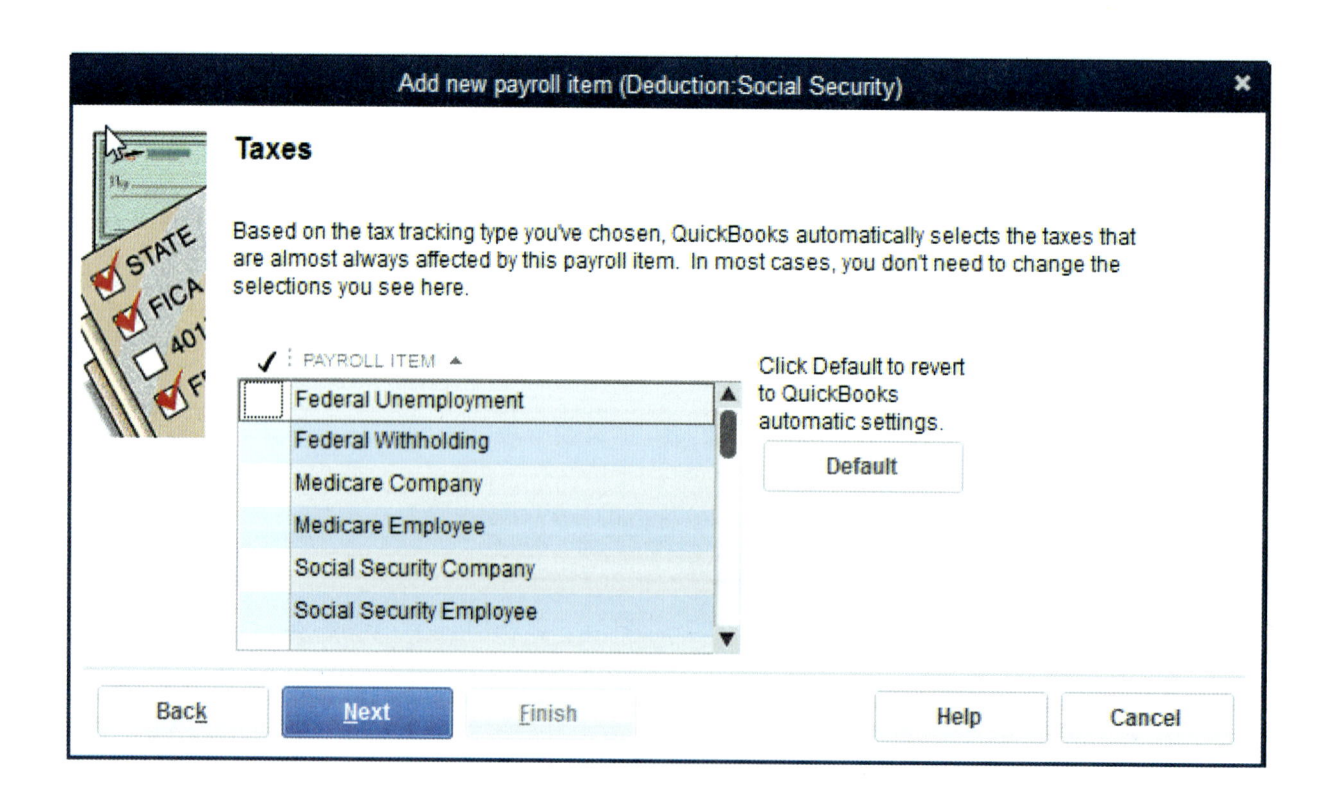

Add new payroll item (Deduction:Social Security)

Taxes

Based on the tax tracking type you've chosen, QuickBooks automatically selects the taxes that are almost always affected by this payroll item. In most cases, you don't need to change the selections you see here.

✓	PAYROLL ITEM ▲
☐	Federal Unemployment
	Federal Withholding
	Medicare Company
	Medicare Employee
	Social Security Company
	Social Security Employee

Click Default to revert to QuickBooks automatic settings.

[Default]

[Back] [Next] [Finish] [Help] [Cancel]

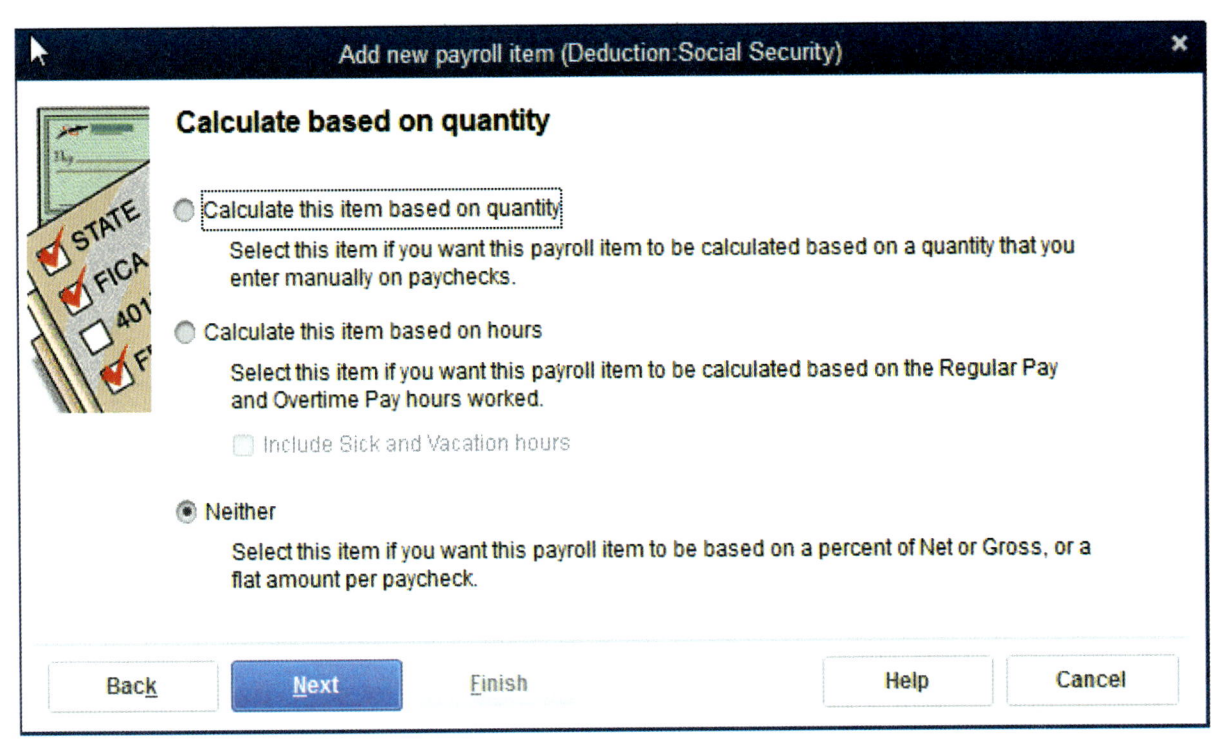

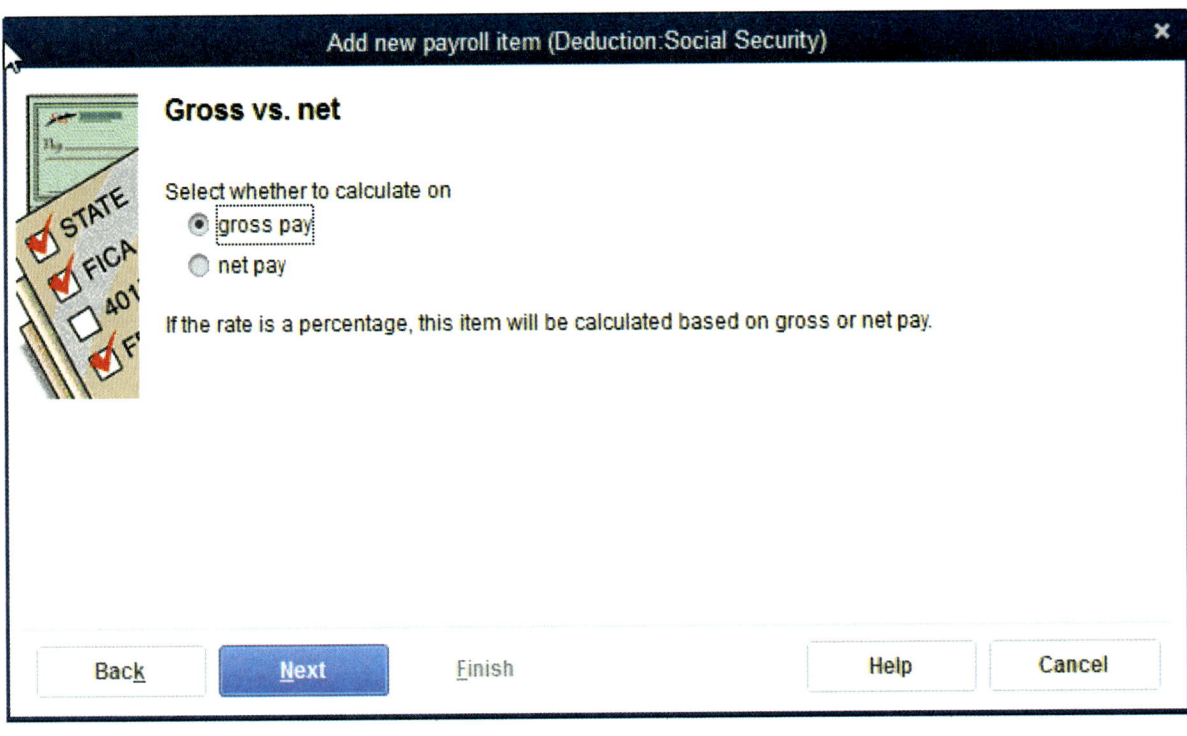

Add new payroll item (Deduction:Social Security)

Calculate based on quantity

○ **Calculate this item based on quantity**
Select this item if you want this payroll item to be calculated based on a quantity that you enter manually on paychecks.

○ **Calculate this item based on hours**
Select this item if you want this payroll item to be calculated based on the Regular Pay and Overtime Pay hours worked.

☐ Include Sick and Vacation hours

⦿ **Neither**
Select this item if you want this payroll item to be based on a percent of Net or Gross, or a flat amount per paycheck.

[Back] [Next] [Finish]   [Help] [Cancel]

Add new payroll item (Deduction:Social Security)

Gross vs. net

Select whether to calculate on
⦿ gross pay
○ net pay

If the rate is a percentage, this item will be calculated based on gross or net pay.

[Back] [Next] [Finish]   [Help] [Cancel]

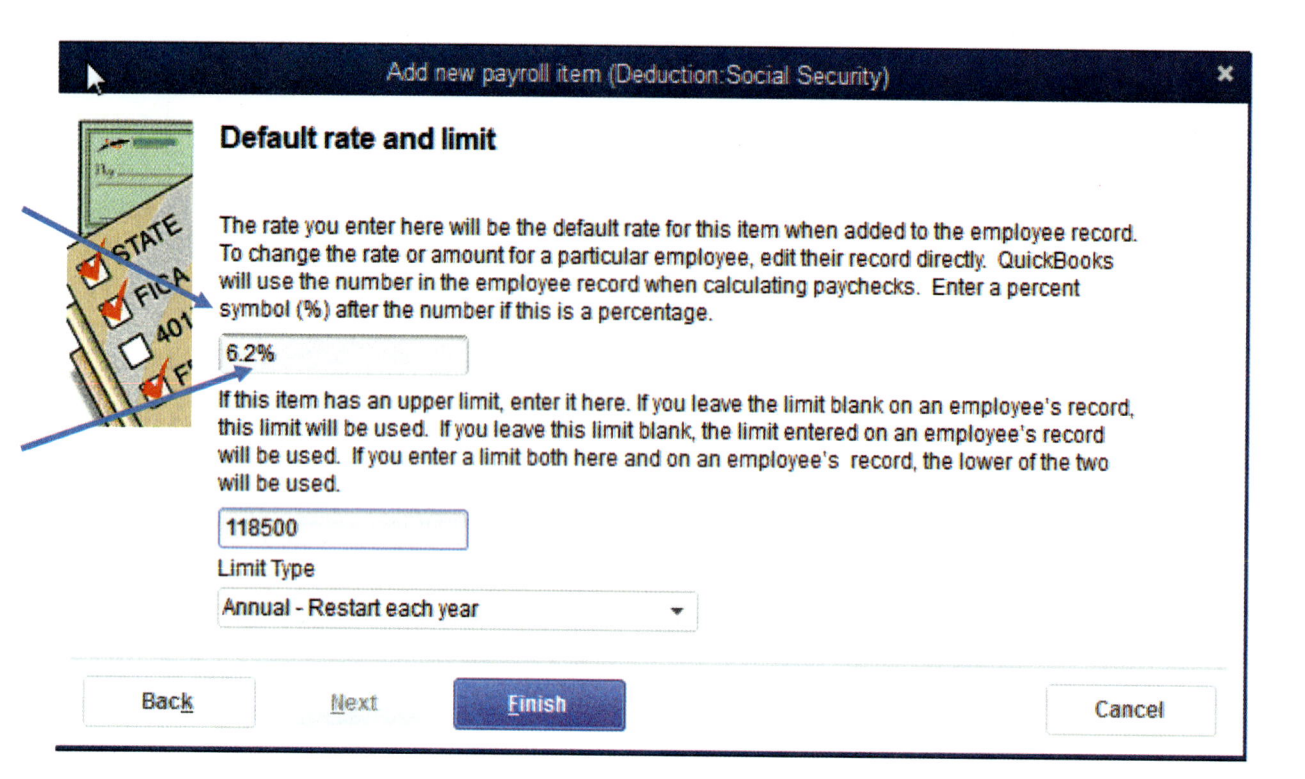

Add new payroll item (Deduction:Social Security)

Default rate and limit

The rate you enter here will be the default rate for this item when added to the employee record. To change the rate or amount for a particular employee, edit their record directly. QuickBooks will use the number in the employee record when calculating paychecks. Enter a percent symbol (%) after the number if this is a percentage.

`6.2%`

If this item has an upper limit, enter it here. If you leave the limit blank on an employee's record, this limit will be used. If you leave this limit blank, the limit entered on an employee's record will be used. If you enter a limit both here and on an employee's record, the lower of the two will be used.

`118500`

Limit Type

Annual - Restart each year

[Back] [Next] [**Finish**] [Cancel]

> Select Finish/OK to schedule payments.
> Screen shot with Social Security Deduction
>   (Note: Deduction will be shown with minus sign):

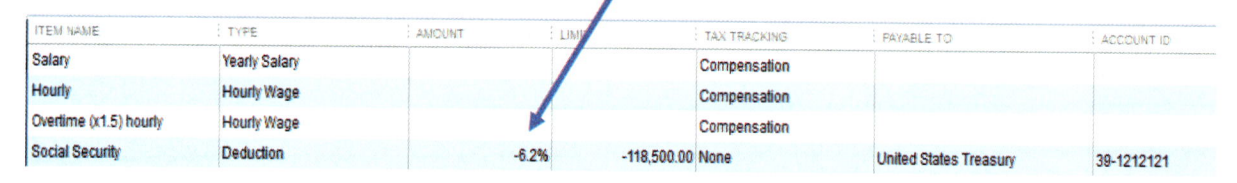

ITEM NAME	TYPE	AMOUNT	LIMIT	TAX TRACKING	PAYABLE TO	ACCOUNT ID
Salary	Yearly Salary			Compensation		
Hourly	Hourly Wage			Compensation		
Overtime (x1.5) hourly	Hourly Wage			Compensation		
Social Security	Deduction	-6.2%	-118,500.00	None	United States Treasury	39-1212121

> Follow the example of the screen shots above; continue to use Custom Set-up to add new payroll items for the following:

  ✓ **Medicare — Employee** (deduction): U.S. Treasury, 39-1212121, FICA Payable, 1.45%, no wage limit, OK to schedule payments

  ✓ **Fed. Withholding** (deduction): U.S. Treasury, 39-1212121, FIT Withholding (new account: Other current liability), no calculation, we will enter this deduction per withholding charts on the following pages, OK

  ✓ **St. Withholding** (deduction): WI Dept. of Revenue, 036-3456789012-04, SWT Payable (new account: Other current liability), 2% of gross wages, no wage limit, OK

- ✓ **Social Security — Employer** (company contribution): U.S. Treasury, 39-1212121, FICA Payable, FICA Tax Expense (new account: Expense), 6.2%, wage limit of $118,500, OK

- ✓ **Medicare — Employer** (company contribution): U.S. Treasury, 39-1212121, FICA Payable and FICA Tax Expense, 1.45%, no wage limit, OK

- ✓ **Fed. Unemployment** (company contribution): U.S. Treasury, 39-1212121, FUTA Payable (new account: Other current liability) and FUTA Tax Expense (Expense new account), .6%, wage limit of $7,000, OK

- ✓ **St. Unemployment** (company contribution): WI Dept. of Workforce Development (new vendor using new account SUTA Payable, other current liability as account setting) 876543-211-1, SUTA Payable and SUTA Tax Expense (new account: Expense), 4.1%, wage limit of $14,000, OK

The item screen after editing will appear as follows:

ITEM NAME	TYPE	AMOUNT	LIMIT	TAX TRACKING	PAYABLE TO	ACCOUNT ID
Salary	Yearly Salary			Compensation		
Hourly	Hourly Wage			Compensation		
Overtime (x1.5) hourly	Hourly Wage			Compensation		
Fed. Withholding	Deduction	0.00		None	United States Treasury	39-1212121
Medicare - Employee	Deduction	-1.45%		None	United States Treasury	39-1212121
Social Security	Deduction	-6.2%	-118,500.00	None	United States Treasury	39-1212121
St. Withholding	Deduction	-2.0%		None	WI Dept of Revenue	036-3456789012-04
Fed. Unemployment	Company Contribution	0.6%	7,000.00	None	United States Treasury	39-1212121
Medicare - Employer	Company Contribution	1.45%		None	United States Treasury	39-1212121
Social Security - Employer	Company Contribution	6.2%	118,500.00	None	United States Treasury	39-1212121
St. Unemployment	Company Contribution	4.1%	14,000.00	None	WI Dept. of Workforce Development	876543-211-1

> ➤ Edit payroll items for salary, hourly, and overtime to these expense accounts, adding new accounts as necessary:

    Salary: Office Wages

    Hourly: Field Wages

    Overtime: Field Wages

> ➤ On your chart of accounts, make the Payroll Liabilities and Payroll Expense accounts inactive.

On to the employee side:

Add these earnings, deductions, and company contributions to *each* employee by first creating an *Employee Default*; in software, defaults are like a master or template.

> Go to Employee Center/Manage Employee Information/Change New Employee Default Settings.

> Add *all* Earnings and *all* Deductions and Company Contributions; the screen shot below is unable to show all items:

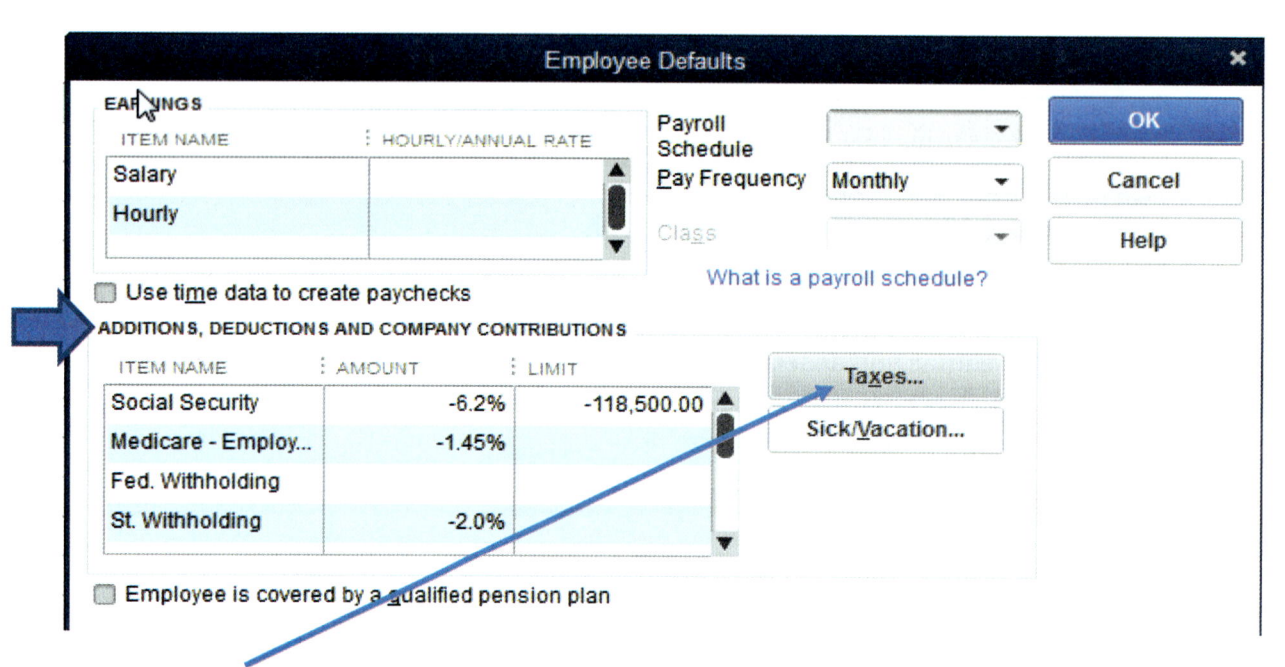

Go to Taxes to enter WI as State Worked and State Subject to Withholding.

As mentioned, we are using WI as an example for state items as we go through this project.

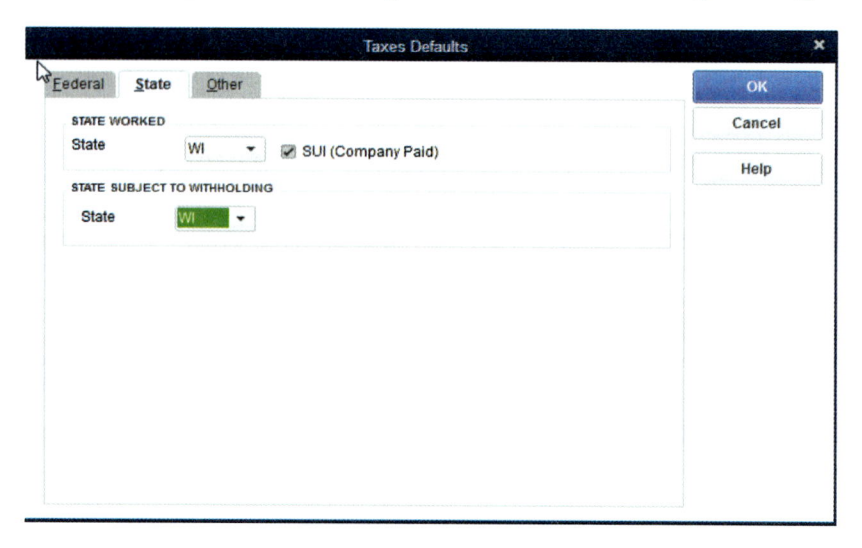

- Go to New Employees:

  [New Employee... | Manage Employee Information ▼ | Print ▼ | Enter Time ▼ | Excel ▼ | Word ▼]

- Enter two employees, Mary and Max, using the information below, no direct deposit, employees will be paid monthly, and wages subject to Social Security, Medicare, federal and state withholding as well as federal and Wisconsin unemployment.

- Mary Martin: Address: 100 Main St., Landscape, WI 53022, regular employee, Social Security #775-13-2222, as office manager at $8/hour. She will handle administrative duties and help you with the accounting functions. She is single, claiming one allowance for both federal and state withholding.

- Max Smith: Address: 200 Main St., Landscape, WI 53022, Social Security #489-78-1234, married claiming three allowances; he will provide the lawn and landscaping labor and be full-time/part-time as seasonal needs require, at $9.50/hour, time and one-half for overtime hours above 160 hours per month.

"Adjust employee" should appear as below (only Mary is shown as an example):

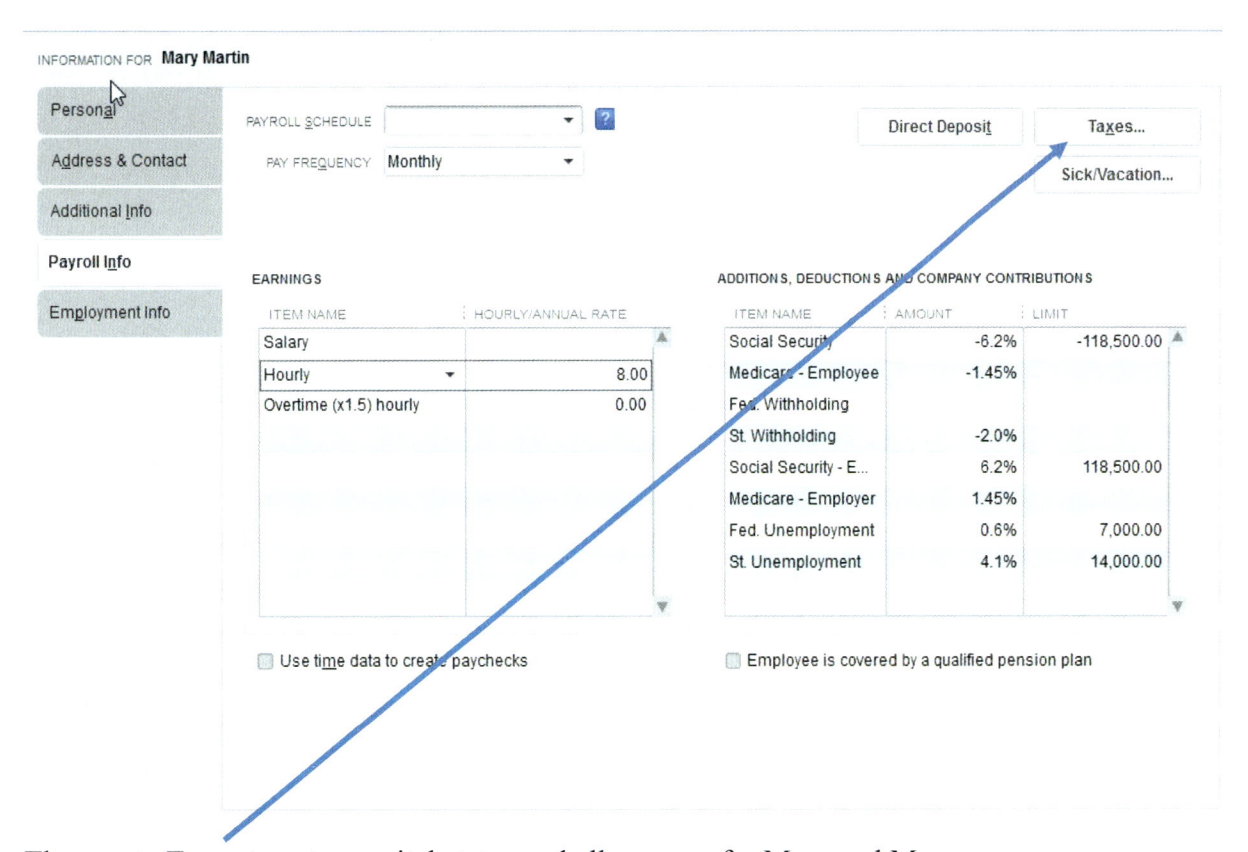

INFORMATION FOR Mary Martin

Personal | PAYROLL SCHEDULE: | Direct Deposit | Taxes...
Address & Contact | PAY FREQUENCY: Monthly | | Sick/Vacation...
Additional Info
Payroll Info
Employment Info

EARNINGS

ITEM NAME	HOURLY/ANNUAL RATE
Salary	
Hourly	8.00
Overtime (x1.5) hourly	0.00

ADDITIONS, DEDUCTIONS AND COMPANY CONTRIBUTIONS

ITEM NAME	AMOUNT	LIMIT
Social Security	-6.2%	-118,500.00
Medicare - Employee	-1.45%	
Fed. Withholding		
St. Withholding	-2.0%	
Social Security - E...	6.2%	118,500.00
Medicare - Employer	1.45%	
Fed. Unemployment	0.6%	7,000.00
St. Unemployment	4.1%	14,000.00

☐ Use time data to create paychecks   ☐ Employee is covered by a qualified pension plan

Then go to Taxes to enter marital status and allowances for Mary and Max:

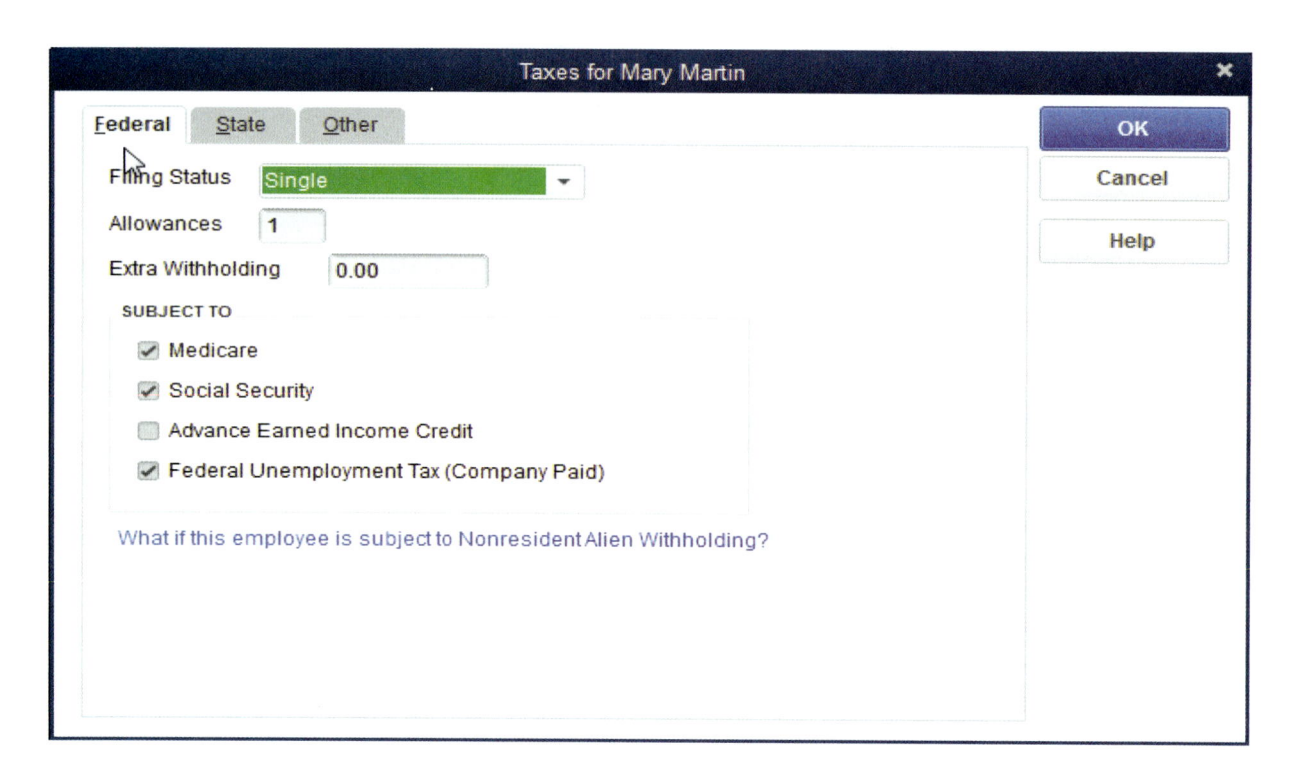

Taxes for Mary Martin (Federal tab)

- **Filing Status:** Single
- **Allowances:** 1
- **Extra Withholding:** 0.00

SUBJECT TO
- ☑ Medicare
- ☑ Social Security
- ☐ Advance Earned Income Credit
- ☑ Federal Unemployment Tax (Company Paid)

What if this employee is subject to Nonresident Alien Withholding?

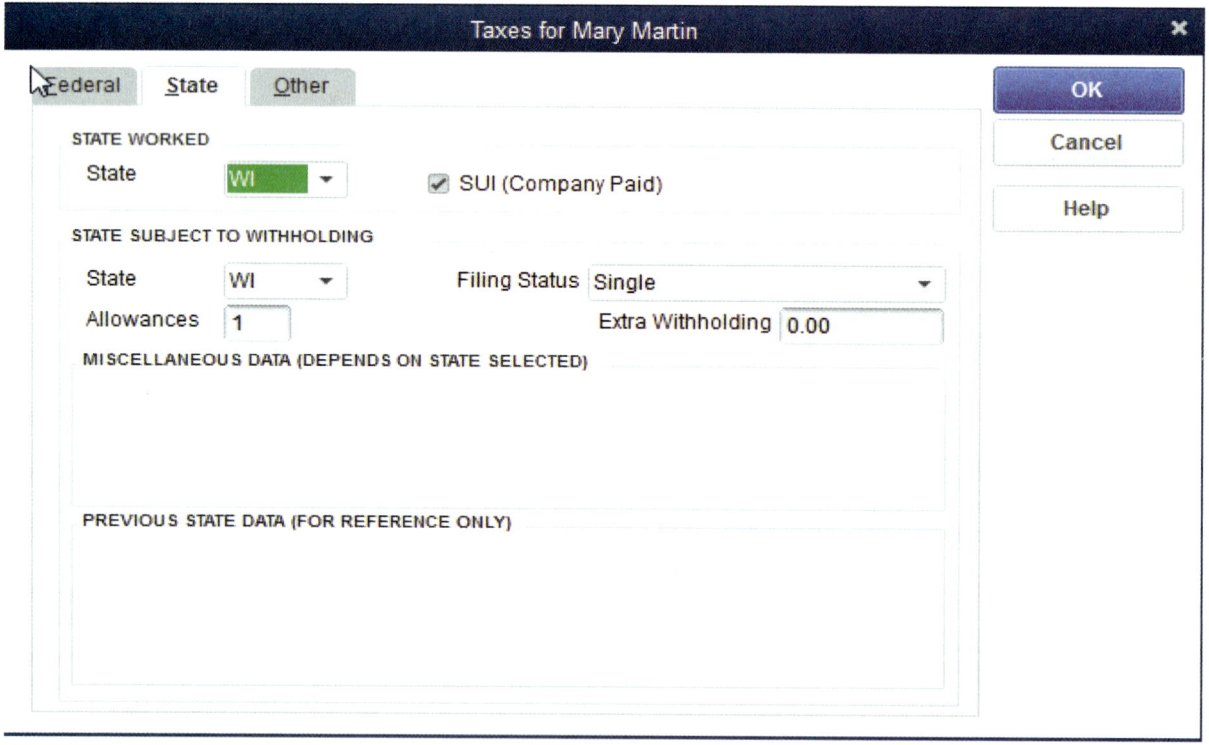

Taxes for Mary Martin (State tab)

STATE WORKED
- State: WI
- ☑ SUI (Company Paid)

STATE SUBJECT TO WITHHOLDING
- State: WI
- Allowances: 1
- Filing Status: Single
- Extra Withholding: 0.00

MISCELLANEOUS DATA (DEPENDS ON STATE SELECTED)

PREVIOUS STATE DATA (FOR REFERENCE ONLY)

✓ "Do you wish to set up payroll information for: *Other or local taxes… *Sick/vacation": *leave as is*.

➤ Review Mary's and Max's employee information, that is, check earnings rates and taxes — federal and state.

4/30   Go to the Home Screen Pay Employees icon *or* Employees pull-down menu/Pay Employees. (Note: There are many options to navigate to a task in QuickBooks; please be flexible to be able to acclimate to other accounting software.)

> Enter pay period ending and check dates. Under Check Options, check Handwrite and Assign check numbers, check Mary, open paycheck detail, and deductions and company contributions will calculate.

   ✓ Enter federal withholding with a minus sign as determined by the following withholding tables.

Mary: 42 hours (ck. #1017)   Max: 80 hours (ck. #1018)

Note: We will use the tables as shown below, regardless of the date:

SINGLE Persons—MONTHLY Payroll Period
(For Wages Paid through December 2013)

And the wages are—		And the number of withholding allowances claimed is—										
At least	But less than	0	1	2	3	4	5	6	7	8	9	10
		The amount of income tax to be withheld is—										
$ 0	$220	$0	$0	$0	$0	$0	$0	$0	$0	$0	$0	$0
220	230	4	0	0	0	0	0	0	0	0	0	0
230	240	5	0	0	0	0	0	0	0	0	0	0
240	250	6	0	0	0	0	0	0	0	0	0	0
250	260	7	0	0	0	0	0	0	0	0	0	0
260	270	8	0	0	0	0	0	0	0	0	0	0
270	280	9	0	0	0	0	0	0	0	0	0	0
280	290	10	0	0	0	0	0	0	0	0	0	0
290	300	11	0	0	0	0	0	0	0	0	0	0
300	320	13	0	0	0	0	0	0	0	0	0	0
320	340	15	0	0	0	0	0	0	0	0	0	0
340	360	17	0	0	0	0	0	0	0	0	0	0
360	380	19	0	0	0	0	0	0	0	0	0	0
380	400	21	0	0	0	0	0	0	0	0	0	0
400	420	23	0	0	0	0	0	0	0	0	0	0
420	440	25	0	0	0	0	0	0	0	0	0	0
440	460	27	0	0	0	0	0	0	0	0	0	0
460	480	29	0	0	0	0	0	0	0	0	0	0
480	500	31	0	0	0	0	0	0	0	0	0	0
500	520	33	0	0	0	0	0	0	0	0	0	0
520	540	35	2	0	0	0	0	0	0	0	0	0
540	560	37	4	0	0	0	0	0	0	0	0	0
560	580	39	6	0	0	0	0	0	0	0	0	0
580	600	41	8	0	0	0	0	0	0	0	0	0
600	640	44	11	0	0	0	0	0	0	0	0	0
640	680	48	15	0	0	0	0	0	0	0	0	0
680	720	52	19	0	0	0	0	0	0	0	0	0
720	760	56	23	0	0	0	0	0	0	0	0	0
760	800	60	27	0	0	0	0	0	0	0	0	0
800	840	64	31	0	0	0	0	0	0	0	0	0
840	880	68	35	3	0	0	0	0	0	0	0	0
880	920	72	39	7	0	0	0	0	0	0	0	0
920	960	76	43	11	0	0	0	0	0	0	0	0
960	1,000	82	47	15	0	0	0	0	0	0	0	0
1,000	1,040	88	51	19	0	0	0	0	0	0	0	0
1,040	1,080	94	55	23	0	0	0	0	0	0	0	0
1,080	1,120	100	59	27	0	0	0	0	0	0	0	0
1,120	1,160	106	63	31	0	0	0	0	0	0	0	0
1,160	1,200	112	67	35	2	0	0	0	0	0	0	0
1,200	1,240	118	71	39	6	0	0	0	0	0	0	0
1,240	1,280	124	76	43	10	0	0	0	0	0	0	0
1,280	1,320	130	82	47	14	0	0	0	0	0	0	0
1,320	1,360	136	88	51	18	0	0	0	0	0	0	0
1,360	1,400	142	94	55	22	0	0	0	0	0	0	0

MARRIED Persons—MONTHLY Payroll Period
(For Wages Paid through December 2013)

And the wages are—		And the number of withholding allowances claimed is—										
At least	But less than	0	1	2	3	4	5	6	7	8	9	10
		The amount of income tax to be withheld is—										
$0	$680	$0	$0	$0	$0	$0	$0	$0	$0	$0	$0	$0
680	720	1	0	0	0	0	0	0	0	0	0	0
720	760	5	0	0	0	0	0	0	0	0	0	0
760	800	9	0	0	0	0	0	0	0	0	0	0
800	840	13	0	0	0	0	0	0	0	0	0	0
840	880	17	0	0	0	0	0	0	0	0	0	0
880	920	21	0	0	0	0	0	0	0	0	0	0
920	960	25	0	0	0	0	0	0	0	0	0	0
960	1,000	29	0	0	0	0	0	0	0	0	0	0
1,000	1,040	33	0	0	0	0	0	0	0	0	0	0
1,040	1,080	37	4	0	0	0	0	0	0	0	0	0
1,080	1,120	41	8	0	0	0	0	0	0	0	0	0
1,120	1,160	45	12	0	0	0	0	0	0	0	0	0
1,160	1,200	49	16	0	0	0	0	0	0	0	0	0
1,200	1,240	53	20	0	0	0	0	0	0	0	0	0
1,240	1,280	57	24	0	0	0	0	0	0	0	0	0
1,280	1,320	61	28	0	0	0	0	0	0	0	0	0
1,320	1,360	65	32	0	0	0	0	0	0	0	0	0
1,360	1,400	69	36	4	0	0	0	0	0	0	0	0
1,400	1,440	73	40	8	0	0	0	0	0	0	0	0
1,440	1,480	77	44	12	0	0	0	0	0	0	0	0
1,480	1,520	81	48	16	0	0	0	0	0	0	0	0
1,520	1,560	85	52	20	0	0	0	0	0	0	0	0
1,560	1,600	89	56	24	0	0	0	0	0	0	0	0
1,600	1,640	93	60	28	0	0	0	0	0	0	0	0
1,640	1,680	97	64	32	0	0	0	0	0	0	0	0
1,680	1,720	101	68	36	3	0	0	0	0	0	0	0
1,720	1,760	105	72	40	7	0	0	0	0	0	0	0
1,760	1,800	109	76	44	11	0	0	0	0	0	0	0

➢ Compare your paycheck details for Mary and Max as shown below:

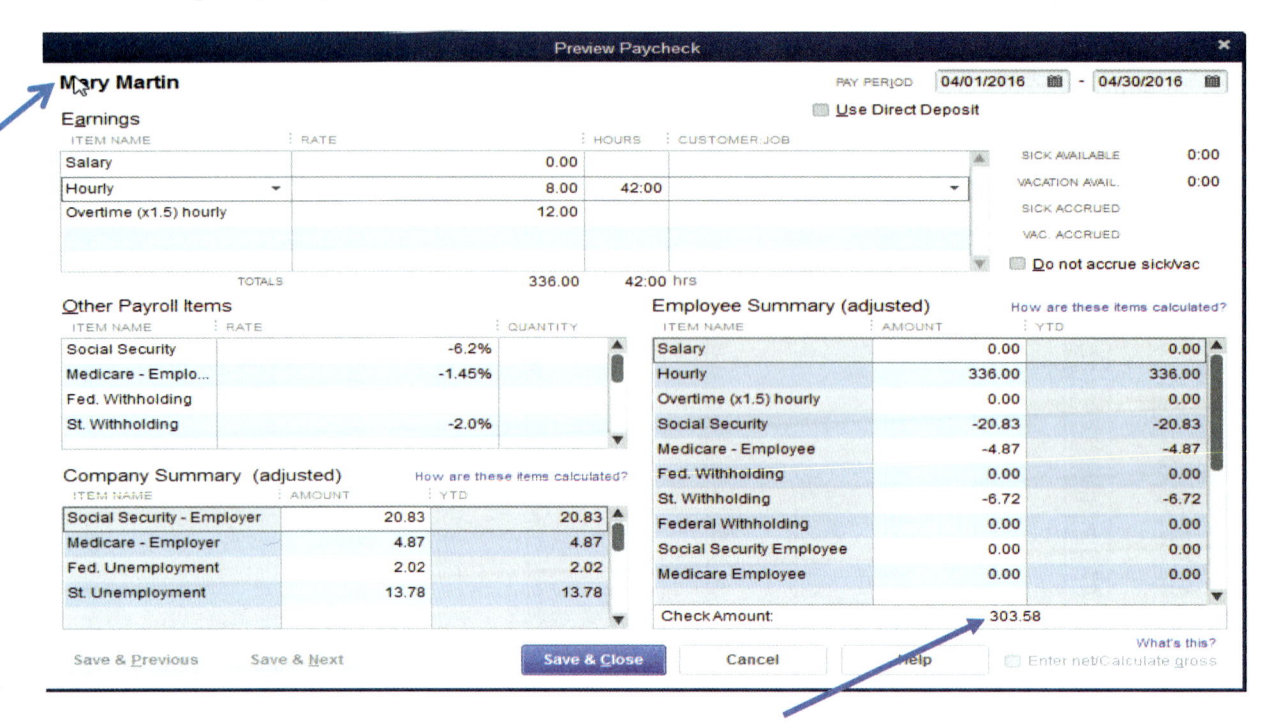

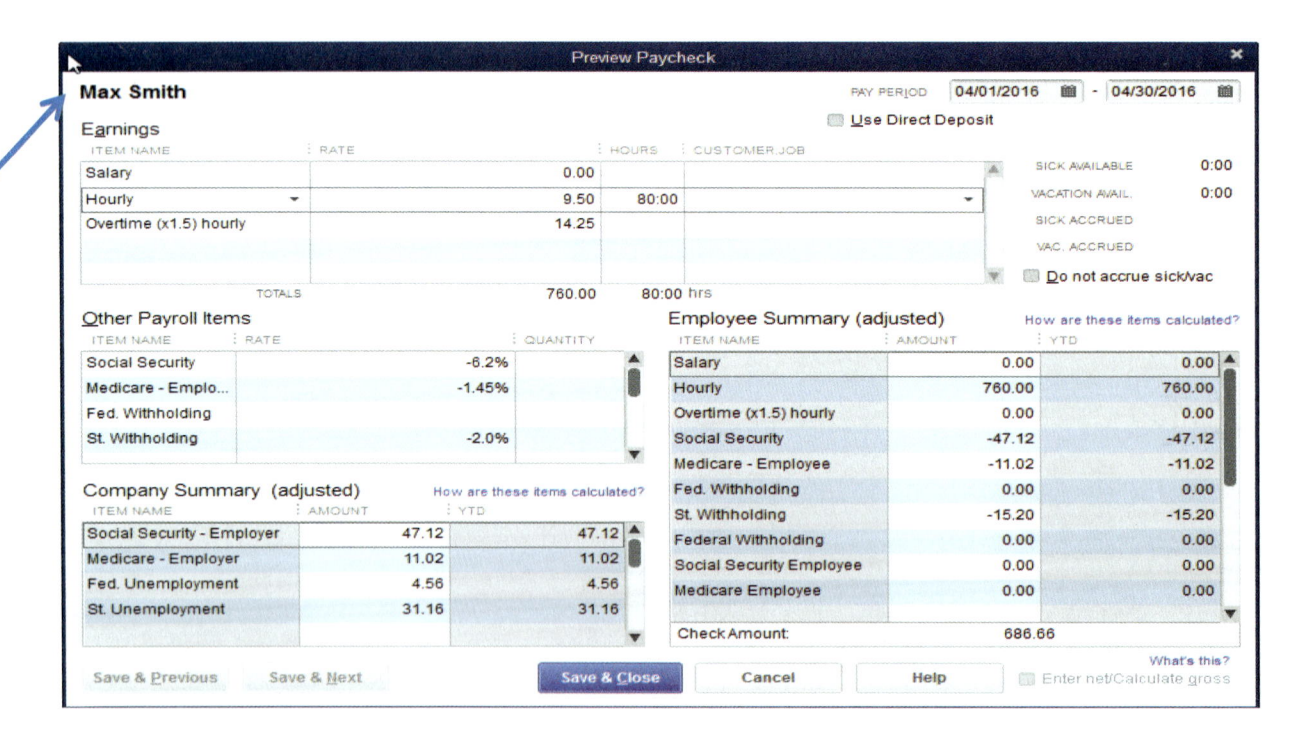

Preview Paycheck — Mary Martin

Pay Period: 04/01/2016 - 04/30/2016

Earnings

Item Name	Rate	Hours	Customer:Job
Salary	0.00		
Hourly	8.00	42:00	
Overtime (x1.5) hourly	12.00		
TOTALS	336.00	42:00 hrs	

Sick Available: 0:00
Vacation Avail.: 0:00
Sick Accrued:
Vac. Accrued:
☐ Do not accrue sick/vac

Other Payroll Items

Item Name	Rate	Quantity
Social Security	-6.2%	
Medicare - Emplo...	-1.45%	
Fed. Withholding		
St. Withholding	-2.0%	

Company Summary (adjusted)

Item Name	Amount	YTD
Social Security - Employer	20.83	20.83
Medicare - Employer	4.87	4.87
Fed. Unemployment	2.02	2.02
St. Unemployment	13.78	13.78

Employee Summary (adjusted)

Item Name	Amount	YTD
Salary	0.00	0.00
Hourly	336.00	336.00
Overtime (x1.5) hourly	0.00	0.00
Social Security	-20.83	-20.83
Medicare - Employee	-4.87	-4.87
Fed. Withholding	0.00	0.00
St. Withholding	-6.72	-6.72
Federal Withholding	0.00	0.00
Social Security Employee	0.00	0.00
Medicare Employee	0.00	0.00
Check Amount:	303.58	

Preview Paycheck — Max Smith

Pay Period: 04/01/2016 - 04/30/2016

Earnings

Item Name	Rate	Hours	Customer:Job
Salary	0.00		
Hourly	9.50	80:00	
Overtime (x1.5) hourly	14.25		
TOTALS	760.00	80:00 hrs	

Sick Available: 0:00
Vacation Avail.: 0:00
Sick Accrued:
Vac. Accrued:
☐ Do not accrue sick/vac

Other Payroll Items

Item Name	Rate	Quantity
Social Security	-6.2%	
Medicare - Emplo...	-1.45%	
Fed. Withholding		
St. Withholding	-2.0%	

Company Summary (adjusted)

Item Name	Amount	YTD
Social Security - Employer	47.12	47.12
Medicare - Employer	11.02	11.02
Fed. Unemployment	4.56	4.56
St. Unemployment	31.16	31.16

Employee Summary (adjusted)

Item Name	Amount	YTD
Salary	0.00	0.00
Hourly	760.00	760.00
Overtime (x1.5) hourly	0.00	0.00
Social Security	-47.12	-47.12
Medicare - Employee	-11.02	-11.02
Fed. Withholding	0.00	0.00
St. Withholding	-15.20	-15.20
Federal Withholding	0.00	0.00
Social Security Employee	0.00	0.00
Medicare Employee	0.00	0.00
Check Amount:	686.66	

Note: For this payroll, both Mary and Max did *not* have any federal withholding; you will have to check the withholding tables *each* payroll.

> Print/PDF pay stubs to submit at month-end. (Also found under File/Print Forms/Pay stubs)

> Create an Excel worksheet to track year-to-date gross wages for Mary and Max for FUTA ($7,000) and SUTA ($14,000) wage limits; QuickBooks should track these limits, but it is always a good idea to double-check!

YTD Gross Pay for Wage Limits: FUTA & SUTA

	Mary	Max	Mary YTD	Max YTD
Apr. 30	336	760	336	760

4/30 Month-end tasks:

> Dave reviews Unpaid Bills Detail report and approves payment for invoices *due*, check #1019. Watch the discount period.

> Prepare *1st quarter* Wisconsin sales tax return (ST-12) and pay tax due.

✓ In preparing the ST-12 or later the payroll forms, the reconciliation process will compare the
   o QuickBooks report(s) to the
   o Profit and Loss Statement and/or trial balance to the
   o ST-12, sales tax return (form to file)

Note: You will include this complete reconciliation in April's monthly questions.

✓ Print/snip the Sales Tax Revenue Summary report for 1st quarter found under the Manage Sales Tax icon:

DM Yard Services - 2016
Sales Tax Revenue Summary
January through March 2016

	Taxable Sales	Non-Taxable Sales	TOTAL
▼ WI Dept of Revenue			
Wisconsin sales tax ▶	762.00 ◀	1,480.00	2,242.00
Total WI Dept of Reve…	762.00	1,480.00	2,242.00
TOTAL	762.00	1,480.00	2,242.00

Note: The non-taxable sales are to Forest Hill School.

- **Agrees** with January – March 2016 Profit and Loss:

DM Yard Services - 2016
Profit & Loss
January through March 2016

	Jan - Mar 16
▼ Income	
Landscaping Services ▶	770.00 ◀
Mulch Sales	1,472.00
Total Income	2,242.00

- **Agrees** with Line 1 of the ST-12 on the following page:

✓ Print/snip 1st quarter Sales Tax Liability report.

DM Yard Services - 2016
Sales Tax Liability
January through March 2016

	Total Sales	Non-Taxable Sales	Taxable Sales	Tax Rate	Tax Collected	Sales Tax Payable As of Mar 31, 16
▼ WI Dept of Revenue						
Wisconsin sales tax	2,242.00	1,480.00	762.00	5.0%	38.10	38.10
Total WI Dept of Reve...	2,242.00	1,480.00	762.00		38.10	38.10
TOTAL	2,242.00	1,480.00	762.00		38.10	38.10

o **Agrees** with March 31, 2016, Trial Balance: Sales Tax Payable:

DM Yard Services - 2016
Trial Balance
As of March 31, 2016

	Mar 31, 16 Debit	Credit
Leasehold Improvements	850.00	
Office Equipment	787.50	
Truck	18,200.00	
Security Deposit	1,000.00	
Accounts Payable		4,700.00
Credit Card Payable		270.00
Sales Tax Payable		38.10

o *Agrees* with ST-12, line 8 on the next page: 38.10.

Note: The objective is to reconcile the a) QuickBooks sales tax reports to b) their respective account balances (per profit and loss, trial balance, etc.) to c) the filed form, the Wisconsin ST-12.

> ➢ Print/PDF complete Wisconsin Sales and Use Tax Return, ST-12 (source: Wisconsin Department of Revenue website). The discount given on line 19 represents a small remuneration for collecting and remitting the sales tax and should be credited to a miscellaneous income account.
>
> ➢ Pay the amount due; follow the screen shots below carefully! Check #1020.

Form ST-12

Wisconsin Department of Revenue

Wisconsin Sales and Use Tax Return
State, County and Stadium Sales and Use Tax
Tab to navigate throughout form.

Please enter 15-digit number (no dashes)
Tax Account Number: 7890785
FEIN / SSN: 391212121

Period Begin Date (MM DD YYYY): 01 01 2016
Period End Date (MM DD YYYY): 03 31 2016
Due Date (MM DD YYYY): 04 30 2016

Use BLACK INK Only

Attention:
Business Name: DM YARD SERVICES
Legal Name:
Mailing Address - Street or PO Box: 900 MAIN ST.
City: LANDSCAPE
State: WI
Zip Code: 53022

____ Check if business discontinued (enter discontinuation date below)
_____ (MM DD YYYY)
____ Check if address or name change (note changes at left)
____ Check if this is an amended return
____ Check if correspondence is included

Step A — Sales Tax – State

1	Total sales 1	2242.00
	Subtractions from total sales:	
2	Sales for which you received exemption certificates 2	1480.00
3	Sales of exempt property and services (sales that occurred outside Wisconsin, real property, groceries and highway fuel, etc.) 3	
4	Sales returns, allowances, and bad debts 4	
5	Other (sales tax included in line 1, etc.) 5	
6	Total subtractions (add lines 2 through 5) 6	1480.00
7	Sales subject to state sales tax (subtract line 6 from line 1) 7	762.00
8	State sales tax (line 7 x .05) 8	38.10

Step D — Discount and Net Sales Tax

18	Total sales tax (fill in amount from line 17) 18	38.10
19	Discount – Applies only if return is filed and tax is paid by due date { If line 18 is $0 to $10, enter the amount from line 18. If line 18 is $10 to $2,000, enter $10. If line 18 is greater than $2,000, multiply line 18 by .005 and enter the result. } 19	10.00
20	Net sales tax (subtract line 19 from line 18) 20	28.10

Pay Sales Tax

Pay From Account	Check Date	Show sales tax due through	Starting Check No.
DM Yard Services Chec...	04/30/2016	03/31/2016	1020

P...	ITEM	VENDOR	AMT. DUE	AMT. PAID
	Wisconsin sales t...	WI Dept of Revenue	38.10	0.00
		Totals	38.10	0.00

Pay All Tax   Adjust   Ending Bank Balance   14,585.16

☐ To be printed   OK   Cancel   Help

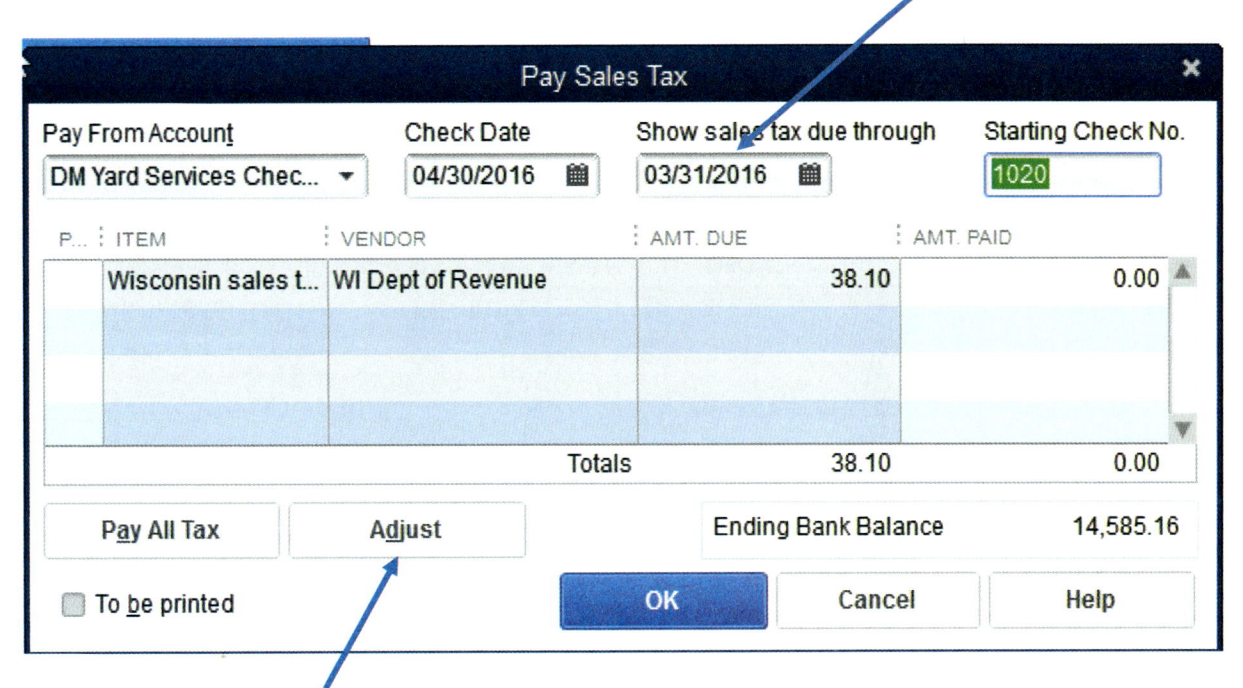

> To account for the $10 discount on line 19 shown on the previous page, click Adjust.

Sales Tax Adjustment

Adjustment Date: 04/30/2016
Entry No.: 4
Sales Tax Vendor: WI Dept of Revenue
Adjustment Account: Miscellaneous Income

ADJUSTMENT
○ Increase Sales Tax By
● Reduce Sales Tax By   Amount 10.00

Memo: Sales Tax Adjustment

OK   Cancel   Help

Select New account

Note: Reduce

Click OK to adjust vendor.

Click **Pay All Tax here**, then click OK.

Pay Sales Tax

Pay From Account	Check Date	Show sales tax due through	Starting Check No.
DM Yard Services Chec... ▼	04/30/2016	03/31/2016	1020

P...	ITEM	VENDOR	AMT. DUE	AMT. PAID
	Wisconsin sales t...	WI Dept of Revenue	38.10	0.00
		WI Dept of Revenue	-10.00	0.00
		Totals	28.10	0.00

Pay All Tax | Adjust | Ending Bank Balance 14,585.16

☐ To be printed | OK | Cancel | Help

Month-end tasks continued:

➢ Prepare monthly draw of $1000, check #1021.

➢ Reconcile cash account for April. Verify ending cash balance equals cash balance on trial balance.

➢ Export trial balance to Excel or PDF and compare to the trial balance below; see the reconciliation process after trial balance and make corrections as needed.

➢ Note: The bank reconciliations and trial balances were included through this first month with payroll. Future reports will not be posted in each month's materials.

DM Yard Services - 2016
Reconciliation Detail
DM Yard Services Checking, Period Ending 04/30/2016

Type	Date	Num	Name	Clr	Amount	Balance
Beginning Balance						18,507.56
Cleared Transactions						
Checks and Payments - 10 items						
Check	02/25/2016	1003	Office City	X	-387.45	-387.45
Bill Pmt -Check	03/15/2016	1009	Tom George	X	-850.00	-1,237.45
Check	03/31/2016	1010	D. Michaels	X	-500.00	-1,737.45
Check	04/01/2016	1011	John Smith	X	-750.00	-2,487.45
Check	04/07/2016	1012	American Insurance	X	-1,410.00	-3,897.45
Check	04/15/2016	1015	IRS	X	-500.00	-4,397.45
Check	04/15/2016	1014	Credit Card Services	X	-342.80	-4,740.25
Check	04/15/2016	1016	WI Dept of Revenue	X	-150.00	-4,890.25
Bill Pmt -Check	04/15/2016	1013	JS Garden Supply	X	-126.91	-5,017.16
Check	04/30/2016			X	-15.00	-5,032.16
Total Checks and Payments					-5,032.16	-5,032.16
Deposits and Credits - 1 item						
Deposit	04/03/2016			X	2,234.50	2,234.50
Total Deposits and Credits					2,234.50	2,234.50
Total Cleared Transactions					-2,797.66	-2,797.66
Cleared Balance					-2,797.66	15,709.90
Uncleared Transactions						
Checks and Payments - 5 items						
Check	04/30/2016	1021	D. Michaels		-1,000.00	-1,000.00
Paycheck	04/30/2016	1018	Max Smith		-686.66	-1,686.66
Paycheck	04/30/2016	1017	Mary Martin		-303.58	-1,990.24
Bill Pmt -Check	04/30/2016	1019	JS Garden Supply		-149.50	-2,139.74
Sales Tax Payment	04/30/2016	1020	WI Dept of Revenue		-28.10	-2,167.84
Total Checks and Payments					-2,167.84	-2,167.84
Total Uncleared Transactions					-2,167.84	-2,167.84
Register Balance as of 04/30/2016					-4,965.50	13,542.06
Ending Balance					-4,965.50	13,542.06

> Review, compare, and reconcile the April trial balance below, particularly noting new payroll accounts:

10:28 AM
01/16/17
Accrual Basis

DM Yard Services - 2016
Trial Balance
As of April 30, 2016

	Apr 30, 16 Debit	Credit
DM Yard Services Checking	13,542.06	
Petty Cash	200.00	
Accounts Receivable	2,288.55	
Inventory Asset	5,030.94	
Prepaid Insurance	1,175.00	
Undeposited Funds	0.00	
Lawn and Landscaping Equipment	4,500.00	
Leasehold Improvements	850.00	
Office Equipment	787.50	
Truck	18,200.00	
Security Deposit	1,000.00	
Accounts Payable		4,700.00
Credit Card Payable		66.87
FICA Payable		167.68
FIT Withholding	0.00	
FUTA Payable		6.58
Payroll Liabilities	0.00	
Sales Tax Payable		95.55
SUTA Payable		44.94
SWT Payable		21.92
D. Michaels, Capital		48,200.00
D. Michaels, Draw	3,340.81	
Fertilizing Income		324.00
Landscaping Services		1,295.00
Lawn Cutting and Trimming		980.00
Mulch Sales		1,702.00
Sales Discounts	45.60	
Seeding Income		134.00
Fertilizing Costs	269.10	
Mulch Costs	1,424.50	
Purchase Discounts		133.79
Seeding Costs	114.26	
Auto and Truck Expenses	195.00	
Bank Service Charges	60.00	
FICA Tax Expense	83.84	
Field Wages	1,096.00	
FUTA Tax Expense	6.58	
Insurance Expense	235.00	
Office Supplies	709.47	
Office Wages	0.00	
Payroll Expenses	0.00	
Rent Expense	1,500.00	
Small Tools and Equipment	923.18	
SUTA Tax Expense	44.94	
Telephone Expense	110.00	
Utilities	150.00	
Miscellaneous Income		10.00
TOTAL	**57,882.33**	**57,882.33**

Note: See the reconciliation process on next page if your trial balance does not agree with that shown above.

> Reconciliation process:
> - Export your trial balance into Excel.
> - Enter the trial balance on the previous page (shown below as Posted Trial Bal.).
> - Calculate account differences where necessary.
> - Compare specific accounts to the general ledger.

STUDENT Yard Services

Trial Balance

As of April 30, 2016

	Apr 30, 16 Debit	Credit	POSTED TRIAL BAL. Debit	Credit	Difference
DM Yard Services Checking	13,542.06		13,542.06		
Petty Cash	200.00		200.00		
Accounts Receivable	2,068.05		2,288.55		−220.5
Inventory Asset	5,030.94		5,030.94		
Prepaid Insurance	1,175.00		1,175.00		
Undeposited Funds	0.00		0.00		
Lawn and Landscaping Equipment	4,500.00		4,500.00		
Leasehold Improvements	850.00		850.00		
Office Equipment	787.50		787.50		
Truck	18,200.00		18,200.00		
Security Deposit	1,000.00		1,000.00		
Accounts Payable		4,700.00		4,700.00	
Credit Card Payable		66.87		66.87	
FICA Payable		167.68		167.68	
FIT Withholding	0.00			0.00	
FUTA Payable		6.58		2.02	
Payroll Liabilities	0.00				
Sales Tax Payable		85.05		95.55	−10.50
SUTA Payable		44.94		44.94	
SWT Payable		21.92		21.92	
D. Michaels, Capital		48,200.00		48,200.00	
D. Michaels, Draw	3,340.81		3,340.81		
Fertilizing Income		324.00		324.00	
Landscaping Services		1,295.00		1,295.00	
Lawn Cutting and Trimming		770.00		980.00	−210.00
Mulch Sales		1,702.00		1,702.00	
Sales Discounts	45.60		45.60		
Seeding Income		134.00		134.00	
Fertilizing Costs	269.10		269.10		
Mulch Costs	1,424.50		1,424.50		
Purchase Discounts		133.79		133.79	

Seeding Costs	114.26	114.26	
Auto and Truck Expenses	195.00	195.00	
Bank Service Charges	60.00	60.00	
FICA Tax Expense	83.84	83.84	
Field Wages	1,096.00	1,096.00	
FUTA Tax Expense	6.58	2.02	
Insurance Expense	235.00	235.00	
Office Supplies Expense	709.47	709.47	
Office Wages	0.00	0.00	
Payroll Expenses	0.00	0.00	
Rent Expense	1,500.00	1,500.00	
Small Tools and Equipment	923.18	923.18	
SUTA Tax Expense	44.94	44.94	
Telephone Expense	110.00	110.00	
Utilities	150.00	150.00	
Miscellaneous Income		10.00	10.00
TOTAL	57,661.83	57,661.83	57,877.77	57,877.77

Below find snip of accounts receivable from the Student General Ledger.

STUDENT Yard Services
General Ledger
As of April 30, 2016

Accrual Basis

Type	Date	Num	Name	Debit	Credit	Balance
Accounts Receivable						0.00
Invoice	03/12/2016	1	Davidson Foods	800.10		800.10
Invoice	03/22/2016	2	Forest Hill School	1,480.00		2,280.10
Invoice	04/02/2016	3	Walter Brown	315.00		2,595.10
Payment	04/03/2016		Forest Hill School		1,480.00	1,115.10
Payment	04/03/2016		Davidson Foods		800.10	315.00
Invoice	04/10/2016	4	Walter Brown	55.65		370.65
Invoice	04/10/2016	5	Joe Calhoun	55.65		426.30
Invoice	04/10/2016	6	Forest Hill School	142.00		568.30
Invoice	04/10/2016	7	Jacksonville Industrial Park	149.10		717.40
Invoice	04/21/2016	8	Larry Laxson	55.65		773.05
Invoice	04/21/2016	9	Paul Garrett	55.65		828.70
Invoice	04/21/2016	10	Nottingham Condominium Complex	437.85		1,266.55
Invoice	04/21/2016	12	Joe Calhoun	110.25		1,376.80
Invoice	04/26/2016	13	Forest Hill School	140.00		1,516.80
Invoice	04/26/2016	15	Larry Laxson	73.50		1,590.30
Invoice	04/26/2016	16	Paul Garrett	110.25		1,700.55
Invoice	04/26/2016	17	Nottingham Condominium Complex	294.00		1,994.55
Invoice	04/26/2016	11	Walter Brown	73.50		2,068.05
Total Accounts Receivable						2,068.05

Note: There is an invoice to Jacksonville on 4/10 but not on 4/26; this *could* be a possible reason for the difference. Review the April invoices.

Credit Card Services, Inc.

DM Yard Services

Statement Date: 4/5/2016

Last Payment: 3/15/2016 $712.51

Amount Due: $342.80

Due Date: 4/15/2016

Charge Summary:

- Deli Stop   12.80
- Gas to Go   52.00
- Cell World   60.00
- Gas to Go   68.00
- Utility Service Corp.   150.00

XYZ Bank

DM Yard Services

Acct. #745-1332   4/1/2016 thru 4/30/2016

Beg. Balance: $1,8507.56

Deposits & CM

4/3 $2,234.50

Checks & DM

#1003	$387.45
#1009	850.00
#1010	500.00
#1011	750.00
#1012	1,410.00
#1013	126.91
#1014	342.80
#1015	500.00
#1016	150.00
4/30 SC	15.00

Ending Balance: $1,5709.90

Receipt: 4/3/2016

ABC Food Store   7.86

This receipt is to support the petty cash disbursement; it should be filed with your petty cash sheet.

April Questions

1. Explain the difference between customer *invoices* and *statements*.

2. As shown in the April transactions, reconcile the QuickBooks sales tax reports (Sales Tax Revenue Summary and Sales Tax Liability) to their respective account balances per the Profit and Loss and trial balance to the Wisconsin ST-12. Use snips of reports.

3. Review financial statements and the Profit & Loss Standard for January through April and Balance Sheet Standard as of 4/30/2016. List three items to edit at year-end when the financial statements are exported into Excel. For example, placement of Sales Discounts in the Income section to calculate Net Sales.

4. Complete a) the Monthly Task List and b) your To Do/Follow-up Question List with at least two items to be addressed by your "manager"/teacher. These may be questions or comments about good or not-so-good business management and internal controls.

CHAPTER PRINT/SUBMISSION SUMMARY

Reminder: Use option to submit reports as a PDF file.

1. _____ Petty Cash Sheet, Excel or Word document (showing activity)

2. _____ 1040-ES and 1-ES

3. _____ Paycheck stubs and Excel file for wage limits

4. _____ Sales Tax Liability and Sales Tax Revenue Summary Reports from QuickBooks & Sales Tax Return: ST-12 (if did not include all snips in question 2 above)

5. _____ Bank Account Reconciliation

6. _____ Trial Balance

7. _____ Profit & Loss Standard for question 3

8. _____ Balance Sheet Standard for question 3

9. _____ Questions 1 – 3

10. _____ Task List/To Do/Question List

APRIL TASK LIST

Check here if completed	Task	Initials
	Review of Unpaid Bills Detail Report	
	Create Excel file for year-to-date payroll amounts	
	Review of Profit and Loss and Balance Sheet	
	Verify cash balance on trial balance equals cash balance on bank reconciliation	
	Review trial balance for completeness and accuracy	
	Back up your monthly transactions to an external destination (e.g., flash drive), changing file name to the month	

To Do/Follow-up/Question List

May Transactions/Activities

Note: As we continue, transactions will not include detailed instructions on how to record the transaction; you are to refer to prior months' transactions or use QuickBooks Help.

Below find a summary of monthly information and tasks to be completed on their respective dates from May through December. These are *not* included in the monthly transactions!

- ✓ Each time you start QuickBooks the prompt to Enter Memorized Transactions will come up; we will only select the one month's insurance adjustment.
- ✓ Pay rent on the 1st of each month, using the memorized transaction set up in April.
- ✓ Review and record the credit card statement on the 5th of each month, payable on the 15th.
- ✓ Dave reviews A/P Aging Detail and approves invoices due for payment on the 15th of each month.

AT MONTH-END:
- ✓ Prepare and calculate monthly payroll as per hours given.
- ✓ Update Excel worksheet for each payroll.
- ✓ Dave reviews A/P Aging Detail or Unpaid Bills Detail and approves invoices due for payment on the 30th/31st of each month.
- ✓ Prepare monthly draw of $1,000, unless otherwise noted.
- ✓ Reconcile cash account.
- ✓ Review trial balance, verifying that the cash balance per trial balance equals the ending balance on the bank reconciliation.

5/2　Returned 2 boxwood bushes to JS Garden Supply for credit on account, credit memo #501.
(If necessary, use QuickBooks Help/"where to record vendor credit.") Follow the policy on *vendor* credit memos per the company information; Dave would initial the A/P Aging Detail 5/15 report for credit memo.

5/2　Changed Mary, office manager, to salaried at $1,280 per month for the busy season of May – September. Note change on Mary's payroll information.

5/3　Hired student, Brian Jones, address 300 Main St., Landscape, WI 53022; SS#: 673-22-8585; *exempt* from federal and state withholding, as part-time summer help at $7.25 an hour. (If necessary, review adding employees from March transactions.)

5/5   Reminder: Upon receipt of credit card statement, enter remaining charges at this time; see March or April transactions, for example. On the 15th, reconcile and pay.

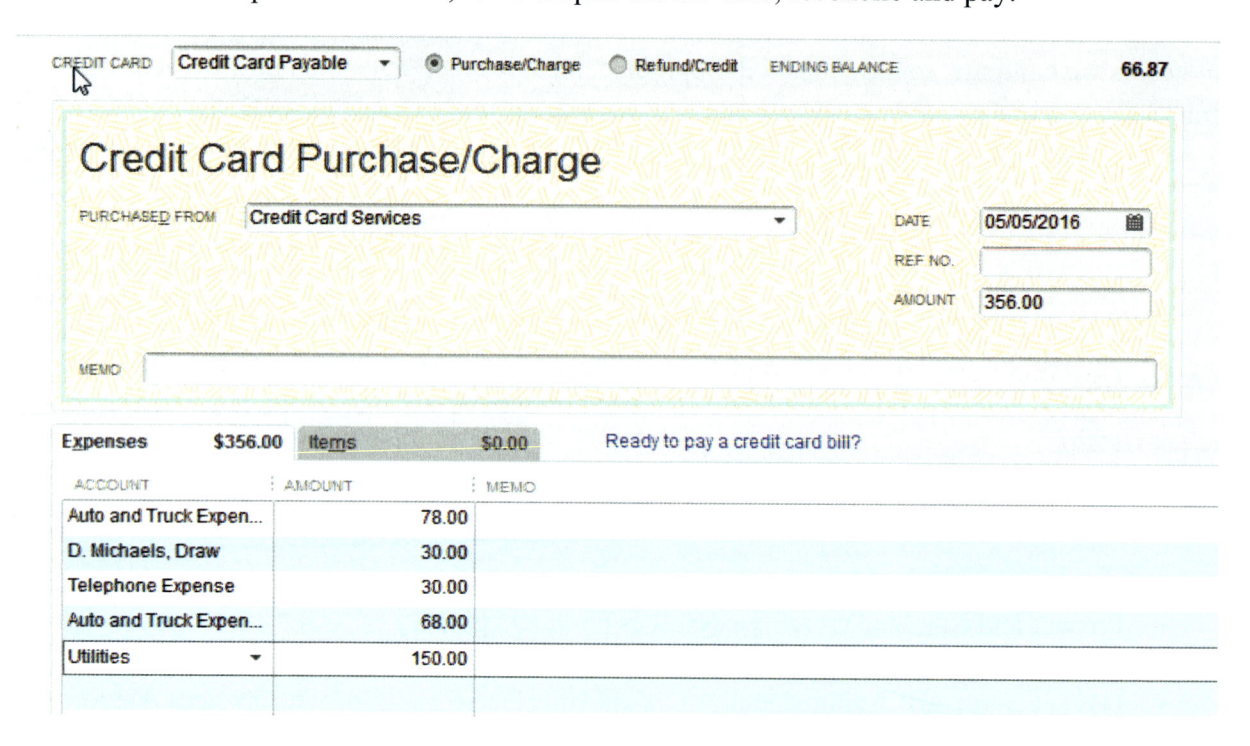

Credit Card Purchase/Charge

PURCHASED FROM: Credit Card Services
DATE: 05/05/2016
REF NO.:
AMOUNT: 356.00

ENDING BALANCE: 66.87

Expenses $356.00

ACCOUNT	AMOUNT	MEMO
Auto and Truck Expen...	78.00	
D. Michaels, Draw	30.00	
Telephone Expense	30.00	
Auto and Truck Expen...	68.00	
Utilities	150.00	

5/7   New section of Jacksonville Industrial Park opened. Spread 4 yards of topsoil, 2 bags of seed, 4 bales of straw, and 15 yards of mulch. Planted 4 boxwood bushes, 4 of the 36" pine trees and 2 of the 5' pine trees, and 16 hours of landscaping services. Invoice for work performed.

5/7   Received payment in full from April's customer statements with the exception of Walter Brown's invoice for mulch job on April 2, still outstanding.

- ✓ Reference number on customer payment may be left blank.

- ✓ Reminder: Discounts: residential n/10 from statement date; commercial 2/10, n/30 from statement date on *each* invoice.

- ✓ Note: There should never be an over- or underpayment on any receipt; watch application of Brown's payment!

- ✓ Record the deposit, using the bank statement on the following pages to verify the correct deposit amount.

5/11 Completed spring clean-up *and* regular lawn maintenance for *all* contracted customers; *additional* time incurred for this invoice is listed below. (Use memorized invoices!) Record all income to Lawn Cutting and Trimming. Create invoices.

Brown: 1 hour (additional); see screen shot below for example

Calhoun: 1 hour (additional)

Forest Hill School: No additional time incurred

Jacksonville Industrial Park: 3 hours (additional)

Laxson: 1 hour (additional)

Garrett: 2 hours (additional)

Nottingham Condominiums: 3 hours (additional)

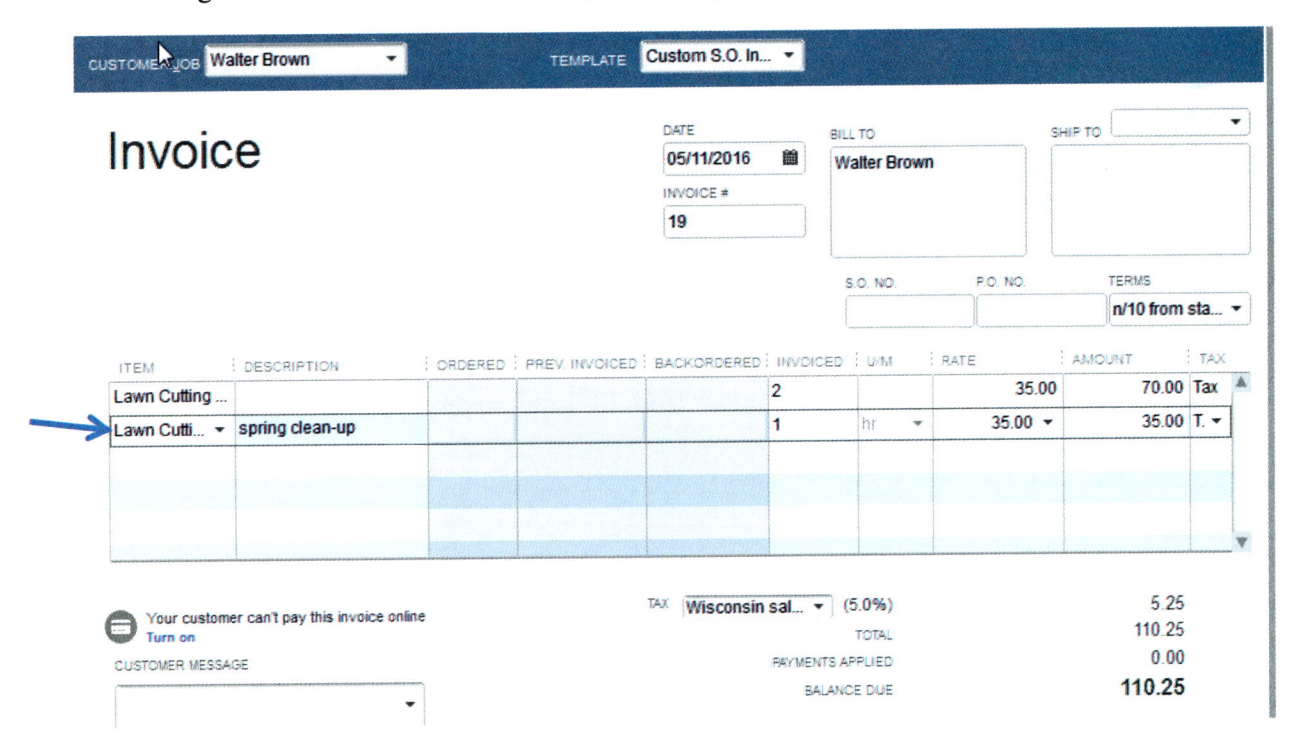

Invoice

| CUSTOMER:JOB | Walter Brown | | TEMPLATE | Custom S.O. In... |

DATE: 05/11/2016
INVOICE #: 19
BILL TO: Walter Brown
TERMS: n/10 from sta...

ITEM	DESCRIPTION	ORDERED	PREV. INVOICED	BACKORDERED	INVOICED	U/M	RATE	AMOUNT	TAX
Lawn Cutting ...					2		35.00	70.00	Tax
Lawn Cutti...	spring clean-up				1	hr	35.00	35.00	T.

TAX: Wisconsin sal... (5.0%) 5.25
TOTAL 110.25
PAYMENTS APPLIED 0.00
BALANCE DUE **110.25**

5/12 Received complaint from Walter Brown about April's mulch work; credited his account for one hour of landscaping services, credit memo #CM3 (relating the credit memo to Brown's invoice #3). Follow policy on credit memos as outlined in company information.

> ➤ Click the "Use credit to apply to invoice" icon to use this credit against the April mulch invoice.

5/15   Reminder: Complete mid-month tasks!

Below is snip of a credit card reconciliation:

Ending Balance	422.87
Cleared Balance	422.87
Difference	0.00

5/18   Completed lawn maintenance for all contracted customers; create invoices. You will not be using any of the estimates or sales orders from here; these invoices should start with 26. Use memorized invoices in the Lists/Memorized Transactions to enter invoices quickly; remember to change the date!

5/25   Due to spring growing season, completed lawn maintenance for *all* contracted customers.

➢ Jacksonville Industrial Park will now require 3 *additional* hours each time, starting with this invoice; replace the memorized transaction for Jacksonville.

➢ Create all invoices.

5/27   Purchased string and oil for trimmer from PP Equipment for $37.80 on credit card. Record purchase.

5/31   Prepare payroll:

Brian: 28 hours (ck. #1024)   Mary — salaried   (ck. #1025)

Max: 162 hours (160 Reg/2 OT) (ck. #1026)

(Note: Mary will have federal withholding this pay period; use the payroll withholding tables found in the last month's activities/transactions.)

➢ Click the Pay Employees Icon and enter a check mark next to Employee, that is, Mary; click Open Paycheck Detail, and enter the federal withholding amount using a "-" sign to indicate the deduction.

- Watch Brian's state withholding; it should be 0. He is exempt from federal *and* state withholding.

- It is not necessary to print paychecks or pay stubs.

- Update the Excel payroll worksheet FUTA and SUTA limits starting with the April payroll.

5/31   Perform month-end tasks. (See list at the beginning of month.)

Credit Card Services, Inc.

DM Yard Services

Statement Date: 5/5/2016

Last Payment: 4/15/2016 $342.80

Amount Due: $422.87

Due Date: 5/15/2016

Charge Summary:

- TV & Appliance   30.45
- Office City   36.42
- Gas to Go   78.00
- Cell World   60.00
- Gas to Go   68.00
- Utility Service Corp.   150.00

XYZ Bank

DM Yard Services

Acct. #745-1332   5/1/2016 thru 5/31/2016

Beg. Balance: $1,5709.90

Deposits & CM

5/7 $1,945.88

Checks & DM

#1017	$303.58	#1021	1,000.00
#1018	686.66	#1022	750.00
#1019	149.50	#1023	422.87
#1020	28.10		
5/31 SC	15.00		

Ending Balance: $1,4300.07

Print the task list below on a separate sheet of brightly colored paper (if possible) to use as a carry-forward schedule, meaning to be brought forward as a reminder to complete these tasks each month.

Below find a summary of monthly information and tasks to be completed on their respective dates from May through December. These are *not* included in the monthly transactions!

- ✓ Each time you start QuickBooks the prompt to Enter Memorized Transactions will come up; we will only select the one month's insurance adjustment.
- ✓ Pay rent on the 1st of each month, using the memorized transaction set up in April.
- ✓ Review and record the credit card statement on the 5th of each month, payable on the 15th.
- ✓ Dave reviews A/P Aging Detail and approves invoices due for payment on the 15th of each month.

At month-end:
- ✓ Prepare and calculate monthly payroll as per hours given.
- ✓ Update the Excel worksheet for each payroll.
- ✓ Dave reviews A/P Aging Detail or Unpaid Bills Detail and approves invoices due for payment on the 30th/31st of each month.
- ✓ Prepare monthly draw of $1,000, unless otherwise noted.
- ✓ Reconcile cash account.
- ✓ Review trial balance, verifying that the cash balance per trial balance equals the ending balance on bank reconciliation.

Note: You could also copy and paste this into a Word document and *add* the quarterly tasks of the subsidiary to control account reconciliations and the quarterly invoice and to check detail reports and review the general ledger!

May Questions

1. There are many QuickBooks Reports:

   ➢ Choose any three you have not used yet; include a snip of the report and briefly describe the information presented.

   ➢ Run the Sales by Customer Summary Report for January through May and customize the report using a filter for Customer Type: Residential, then Commercial; include snips of reports.

2. Complete a) the Monthly Task List and b) your To Do/Follow-up Question List with at least two items to be addressed by your "manager"/teacher.

CHAPTER PRINT/SUBMISSION SUMMARY

1. ____ Customer Balance Detail with credit memo approval (export to Excel or PDF to enter initials)

2. ____ Bank Reconciliation

3. ____ Trial Balance

4. ____ Question 1

5. ____ Task List/To Do/Question List

MAY TASK LIST

Check here if completed	Task	Initials
	Review of Unpaid Bills Detail Report	
	Credit memo prepared and approved	
	Verify cash balance on trial balance equals cash balance on bank reconciliation	
	Review trial balance for completeness and accuracy	
	Back up your monthly transactions to an external destination (e.g., flash drive), changing file name to the month	
	Reminder: Complete month-end tasks	

To Do/Follow-up/Question List

June Transactions/Activities

Reminder: Complete monthly tasks!

6/1 Dave and Sue inherited $10,000 from Sue's uncle; this total amount was invested into the business.

6/1 Completed lawn maintenance for *all* contracted customers; create invoices using the shortcut below.

Shortcut Tip: Group contracted customers in memorized transactions:

- Select Lists/Memorized Transactions, right click on New Group, and enter "Contracted Customers" (this is the name of your group); select Do Not Remind Me.

- Right Click on *each* contracted customer and select Edit Memorized Transaction/Add to Group/Select Contracted Customers Group.

- Right click on Contracted Customer Group/Enter Group Transactions and select 6/1/2016. Click OK. All customers are invoiced!

> The screen shot below is a snip of accounts receivable from the General Ledger for 06/01/2016:

Invoice	06/01/2016	40	Forest Hill School	-SPLIT-	140.00	5,791.73
Invoice	06/01/2016	41	Jacksonville Indus…	-SPLIT-	330.75	6,122.48
Invoice	06/01/2016	42	Joe Calhoun	-SPLIT-	110.25	6,232.73
Invoice	06/01/2016	43	Larry Laxson	-SPLIT-	73.50	6,306.23
Invoice	06/01/2016	44	Nottingham Condo…	-SPLIT-	294.00	6,600.23
Invoice	06/01/2016	45	Paul Garrett	-SPLIT-	110.25	6,710.48
Invoice	06/01/2016	46	Walter Brown	-SPLIT-	73.50	6,783.98

6/4 Spread 1 yard of topsoil and a bag of seed. Planted 2 of the boxwood bushes at Davidson Foods, 3 hours of landscaping services; create invoice.

6/7 Completed general yard clean-up at Forest Hill School, 20 hours of landscaping services. Create invoice.

6/8 Completed lawn maintenance for *all* contracted customers; prepare invoices. Follow the instructions for entering group transactions as explained in the 6/1 transaction.

6/10 Received full payment from customers from their May statements *except* for Brown's April invoice *and* Jacksonville Industrial Park (no payment received).

Note: Watch applying payment on Brown's account; QuickBooks will always apply payments to the earliest invoice!

6/12 Paid PP Equipment $309.50 for oil change on tractor; issued check #1029. (Charge Repairs and Maintenance for this expense.)

6/15 Completed lawn maintenance for all contracted customers; prepare invoices.

6/15 Make federal and Wisconsin estimated tax payments, checks 1031 and 1032. Complete 1040-ES and WI 1-ES for 2nd quarter.

6/16   Received full payment from Jacksonville Industrial Park for May statement.

6/17   Purchased snacks and drinks for office with petty cash, $32.45.

6/22   Completed lawn maintenance for *all* contracted customers; prepare invoices.

6/25   Spread 10 yards of topsoil in the Jacksonville Industrial Park, 5 hours of landscaping services.

6/30   Prepare payroll.

        Brian: 65 hours (ck. #1033)   Mary: salaried (ck. #1034)

        Max: 164 hours (ck. #1035)

6/30   Perform month-end tasks.

Credit Card Services, Inc.

DM Yard Services

Statement Date: 6/5/2016

Last Payment: 5/15/2016 $422.87

Amount Due: $581.70

Due Date: 6/15/2016

Charge Summary

- ABC Food Store   124.72
- Max's Drug Store   15.18
- Gas To Go   120.00
- Cell World   60.00
- Gas to Go   74.00
- Utility Service Corp.   150.00
- PP Equipment   37.80

XYZ Bank

DM Yard Services

Acct. #745-1332   6/1/2016 thru 6/30/2016

Beg. Balance: $1,4300.07

Deposits & CM

6/1 $10,000.00

6/10   2,670.25

6/16   2,674.98

Checks & DM

#1024	$187.47	#1029	309.50
#1025	1,074.48	#1030	581.70
#1026	1,399.07	#1031	500.00
#1027	1,000.00	#1032	150.00
#1028	750.00		

6/30   SC   15.00

Ending Balance: $2,3678.08

Receipt for petty cash disbursement   6/17/2016

ABC Food Store

Snacks   32.45

June Questions

1. Determine if the inheritance received by Dave and Sue is taxable income on their personal income tax return; copy and paste the answer as found in an IRS publication in your Word document. Highlight a specific answer if possible. Then state *your* conclusion to the information presented, that is, "this inheritance is …."

2. Quarterly tasks:

    ➢ Verify the A/R, Inventory, and A/P subsidiary ledger balances agree with the trial balance; document this in your Word document. See example in March questions.

    ➢ As measures of internal control,

    a) Print a report of *quarterly* numerically sorted invoices to ensure all invoices are accounted for.

    b) Print a quarterly check detail report for Dave's review for reasonableness of payees and amounts; Dave initials report.

    c) Review general ledger on screen *only* — no printing; note the review in your Word document of monthly questions.

3. Identify and list two managerial/business-related (e.g., address controls to safeguard inventory) and three financial-related (e.g., current ratio is …) observations through June for your landscaping business.

4. Complete a) the Monthly Task List and b) your To Do/Follow-up Question List with at least two items to be addressed by your "manager"/teacher.

CHAPTER PRINT/SUBMISSION SUMMARY

1. ____ 1040-ES and WI 1-ES

2. ____ Subsidiary ledger reports for A/R, A/P, and Inventory used in question 2 (if not shown in question 2)

3. ____ Report of numerically sorted invoices for quarter (if not shown in question 2)

4. ____ Check Register for April – June with Dave's initials to indicate review (if not shown in question 2)

5. ____ Bank Account Reconciliation

6. ____ Trial Balance

7. ____ Questions 1 – 3

8. ____ Task List/To Do/Question List

JUNE TASK LIST

Check here if completed	Task	Initials
	Review of Unpaid Bills Detail Reports	
	Compare A/R control account balance (A/R on trial balance) to a detail report of the A/R subsidiary ledger	
	Compare A/P control account balance (A/P on trial balance) to a detail report of the A/P subsidiary ledger	
	Compare Inventory control account balance (Inventory on trial balance) to a detail report of the Inventory subsidiary ledger	
	Prepare report of numerically sorted invoices	
	Review check detail for April – June; Dave indicates review with his initials on report (see cash-related information at the beginning of project)	
	Verify cash balance on trial balance equals cash balance on bank reconciliation	
	Review trial balance for completeness and accuracy	
	Back up your monthly transactions to an external destination (e.g., flash drive), changing file name to the month	

To Do/Follow-up/Question List

July Transactions/Activities

Reminder: Complete monthly tasks!

7/1 Offer health insurance and traditional 401k to Mary and Max. The health insurance is a 50/50 plan (*not* a cafeteria or flexible spending plan), 50% employee paid, and 50% employer paid; the married plan is $400 per month in *total*; the single plan is $180 per month in *total*.

For the 401k, Mary and Max will contribute 2% of their gross monthly pay and DM will match these contributions.

Both Mary and Max will take advantage of both of these benefits.

Update payroll setup for these benefits.

> Employees/Payroll Setup/Company Setup/Employee Benefits/Insurance Benefits:

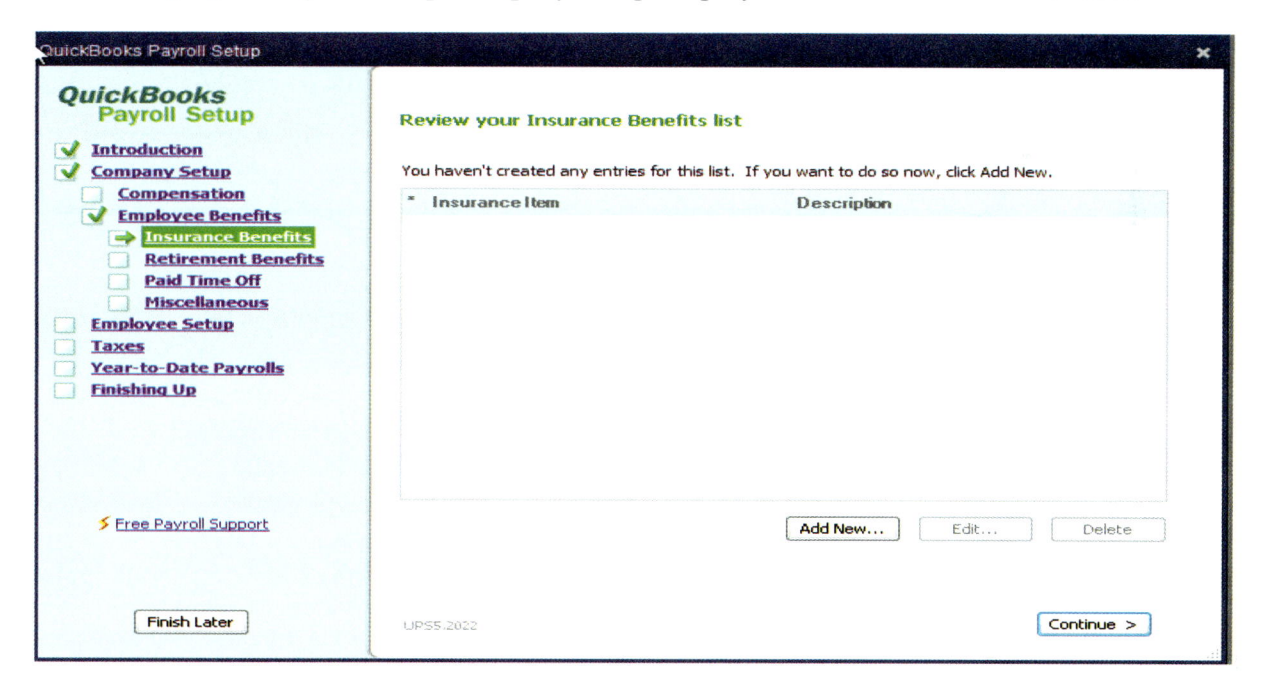

- Once you click on insurance benefits you will see "Set up insurance benefits."
- Check health insurance:

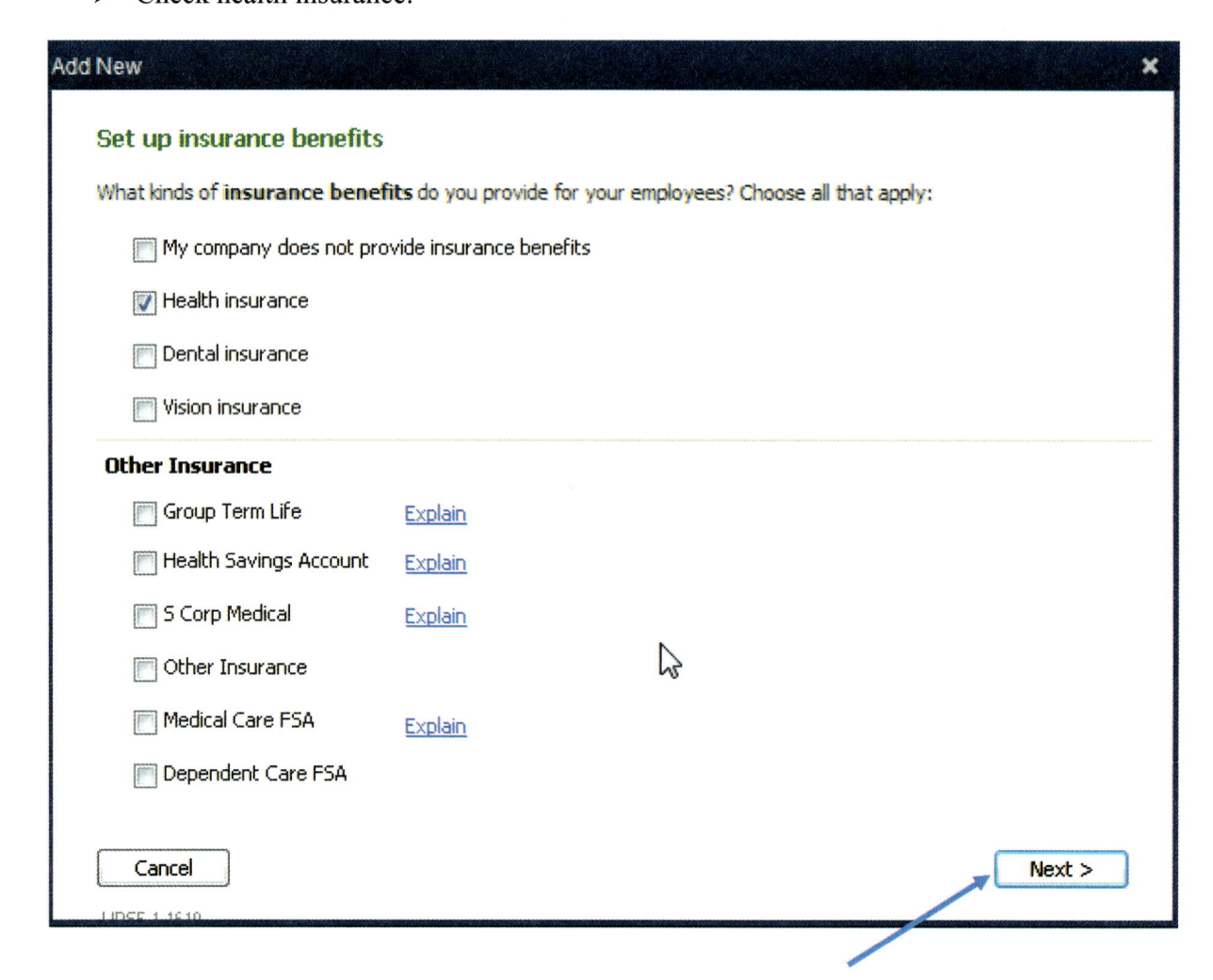

Set up insurance benefits

What kinds of **insurance benefits** do you provide for your employees? Choose all that apply:

- [ ] My company does not provide insurance benefits
- [x] Health insurance
- [ ] Dental insurance
- [ ] Vision insurance

Other Insurance

- [ ] Group Term Life — Explain
- [ ] Health Savings Account — Explain
- [ ] S Corp Medical — Explain
- [ ] Other Insurance
- [ ] Medical Care FSA — Explain
- [ ] Dependent Care FSA

[Cancel] [Next >]

➢ Select "Both the employee and company pay portions," then click Next:

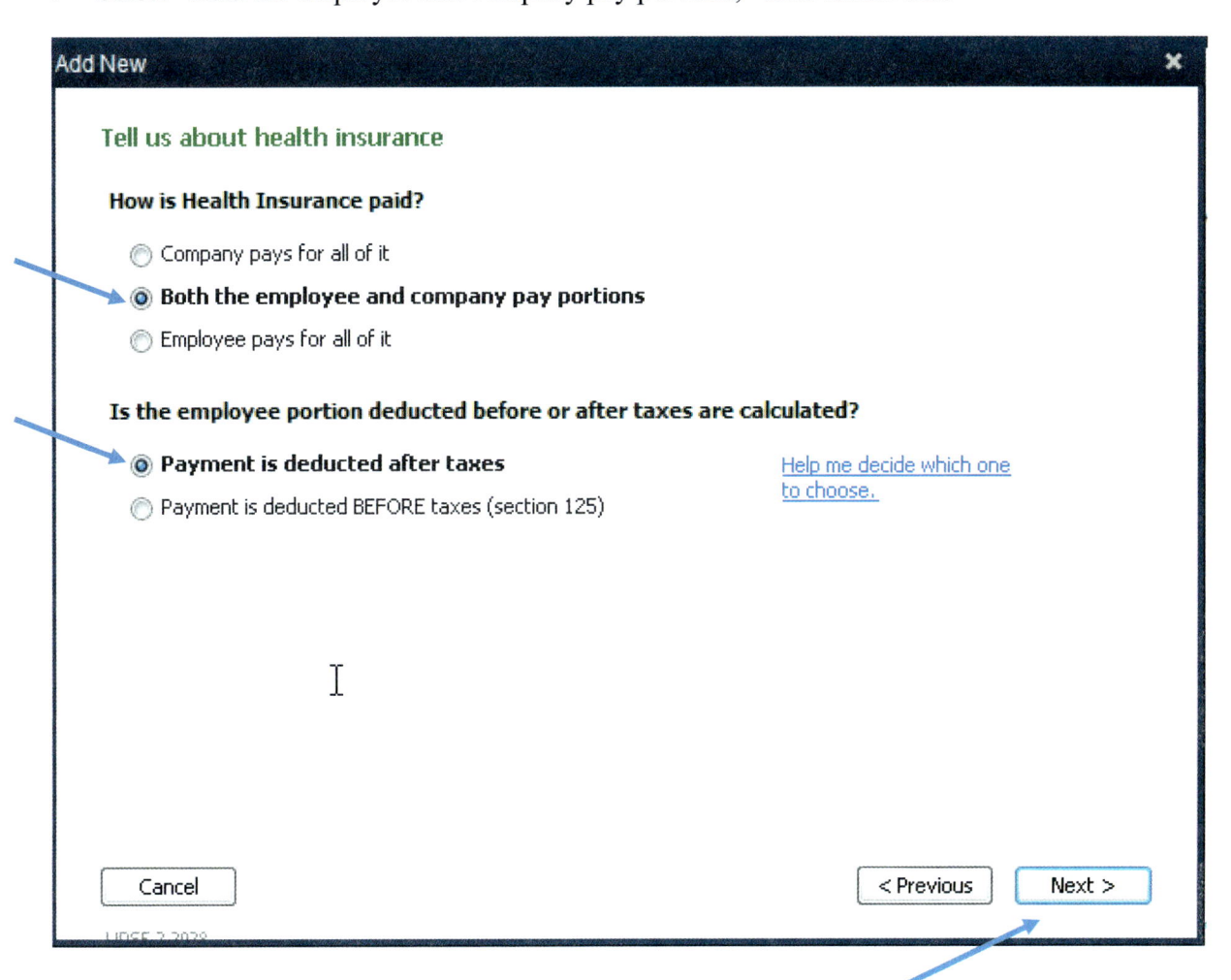

Add New

Tell us about health insurance

How is Health Insurance paid?
- ○ Company pays for all of it
- ◉ Both the employee and company pay portions
- ○ Employee pays for all of it

Is the employee portion deducted before or after taxes are calculated?
- ◉ Payment is deducted after taxes
- ○ Payment is deducted BEFORE taxes (section 125)

Help me decide which one to choose.

[Cancel] [< Previous] [Next >]

> Vendor information: Healthcare Insurance (account #: 12345) and Investors, Inc. (account #: 67890), and *no* regular payment schedule. Health insurance will be a flat amount; the 401k will be a percentage.

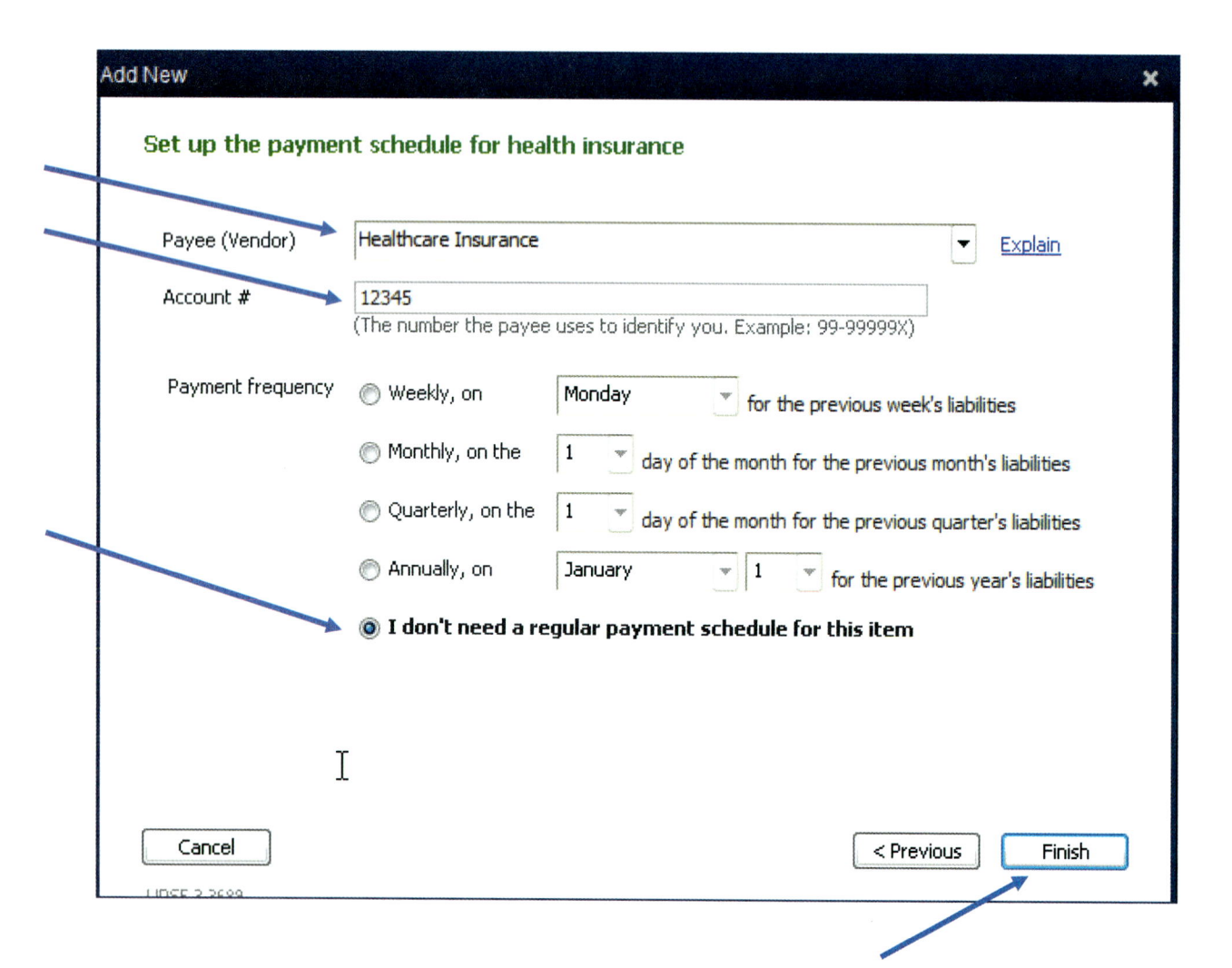

Add New

Set up the payment schedule for health insurance

- Payee (Vendor): Healthcare Insurance
- Account #: 12345
  (The number the payee uses to identify you. Example: 99-99999X)

Payment frequency:
- ○ Weekly, on Monday for the previous week's liabilities
- ○ Monthly, on the 1 day of the month for the previous month's liabilities
- ○ Quarterly, on the 1 day of the month for the previous quarter's liabilities
- ○ Annually, on January 1 for the previous year's liabilities
- ● I don't need a regular payment schedule for this item

[Cancel] [< Previous] [**Finish**]

➢ Next, set up the 401k retirement benefit using the information given in the 7/1 transaction on the previous page. See the screen shot when completed:

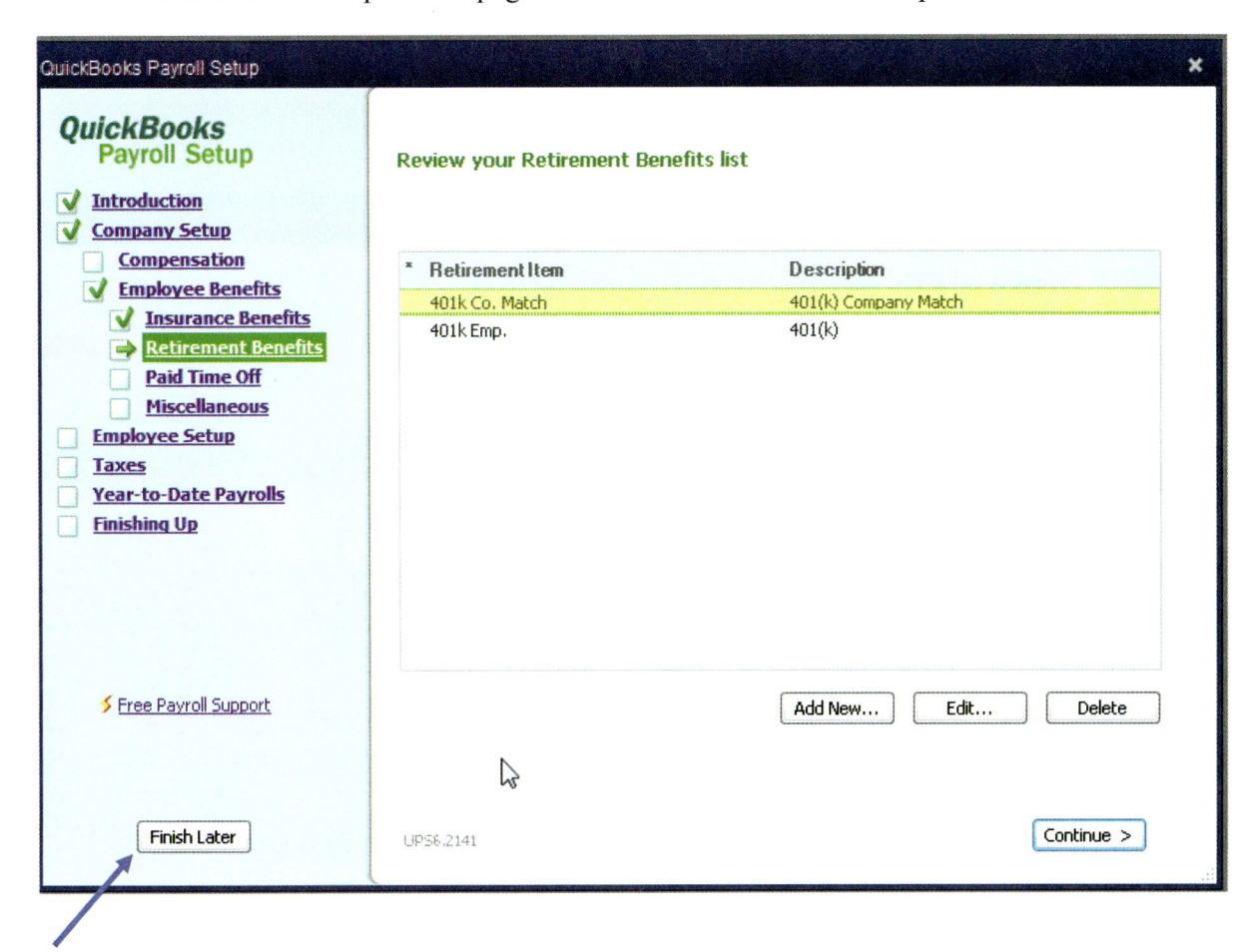

QuickBooks Payroll Setup

Review your Retirement Benefits list

Retirement Item	Description
401k Co. Match	401(k) Company Match
401k Emp.	401(k)

- ✓ Introduction
- ✓ Company Setup
  - ☐ Compensation
  - ✓ Employee Benefits
    - ✓ Insurance Benefits
    - ➡ Retirement Benefits
    - ☐ Paid Time Off
    - ☐ Miscellaneous
- ☐ Employee Setup
- ☐ Taxes
- ☐ Year-to-Date Payrolls
- ☐ Finishing Up

Add New... | Edit... | Delete

Finish Later | Continue >

➢ Next, edit payroll items (Employees/Manage Payroll Items/View/Edit Payroll Item List) for *accounts* and *amounts* and *percentages*:

- ✓ Right click on Health Insurance (taxable) Deduction/Edit Payroll Item:

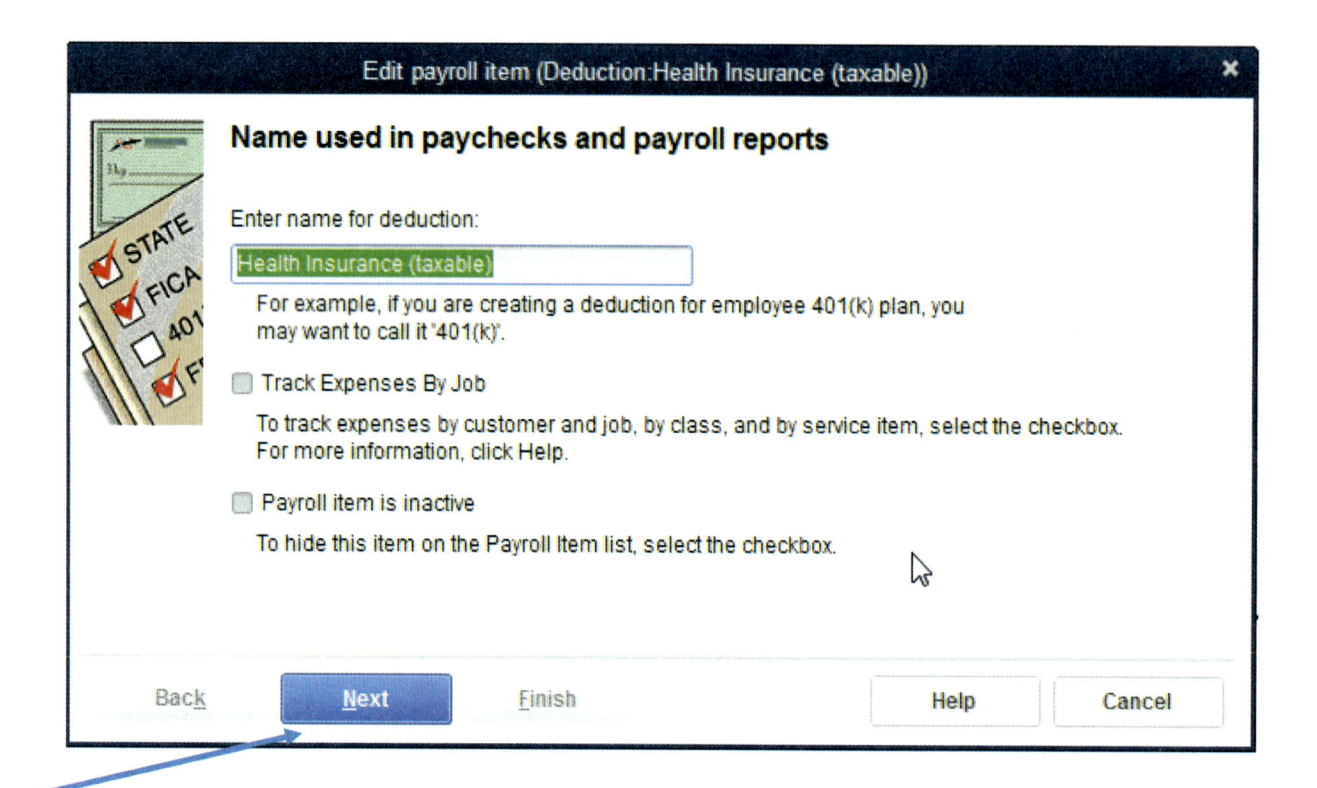

➢ Add a new account for Health Insurance Payable; click Next:

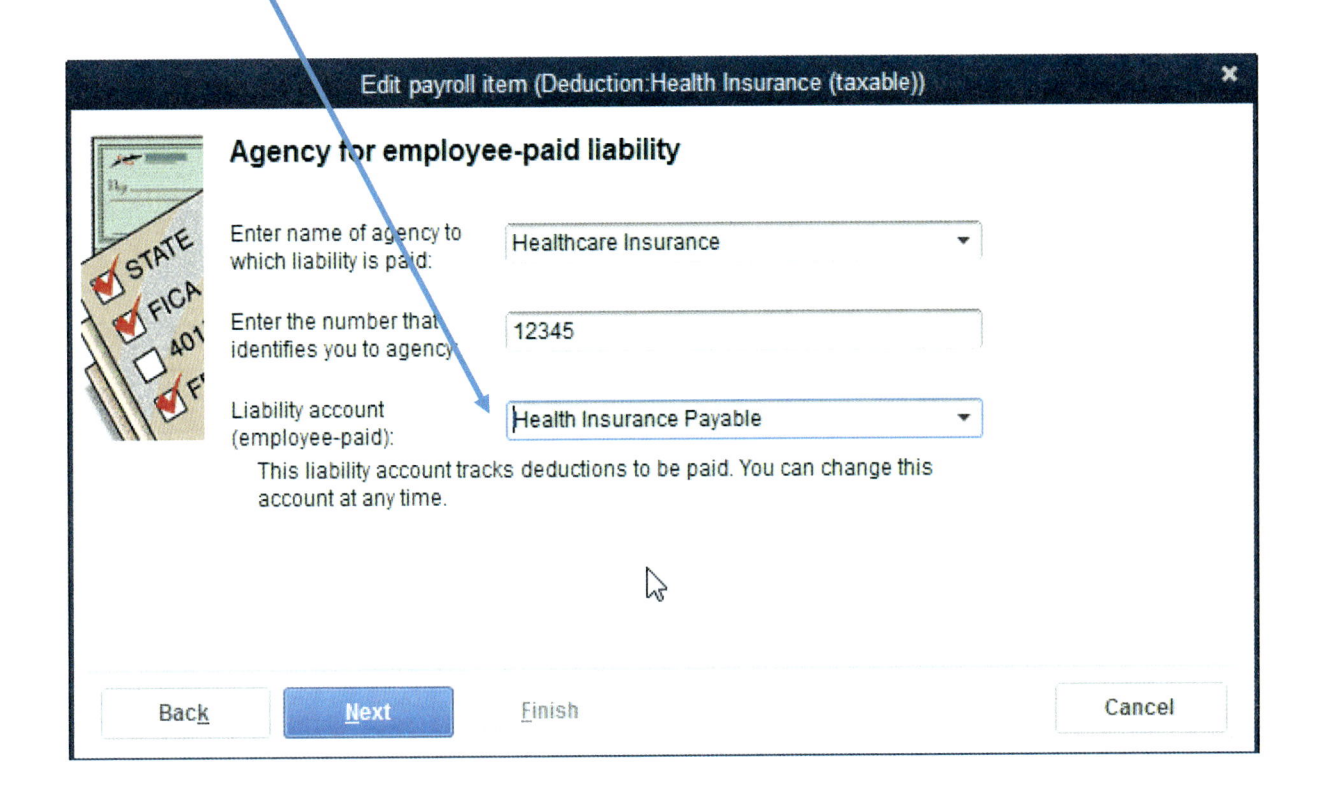

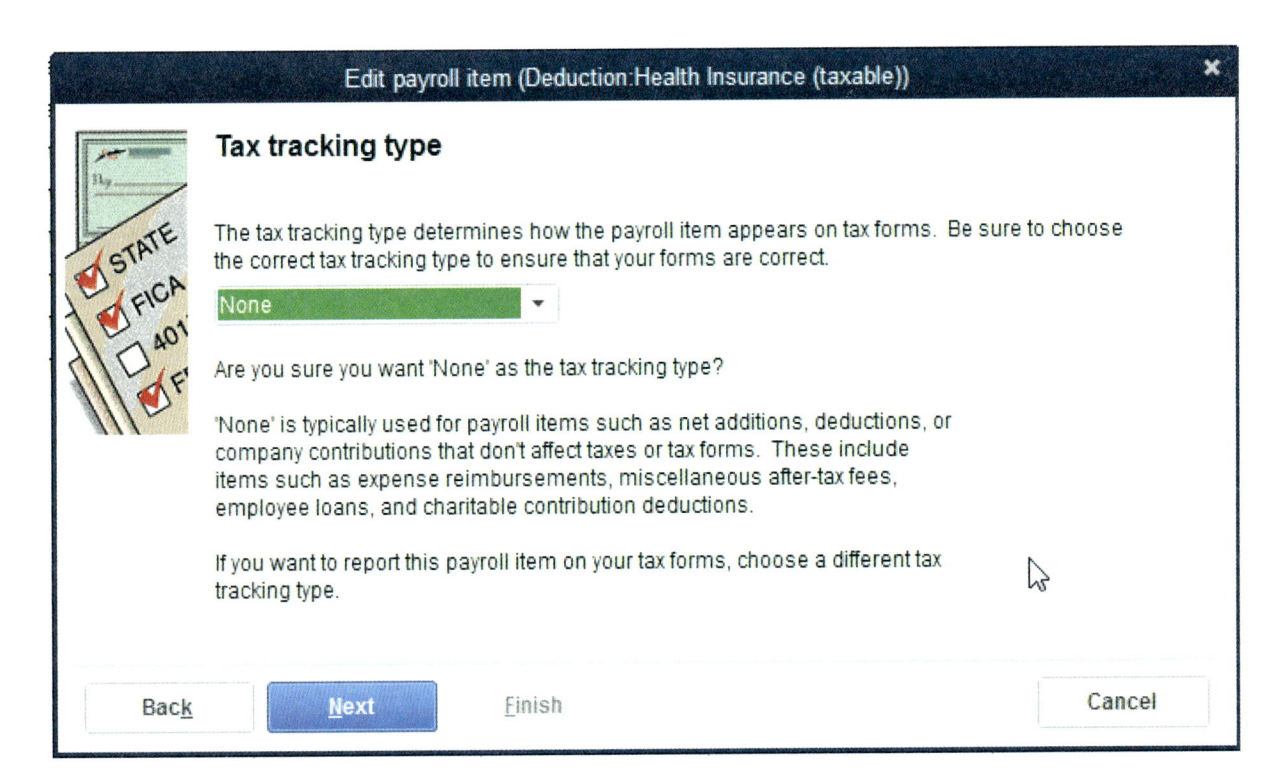

Edit payroll item (Deduction:Health Insurance (taxable))

Agency for employee-paid liability

Enter name of agency to which liability is paid: Healthcare Insurance

Enter the number that identifies you to agency: 12345

Liability account (employee-paid): Health Insurance Payable

This liability account tracks deductions to be paid. You can change this account at any time.

Back | Next | Finish | Cancel

Edit payroll item (Deduction:Health Insurance (taxable))

Tax tracking type

The tax tracking type determines how the payroll item appears on tax forms. Be sure to choose the correct tax tracking type to ensure that your forms are correct.

None

Are you sure you want 'None' as the tax tracking type?

'None' is typically used for payroll items such as net additions, deductions, or company contributions that don't affect taxes or tax forms. These include items such as expense reimbursements, miscellaneous after-tax fees, employee loans, and charitable contribution deductions.

If you want to report this payroll item on your tax forms, choose a different tax tracking type.

Back | Next | Finish | Cancel

➤ Ensure nothing is checked here; click Next:

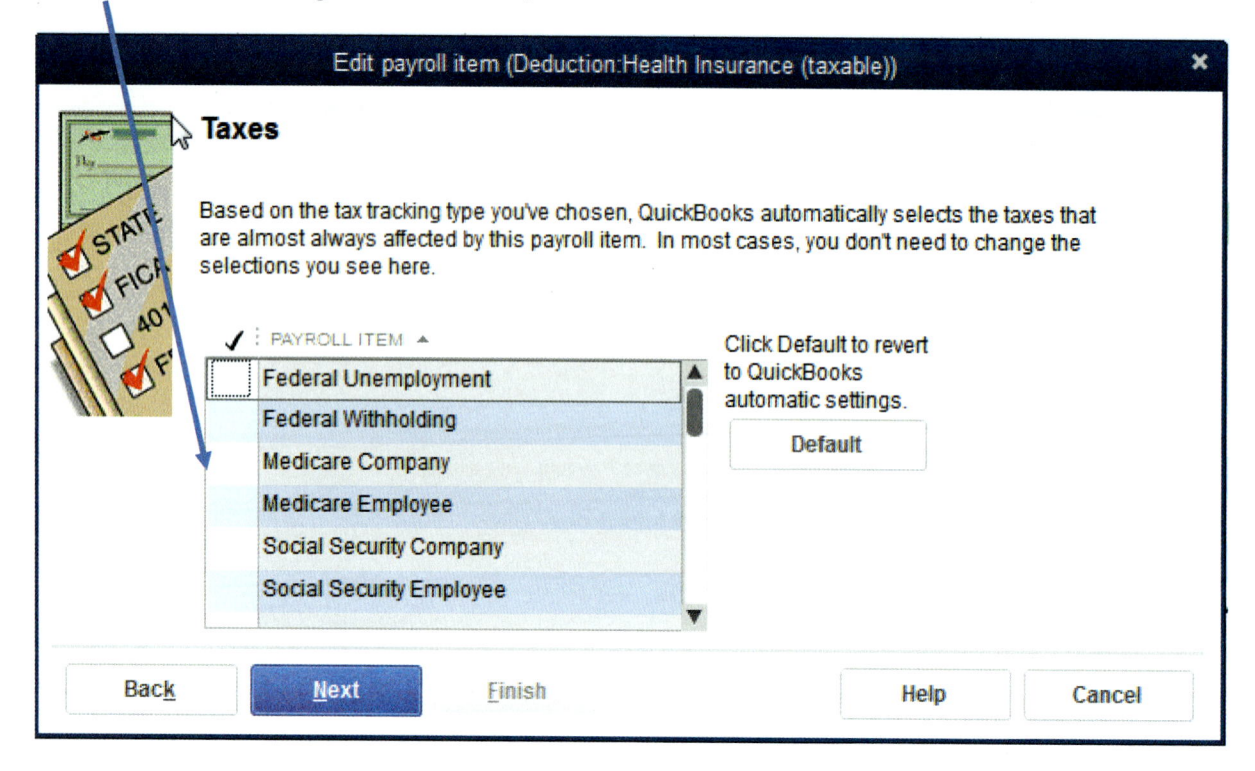

Taxes

Based on the tax tracking type you've chosen, QuickBooks automatically selects the taxes that are almost always affected by this payroll item. In most cases, you don't need to change the selections you see here.

✓	PAYROLL ITEM ▲
	Federal Unemployment
	Federal Withholding
	Medicare Company
	Medicare Employee
	Social Security Company
	Social Security Employee

Click Default to revert to QuickBooks automatic settings.

[Default]

[Back] [Next] [Finish] [Help] [Cancel]

Note: Our health insurance is a flat deduction amount, not calculated on either gross or net pay.

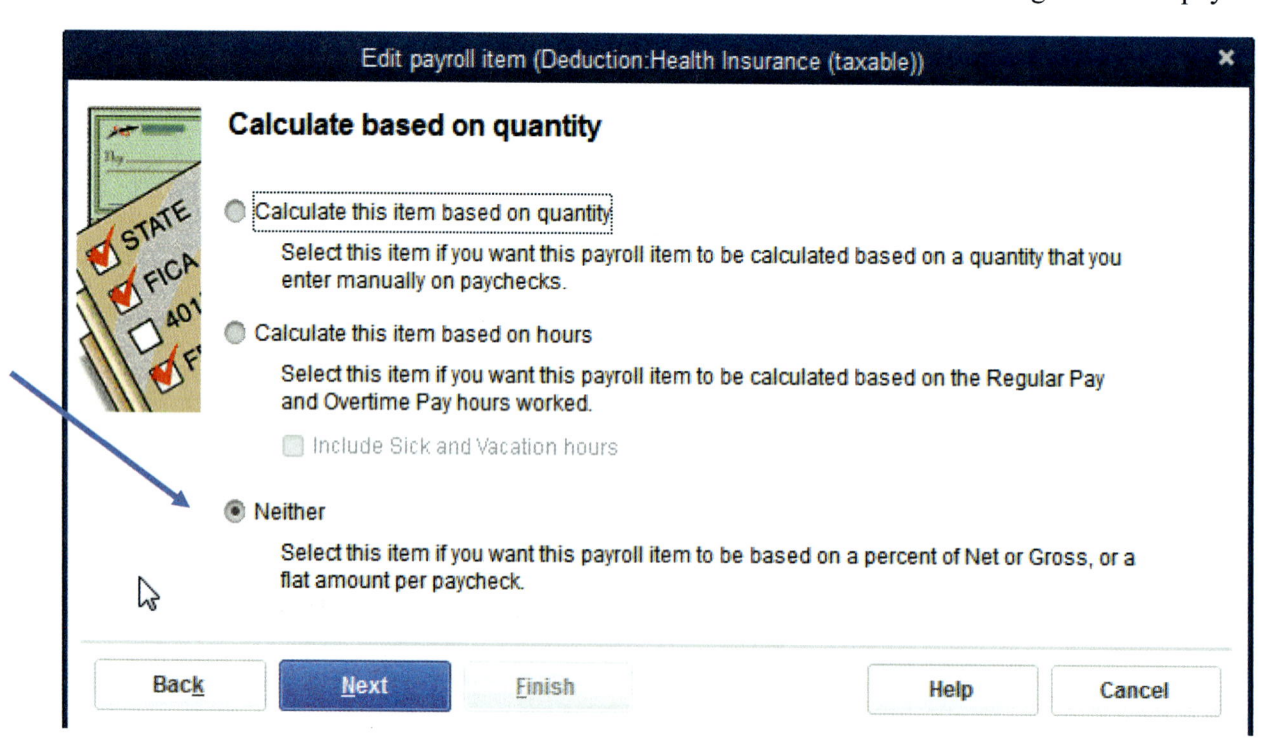

Calculate based on quantity

○ Calculate this item based on quantity
    Select this item if you want this payroll item to be calculated based on a quantity that you enter manually on paychecks.

○ Calculate this item based on hours
    Select this item if you want this payroll item to be calculated based on the Regular Pay and Overtime Pay hours worked.
    ☐ Include Sick and Vacation hours

● Neither
    Select this item if you want this payroll item to be based on a percent of Net or Gross, or a flat amount per paycheck.

[Back] [Next] [Finish] [Help] [Cancel]

Because this benefit is not part of a cafeteria plan or flexible spending plan, it will simply be a deduction to arrive at net pay.

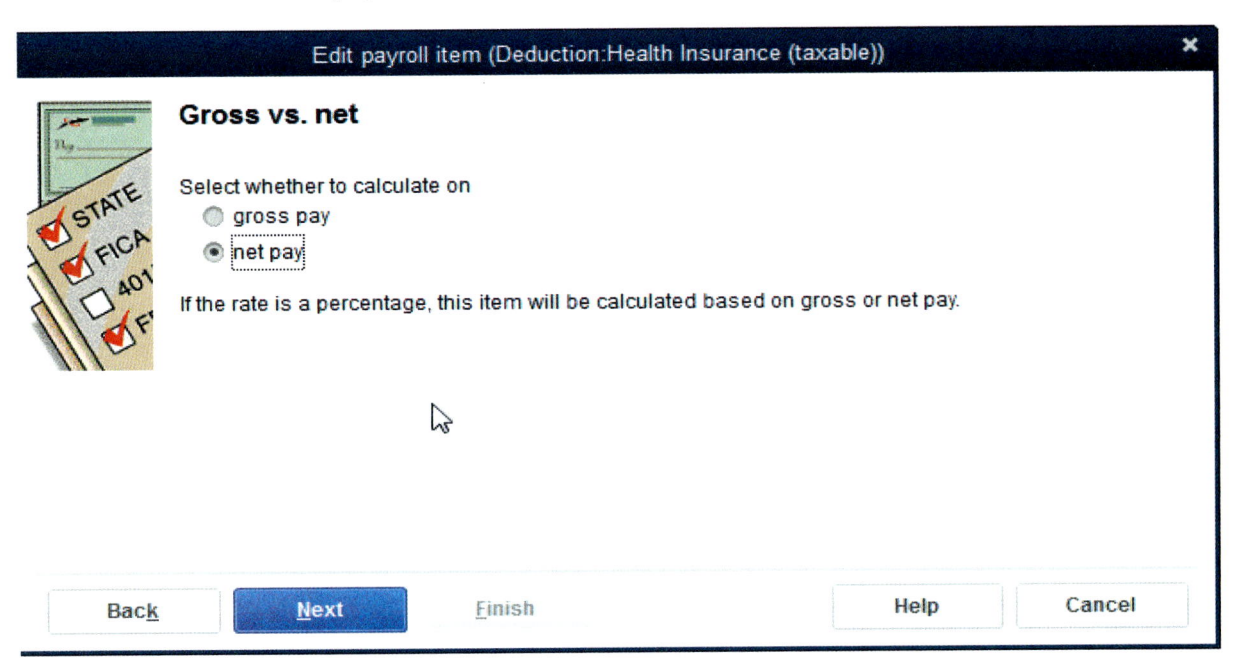

Edit payroll item (Deduction:Health Insurance (taxable))

Gross vs. net

Select whether to calculate on
- ○ gross pay
- ● net pay

If the rate is a percentage, this item will be calculated based on gross or net pay.

[Back] [Next] [Finish]   [Help] [Cancel]

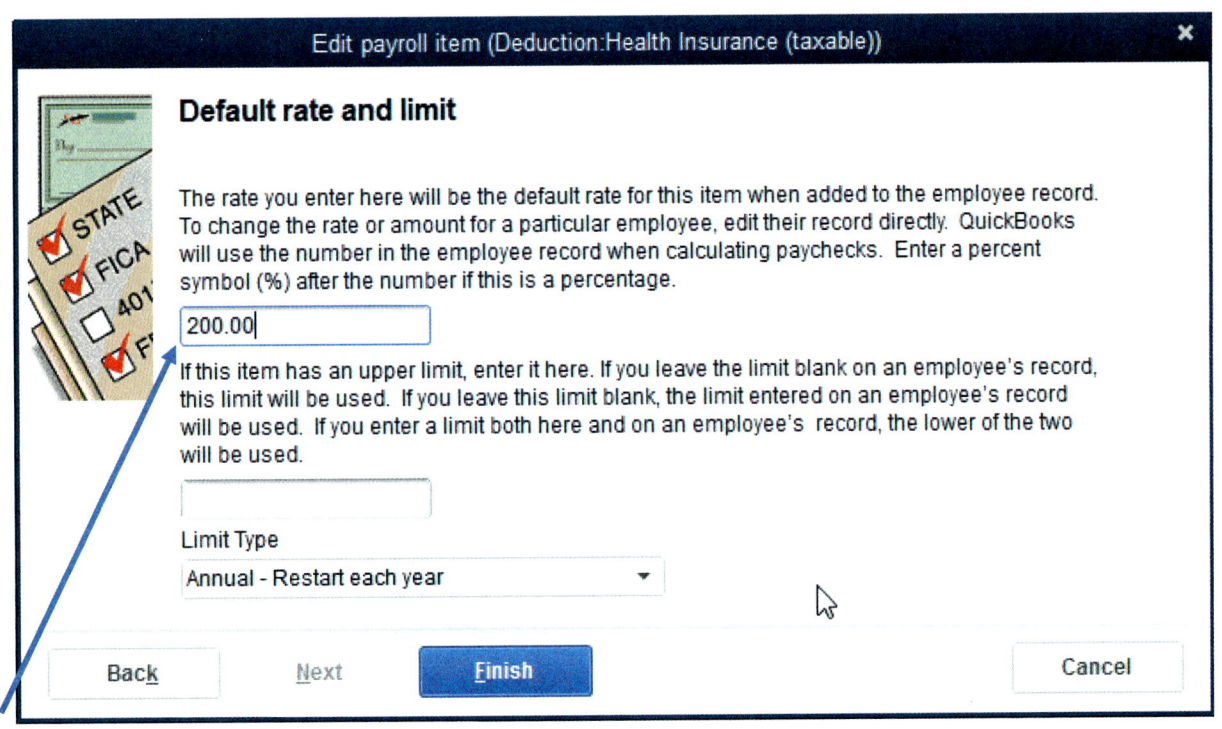

Edit payroll item (Deduction:Health Insurance (taxable))

Default rate and limit

The rate you enter here will be the default rate for this item when added to the employee record. To change the rate or amount for a particular employee, edit their record directly. QuickBooks will use the number in the employee record when calculating paychecks. Enter a percent symbol (%) after the number if this is a percentage.

`200.00`

If this item has an upper limit, enter it here. If you leave the limit blank on an employee's record, this limit will be used. If you leave this limit blank, the limit entered on an employee's record will be used. If you enter a limit both here and on an employee's record, the lower of the two will be used.

Limit Type
`Annual - Restart each year`

[Back] [Next] [Finish]   [Cancel]

Note: An amount is needed here, whether you choose this employee deduction for a married plan or $90 for the single plan; the amount will need to be edited for the other employee. Click Finish.

➢ Next: Edit Health Insurance (Company Contribution), adding a new account. See the screen shot below, noting use of the same dollar amount you used on the previous page.

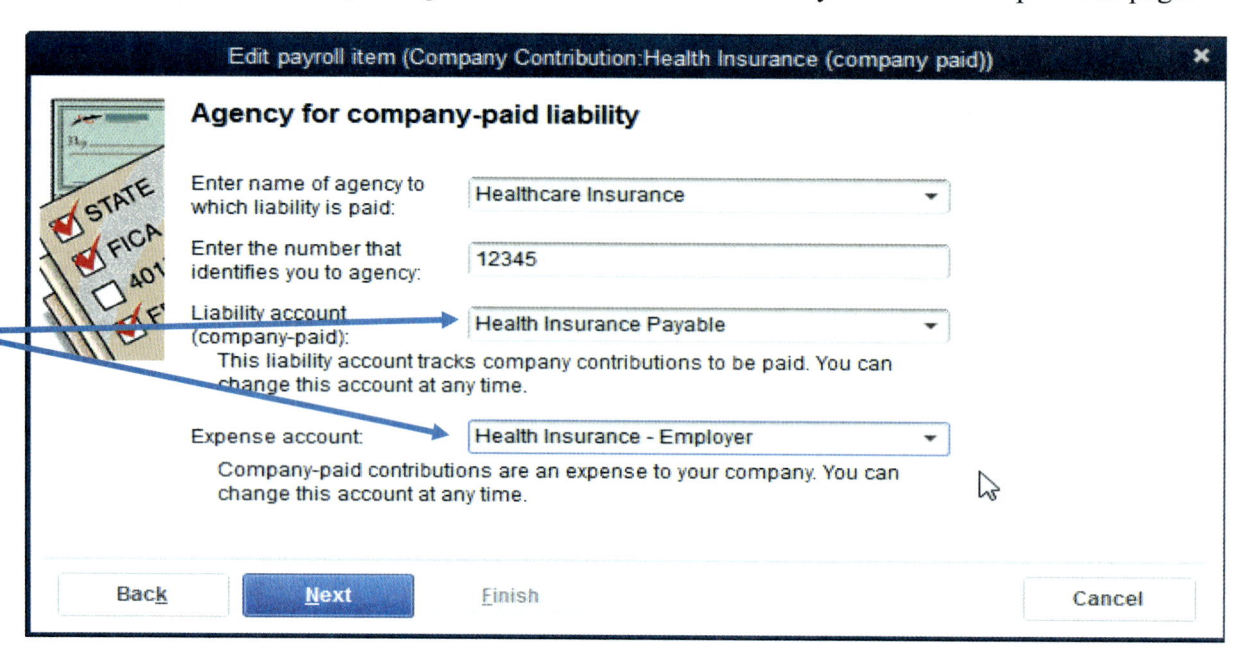

Edit payroll item (Company Contribution:Health Insurance (company paid))

Agency for company-paid liability

Enter name of agency to which liability is paid:	Healthcare Insurance
Enter the number that identifies you to agency:	12345
Liability account (company-paid):	Health Insurance Payable

This liability account tracks company contributions to be paid. You can change this account at any time.

Expense account:	Health Insurance - Employer

Company-paid contributions are an expense to your company. You can change this account at any time.

[Back] [Next] [Finish] [Cancel]

➢ Next: Enter employee and employer health insurance at the employee level. Because these benefits only effect Mary and Max and because of the different dollar amounts of health insurance for the married and single plans, we will add these deductions and company contributions at the employee level versus at the employee default level.

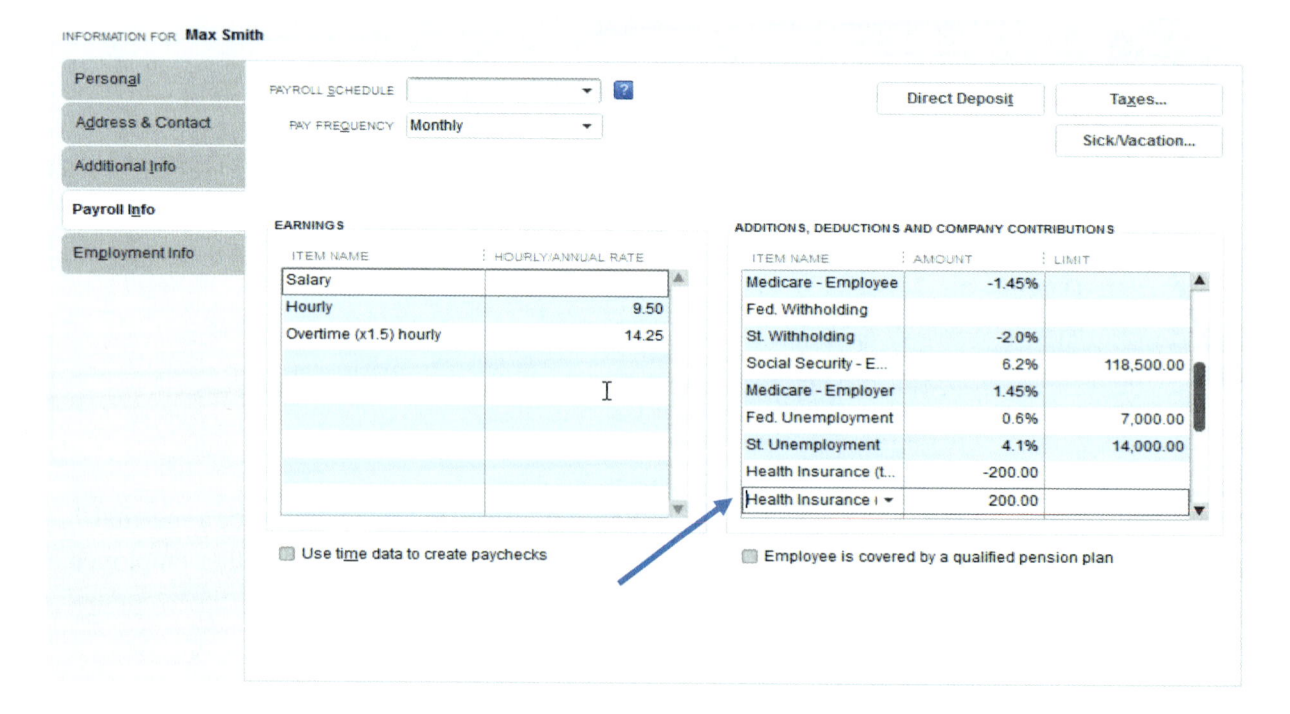

INFORMATION FOR **Max Smith**

Tabs: Personal | Address & Contact | Additional Info | Payroll Info | Employment Info

PAYROLL SCHEDULE:
PAY FREQUENCY: Monthly

[Direct Deposit] [Taxes...] [Sick/Vacation...]

EARNINGS

ITEM NAME	HOURLY/ANNUAL RATE
Salary	
Hourly	9.50
Overtime (x1.5) hourly	14.25

ADDITIONS, DEDUCTIONS AND COMPANY CONTRIBUTIONS

ITEM NAME	AMOUNT	LIMIT
Medicare - Employee	-1.45%	
Fed. Withholding		
St. Withholding	-2.0%	
Social Security - E...	6.2%	118,500.00
Medicare - Employer	1.45%	
Fed. Unemployment	0.6%	7,000.00
St. Unemployment	4.1%	14,000.00
Health Insurance (t...	-200.00	
Health Insurance (	200.00	

☐ Use time data to create paychecks   ☐ Employee is covered by a qualified pension plan

> Also add to Mary, noting to change the deduction amount (use minus sign) and employer portion amount!

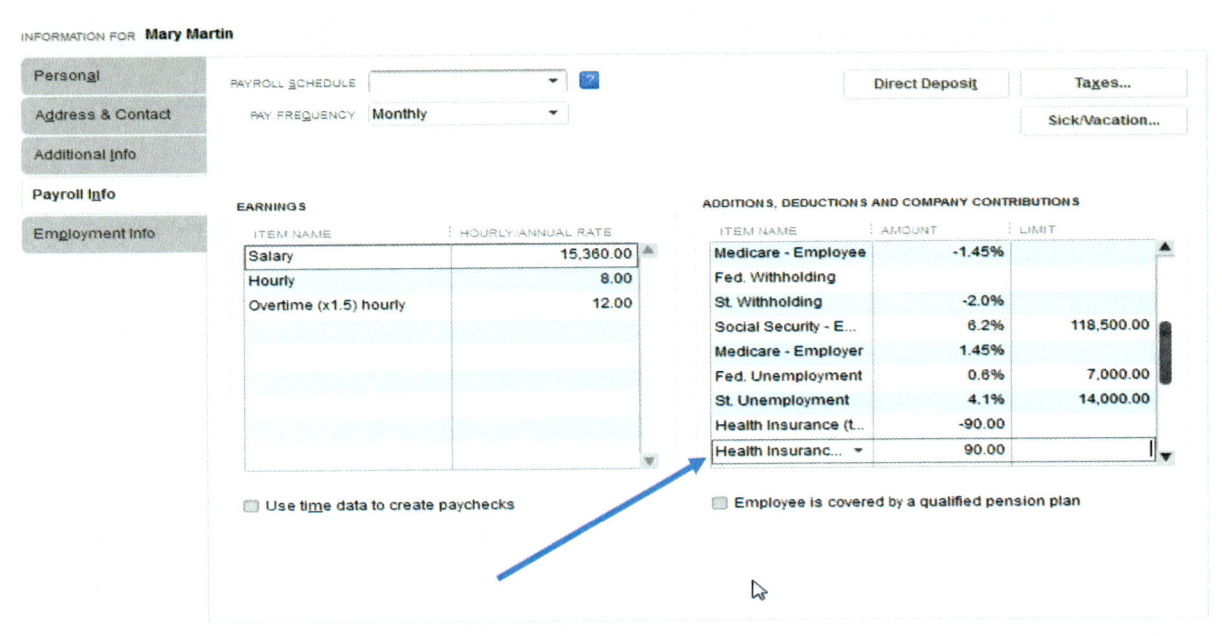

INFORMATION FOR Mary Martin

Personal	PAYROLL SCHEDULE
Address & Contact	PAY FREQUENCY Monthly
Additional Info	
Payroll Info	
Employment Info	

Direct Deposit | Taxes...
Sick/Vacation...

EARNINGS

ITEM NAME	HOURLY/ANNUAL RATE
Salary	15,360.00
Hourly	8.00
Overtime (x1.5) hourly	12.00

ADDITIONS, DEDUCTIONS AND COMPANY CONTRIBUTIONS

ITEM NAME	AMOUNT	LIMIT
Medicare - Employee	-1.45%	
Fed. Withholding		
St. Withholding	-2.0%	
Social Security - E...	6.2%	118,500.00
Medicare - Employer	1.45%	
Fed. Unemployment	0.6%	7,000.00
St. Unemployment	4.1%	14,000.00
Health Insurance (t...	-90.00	
Health Insuranc...	90.00	

☐ Use time data to create paychecks   ☐ Employee is covered by a qualified pension plan

> Complete the entire process given above to edit payroll items for the 401k employee *and* employer portions (not all screen shots are shown below):

  ✓ Add 401k Payable and 401k Employer Contribution accounts.

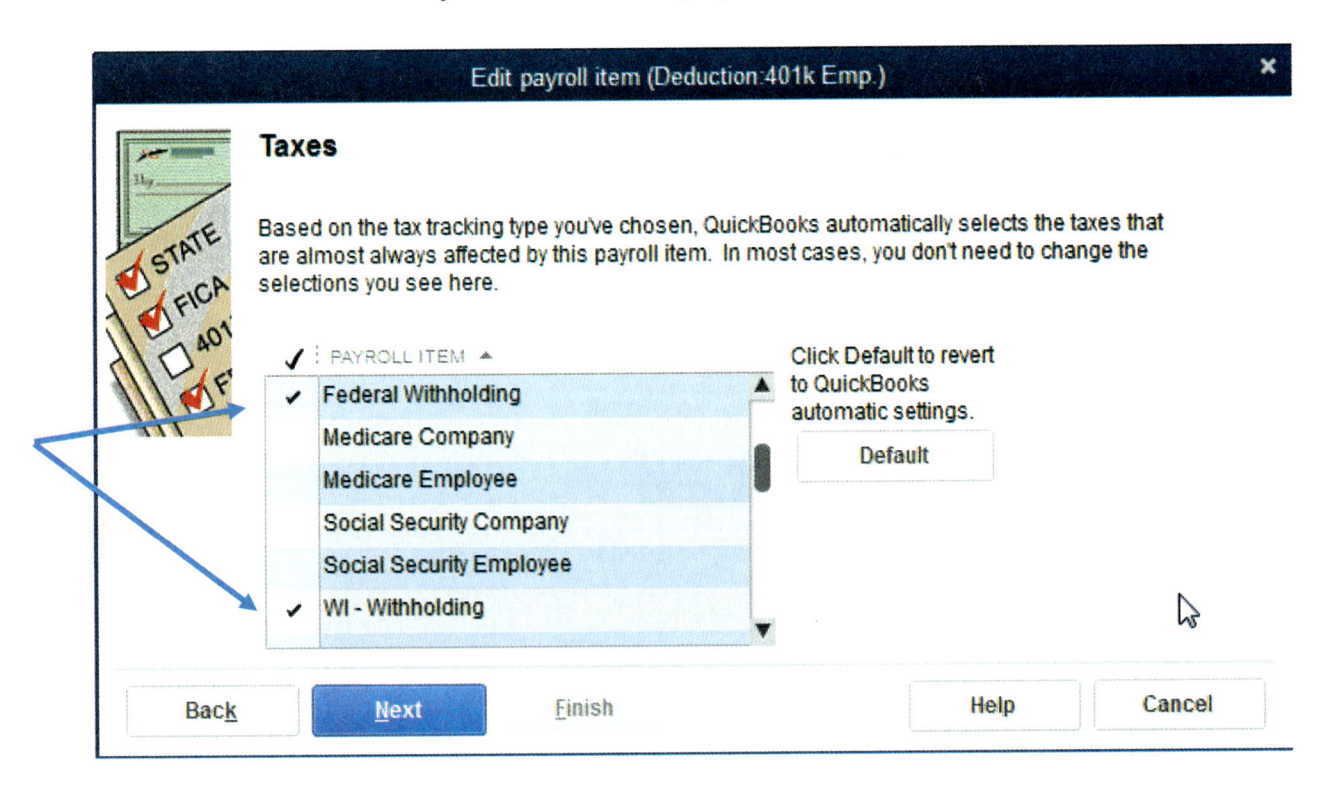

Edit payroll item (Deduction:401k Emp.)

Taxes

Based on the tax tracking type you've chosen, QuickBooks automatically selects the taxes that are almost always affected by this payroll item. In most cases, you don't need to change the selections you see here.

✓	PAYROLL ITEM ▲
✓	Federal Withholding
	Medicare Company
	Medicare Employee
	Social Security Company
	Social Security Employee
✓	WI - Withholding

Click Default to revert to QuickBooks automatic settings.

[Default]

[Back] [Next] [Finish]   [Help] [Cancel]

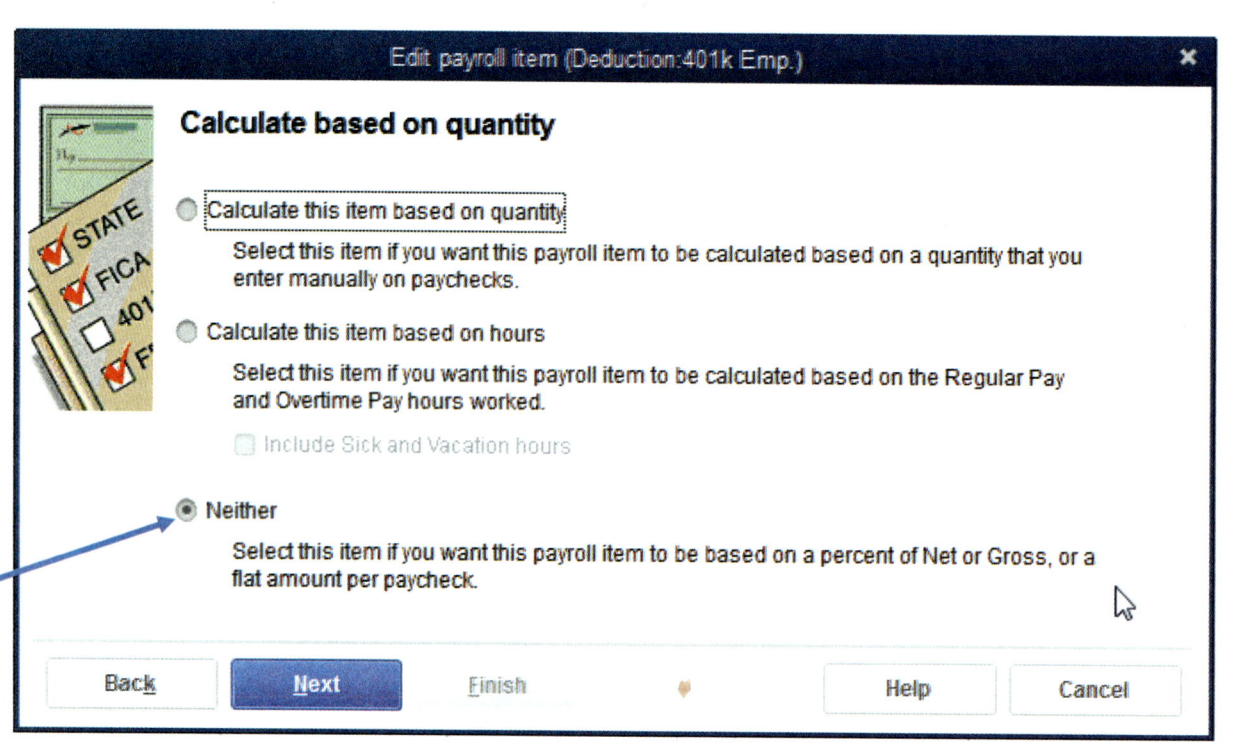

Edit payroll item (Deduction:401k Emp.)

Calculate based on quantity

○ Calculate this item based on quantity

Select this item if you want this payroll item to be calculated based on a quantity that you enter manually on paychecks.

○ Calculate this item based on hours

Select this item if you want this payroll item to be calculated based on the Regular Pay and Overtime Pay hours worked.

☐ Include Sick and Vacation hours

◉ Neither

Select this item if you want this payroll item to be based on a percent of Net or Gross, or a flat amount per paycheck.

[Back] [Next] [Finish] [Help] [Cancel]

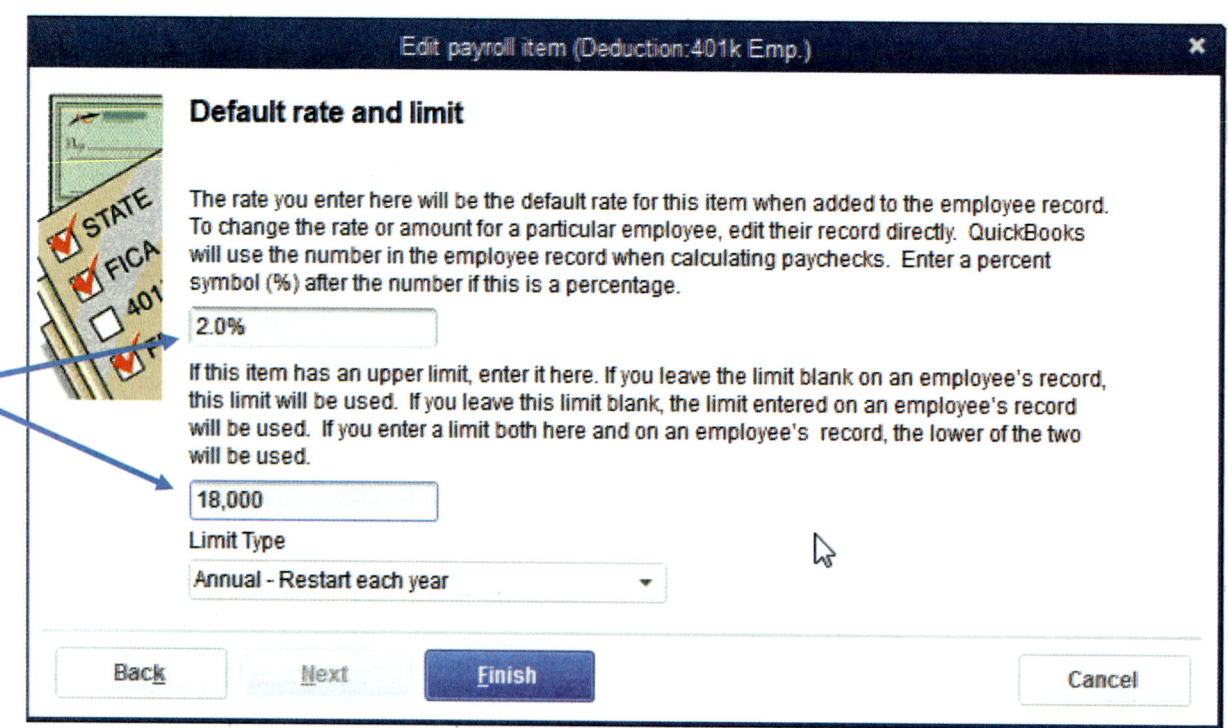

Edit payroll item (Deduction:401k Emp.)

Default rate and limit

The rate you enter here will be the default rate for this item when added to the employee record. To change the rate or amount for a particular employee, edit their record directly. QuickBooks will use the number in the employee record when calculating paychecks. Enter a percent symbol (%) after the number if this is a percentage.

2.0%

If this item has an upper limit, enter it here. If you leave the limit blank on an employee's record, this limit will be used. If you leave this limit blank, the limit entered on an employee's record will be used. If you enter a limit both here and on an employee's record, the lower of the two will be used.

18,000

Limit Type

Annual - Restart each year

[Back] [Next] [Finish] [Cancel]

> Payroll items after editing should appear as follows:

ITEM NAME	TYPE	AMOUNT	LIMIT	TAX TRACKING	PAYABLE TO	ACCOUNT ID
Salary	Yearly Salary			Compensation		
Hourly	Hourly Wage			Compensation		
Overtime (x1.5) hourly	Hourly Wage			Compensation		
401k Emp.	Deduction	-2.0%	-18,000.00	401(k)	Investors, Inc.	67890
Fed. Withholding	Deduction	0.00		None	United States Treasury	39-1212121
Health Insurance (taxable)	Deduction	-200.00		None	Healthcare Insurance	12345
Medicare - Employee	Deduction	-1.45%		None	United States Treasury	39-1212121
Social Security	Deduction	-6.2%	-118,500.00	None	United States Treasury	39-1212121
St. Withholding	Deduction	-2.0%		None	WI Dept of Revenue	036-3456789012-04
401k Co. Match	Company Contribution	2.0%	18,000.00	401(k) Co. Match	Investors, Inc.	67890
Fed. Unemployment	Company Contribution	0.6%	7,000.00	None	United States Treasury	39-1212121
Health Insurance (company...)	Company Contribution	200.00		None	Healthcare Insurance	12345
Medicare - Employer	Company Contribution	1.45%		None	United States Treasury	39-1212121
Social Security - Employer	Company Contribution	6.2%	118,500.00	None	United States Treasury	39-1212121
St. Unemployment	Company Contribution	4.1%	14,000.00	None	WI Dept. of Workforce Development	876543-211-1

Reminder: Add 401k employee and employer to Max's *and* Mary's individual payroll information just as you did the health insurance above.

7/3 Spread 10 yards of topsoil and 3 bags of seed at Forest Hill School; 12 hours of landscaping services; create invoice.

7/10 Received full payment from *all* customers from June statements except for Brown's April invoice. (You will have to scroll down to see all invoices on the receive payments screen). Reminder: Discount is calculated on *each* invoice.

7/13 Paid $1,000 on balance owed to ABC Equipment for equipment previously purchased; pay bill. (Note: Unpaid balance will start accruing interest on 7/15 at a 9% annual rate; interest will be paid when the next payment is made; when to pay all future payments will be specifically identified in the monthly transactions.)

7/13 Completed lawn maintenance for *all* contracted customers; create invoices.

7/14 Purchased printer paper, envelopes, ink, and other miscellaneous office supplies from Office City, charged $65.63 to credit card.

7/15 Review Unpaid Bills Detail; pay any amounts due (payments to ABC Equipment will be specifically identified, no additional payment here).

- Prepare WT-6, Wisconsin state withholding report, from the Wisconsin Department of Revenue website and pay the amount due for *2nd* quarter Wisconsin withholding.

    - ✓ As we did for sales tax in April, reconcile a) the QuickBooks report, here the Payroll Summary for the quarter, to b) SWT Payable per the trial balance, to c) the WT-6. You will include this complete reconciliation in July's monthly questions.

    - ✓ Mary Martin, our office manager, will file these reports; you as the accountant will review them.

Note: This *2nd* quarter payroll summary was exported into Excel, and then the individual employee columns were edited to just show the total column.

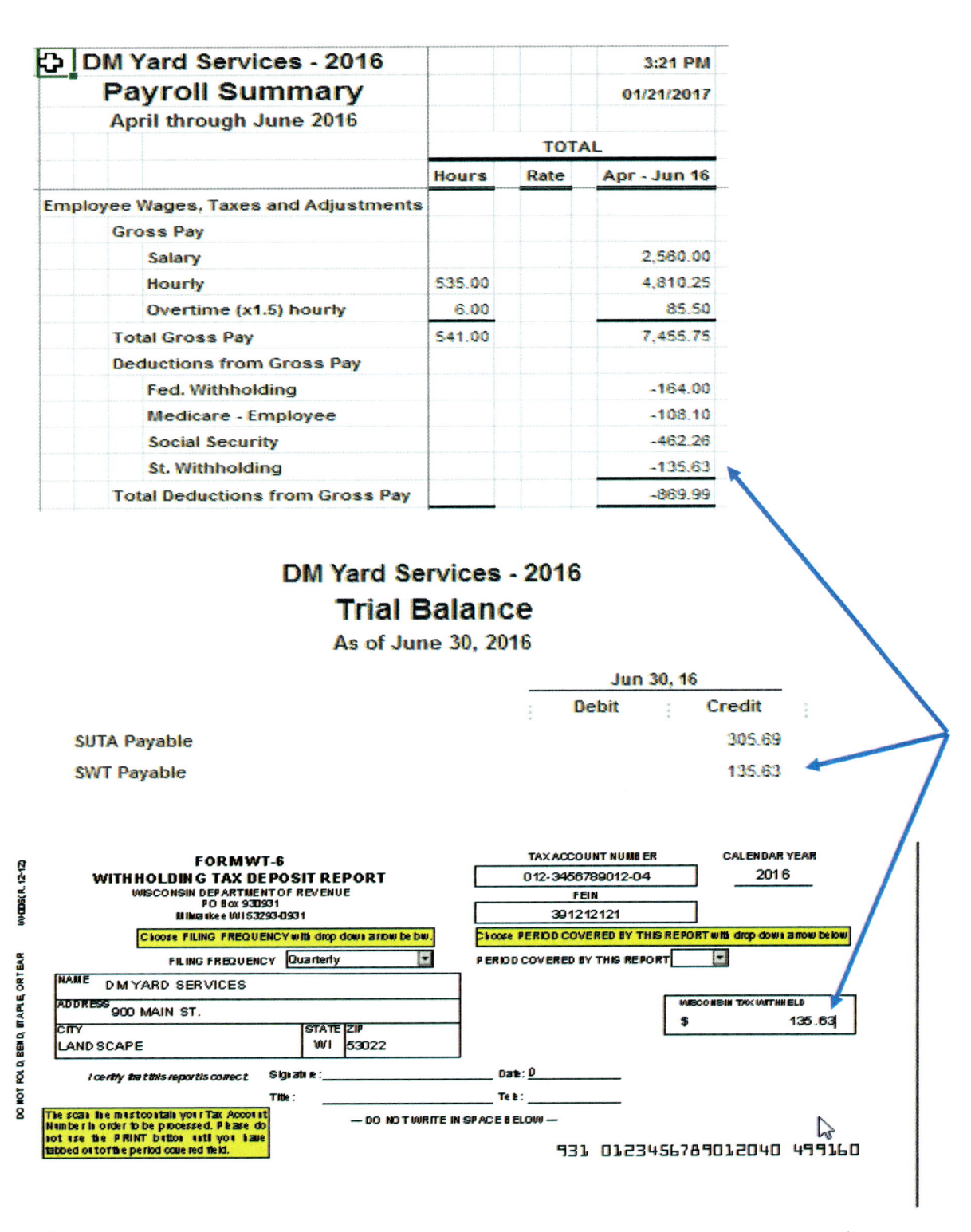

DM Yard Services - 2016
Payroll Summary
April through June 2016

	Hours	Rate	Apr - Jun 16
Employee Wages, Taxes and Adjustments			
Gross Pay			
Salary			2,560.00
Hourly	535.00		4,810.25
Overtime (x1.5) hourly	6.00		85.50
Total Gross Pay	541.00		7,455.75
Deductions from Gross Pay			
Fed. Withholding			-164.00
Medicare - Employee			-108.10
Social Security			-462.26
St. Withholding			-135.63
Total Deductions from Gross Pay			-869.99

Report time: 3:21 PM, 01/21/2017

DM Yard Services - 2016
Trial Balance
As of June 30, 2016

	Debit	Credit
SUTA Payable		305.69
SWT Payable		135.63

FORM WT-6
WITHHOLDING TAX DEPOSIT REPORT
WISCONSIN DEPARTMENT OF REVENUE
PO Box 930931
Milwaukee WI 53293-0931

TAX ACCOUNT NUMBER: 012-3456789012-04
CALENDAR YEAR: 2016
FEIN: 391212121

Choose FILING FREQUENCY with drop down arrow below.
FILING FREQUENCY: Quarterly

Choose PERIOD COVERED BY THIS REPORT with drop down arrow below.
PERIOD COVERED BY THIS REPORT:

NAME: DM YARD SERVICES
ADDRESS: 900 MAIN ST.
CITY: LANDSCAPE
STATE: WI
ZIP: 53022

WISCONSIN TAX WITHHELD: $ 135.63

I certify that this report is correct.
Signature: _____ Date: 0
Title: _____ Tel: _____

— DO NOT WRITE IN SPACE BELOW —

931 01234567890012040 499160

The scanner must contain your Tax Account Number in order to be processed. Please do not use the PRINT button until you have tabbed out of the period covered field.

Note: The WT-6 is most commonly prepared monthly; for our purposes we will prepare it quarterly and use the last month for the period covered by this report.

- ✓ Use Pay Liabilities from the Employee Center of the Home screen or from pull-down menus Employees/Payroll Taxes and Liabilities/Pay Payroll Liabilities; verify amount as shown below.

- ✓ Uncheck "To be printed" box and enter check number on check.

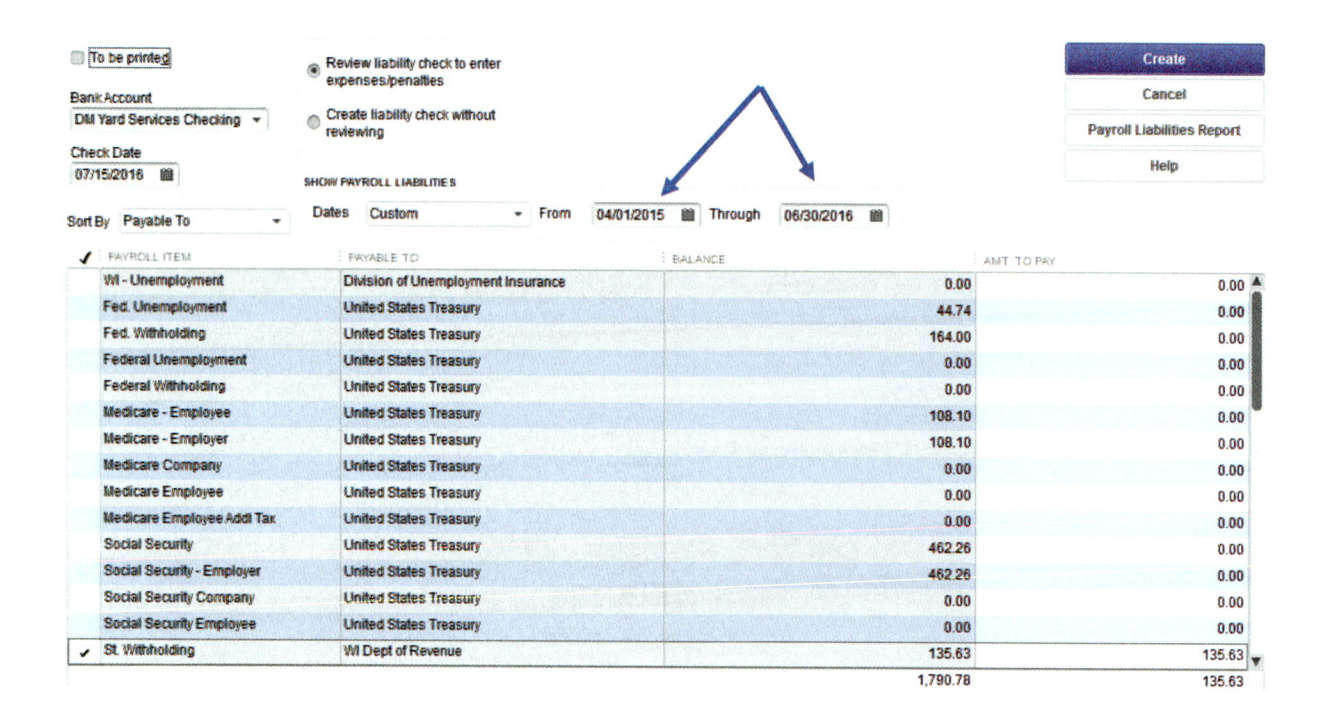

Payroll Item	Payable To	Balance	Amt To Pay
WI - Unemployment	Division of Unemployment Insurance	0.00	0.00
Fed. Unemployment	United States Treasury	44.74	0.00
Fed. Withholding	United States Treasury	164.00	0.00
Federal Unemployment	United States Treasury	0.00	0.00
Federal Withholding	United States Treasury	0.00	0.00
Medicare - Employee	United States Treasury	108.10	0.00
Medicare - Employer	United States Treasury	108.10	0.00
Medicare Company	United States Treasury	0.00	0.00
Medicare Employee	United States Treasury	0.00	0.00
Medicare Employee Addl Tax	United States Treasury	0.00	0.00
Social Security	United States Treasury	462.26	0.00
Social Security - Employer	United States Treasury	462.26	0.00
Social Security Company	United States Treasury	0.00	0.00
Social Security Employee	United States Treasury	0.00	0.00
✓ St. Withholding	WI Dept of Revenue	135.63	135.63
		1,790.78	135.63

- ➢ Reminder: Go to check, use the Reports tab, and review the Transaction Journal to ensure SWT Payable is being debited.

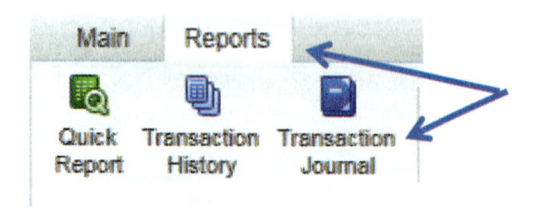

DM Yard Services - 2016
Transaction Journal
All Transactions

Trans #	Type	Date	Num	Name	Memo	Account	Class	Debit	Credit
194	Liability Check	07/15/2016	1040	WI Dept of Revenue	036-345678...	DM Yard Services...			135.63
				WI Dept of Revenue	036-345678...	SWT Payable		135.63	
								135.63	135.63
TOTAL								**135.63**	**135.63**

7/17 Planted 4 36" pine trees, 2 5' pine trees; laid 20 yards of topsoil and 25 yards of mulch at the Nottingham Condominium Complex, 30 hours of landscaping services; create invoice.

7/25 Bought oil and miscellaneous equipment supplies (charge to Repairs and Maintenance) from PP Equipment, $43.05 charged to credit card.

7/31 Brian: 42 hours (#1041) Mary: (#1042) Max: 167 hours (160, 7 OT) (#1043)

> Payroll Reminder: 401k employee/employer and health insurance employee/employer start in July. Note: Federal *and* state withholding are calculated *after* the 401k deduction; you will have to *re-calculate* state withholding!

   ✓ You may have to enter the health insurance deduction; don't forget the minus sign.

   ✓ Review the Company Summary section of the paycheck detail for the employer portions of the health insurance and 401k.

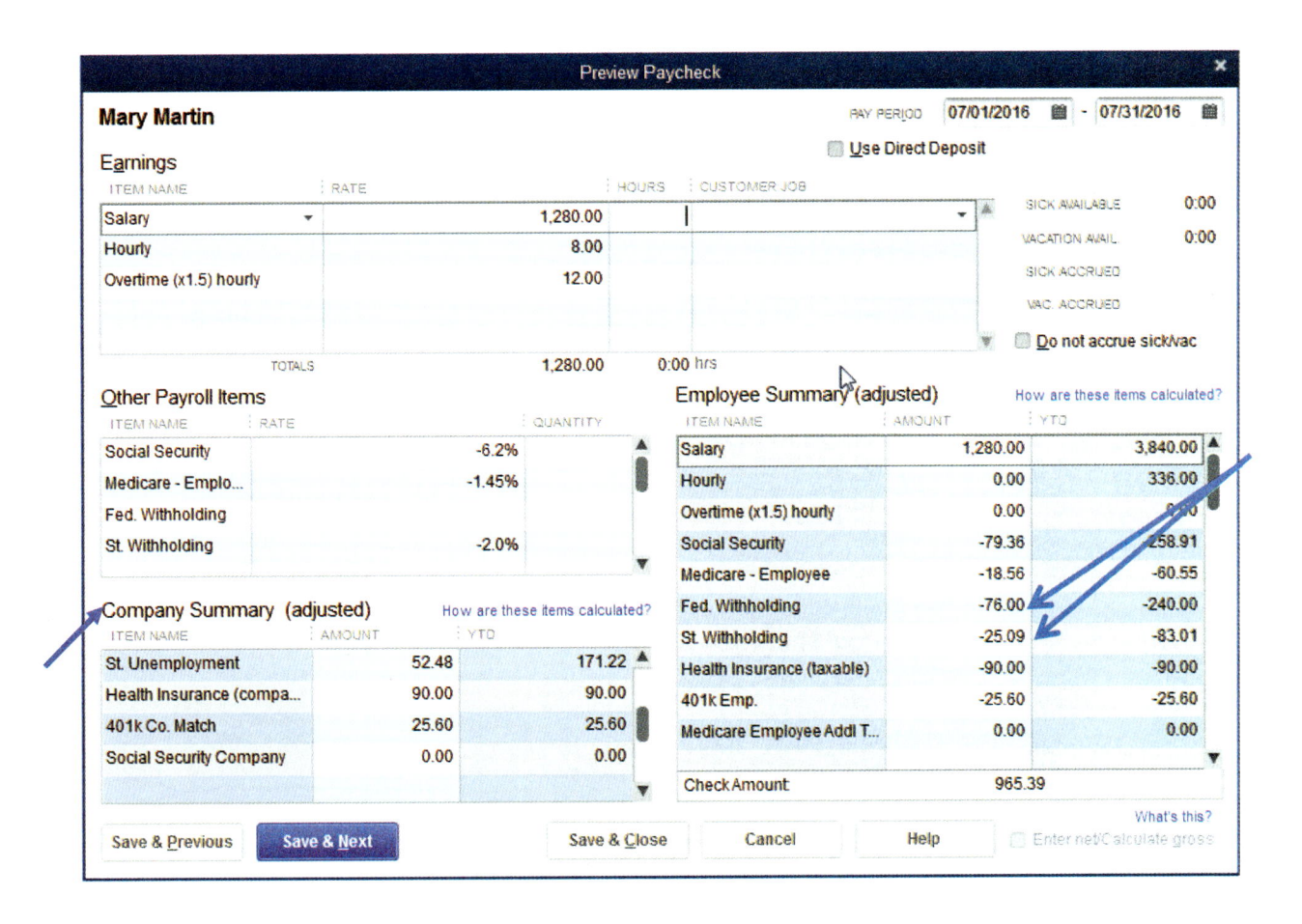

Preview Paycheck — Mary Martin
Pay Period: 07/01/2016 – 07/31/2016

Earnings

Item Name	Rate	Hours	Customer Job
Salary	1,280.00		
Hourly	8.00		
Overtime (x1.5) hourly	12.00		
TOTALS	1,280.00	0:00 hrs	

Sick Available: 0:00
Vacation Avail: 0:00

Other Payroll Items

Item Name	Rate	Quantity
Social Security	-6.2%	
Medicare - Emplo...	-1.45%	
Fed. Withholding		
St. Withholding	-2.0%	

Company Summary (adjusted)

Item Name	Amount	YTD
St. Unemployment	52.48	171.22
Health Insurance (compa...	90.00	90.00
401k Co. Match	25.60	25.60
Social Security Company	0.00	0.00

Employee Summary (adjusted)

Item Name	Amount	YTD
Salary	1,280.00	3,840.00
Hourly	0.00	336.00
Overtime (x1.5) hourly	0.00	
Social Security	-79.36	258.91
Medicare - Employee	-18.56	-60.55
Fed. Withholding	-76.00	-240.00
St. Withholding	-25.09	-83.01
Health Insurance (taxable)	-90.00	-90.00
401k Emp.	-25.60	-25.60
Medicare Employee Addl T...	0.00	0.00

Check Amount: 965.39

7/31   Perform month-end and 2nd quarter reports and reconciliations.

> Complete Wisconsin sales tax return (ST-12) and pay 2nd quarter sales tax (#1045). Follow *complete* reconciliation process with both QuickBooks reports as done in April transactions; this will be documented in question 1 at month-end. Reminder: Click Pay All Tax to complete the payment.

> Complete 2nd quarter 941 (Federal withholding, FICA and Medicare, employee and employer), pay amount due for 2nd quarter under Pay Liabilities (#1046).

- Find Form 941 on the IRS website.

- Complete the reconciliation process as was done for WT-6 on 7/15.

    o Objective: Reconcile Payroll Summary (QuickBooks) report to Trial Balance to form. This reconciliation will be documented in question 2 at month-end. Since this is the 1st quarter for payroll tax forms and reconciliation, detailed steps are provided here.

Payroll Summary
April through June 2016   01/21/2017

	Hours	Rate	Apr - Jun 16
Employee Wages, Taxes and Adjustments			
Gross Pay			
Salary			2,560.00
Hourly	535.00		4,810.25
Overtime (x1.5) hourly	6.00		85.50
Total Gross Pay	541.00		7,455.75
Deductions from Gross Pay			
Fed. Withholding			-164.00
Medicare - Employee			-108.10
Social Security			-462.26
St. Withholding			-135.63
Total Deductions from Gross Pay			-869.99
Employer Taxes and Contributions			
Fed. Unemployment			44.74
Medicare - Employer			108.10
Social Security - Employer			462.26
St. Unemployment			305.69
Total Employer Taxes and Contributions			920.79

Total Gross Pay used on 941 and UCT 101 (Note: also referred to as UCT-101E) is as follows:

941 Taxes: Fed. Withholding   164.00

  Medicare — Employee   108.10
  Social Security (deduction)   462.26
  Medicare — Employer   108.10
  Soc. Sec. — Employer   <u>462.26</u>
    TOTAL: $1,304.72

941 Taxes per Trial Balance:

DM Yard Services - 2016
Trial Balance
As of June 30, 2016

	Jun 30, 16 Debit	Credit
Credit Card Payable	0.00	
FICA Payable		1,140.72
FIT Withholding		164.00

TOTAL: $1,304.72

To 941:

1	Number of employees who received wages, tips, or other compensation for the pay period including: *Mar. 12* (Quarter 1), *June 12* (Quarter 2), *Sept. 12* (Quarter 3), or *Dec. 12* (Quarter 4)	1	3
2	Wages, tips, and other compensation	2	7455 . 75
3	Federal income tax withheld from wages, tips, and other compensation	3	164 . 00
4	If no wages, tips, and other compensation are subject to social security or Medicare tax		☐ Check and go to line 6.

		Column 1		Column 2	
5a	Taxable social security wages	.	× .124 =	924 . 51	
5b	Taxable social security tips	.	× .124 =	.	
5c	Taxable Medicare wages & tips	.	× .029 =	216 . 22	
5d	Taxable wages & tips subject to Additional Medicare Tax withholding	.	× .009 =	.	

5e	Add Column 2 from lines 5a, 5b, 5c, and 5d	5e	1140 . 73
5f	Section 3121(q) Notice and Demand—Tax due on unreported tips (see instructions)	5f	.
6	Total taxes before adjustments. Add lines 3, 5e, and 5f	6	1304 . 73
7	Current quarter's adjustment for fractions of cents	7	. 01
8	Current quarter's adjustment for sick pay	8	.
9	Current quarter's adjustments for tips and group-term life insurance	9	.
10	Total taxes after adjustments. Combine lines 6 through 9	10	1304 . 72
11	Total deposits for this quarter, including overpayment applied from a prior quarter and overpayments applied from Form 941-X, 941-X (PR), 944-X, or 944-X (SP) filed in the current quarter	11	1304 . 72
12	Balance due. If line 10 is more than line 11, enter the difference and see instructions	12	. 00

- Note that Total deposits (line 11) for the quarter should equal the balance in the FICA Payable and FIT Withholding accounts per your 6/30/2016 trial balance, the amount you will pay ($1,304.72).

    - ✓ You complete the 941 up to line 6, enter deposits on line 11, then work back *up* to enter "Current quarter's adjustment for fraction of cents" on line 7, so that your "Total taxes before adjustments" plus/minus the small adjustment equals your deposits (your payable accounts on the trial balance). This small difference is due to calculating Social Security and Medicare *per paycheck* versus in *total* for the quarter here on lines 5a and c.

- Go to Pay Liabilities under the Employee Section of the Home screen and make the 2nd quarter deposit (check #1046). Review the transaction journal for the correct journal entry.

- Complete 2nd quarter state unemployment: Wisconsin Form UCT-101.

    - Reconcile Payroll Summary (QuickBooks) report to Trial Balance to form.

    - Prepare first page of UCT-101 found on the Department of Workforce Development website. Use any year form.

1) Payroll Summary:

Payroll Summary
01/21/2017
April through June 2016

	Hours	Rate	Apr - Jun 16
Employer Taxes and Contributions			
Fed. Unemployment			44.74
Medicare - Employer			108.10
Social Security - Employer			462.26
St. Unemployment			305.69
Total Employer Taxes and Contributions			920.79

2) *Agrees* with 6/30/2016 SUTA Payable per trial balance:

DM Yard Services - 2016
Trial Balance
As of June 30, 2016

	Jun 30, 16 Debit	Jun 30, 16 Credit
SUTA Payable		305.69

3) *Agrees* with UCT-101:

QUARTERLY CONTRIBUTION REPORT TO BE FILED WITH QUARTERLY WAGE REPORT
INSTRUCTIONS ON REVERSE SIDE

1. U.I. ACCOUNT NUMBER: 876543-211-1
2. QUARTER: 2 YEAR: 16
1b. INTERNET ACCESS NUMBER: http://dwd.wisconsin.gov/uitax
3. REPORT AND PAYMENT DUE
4. ACCOUNT NUMBER
5. FEIN: 39-1212121
6. EMPLOYER TELEPHONE NO./EMAIL
7. EMPLOYER NAME AND ADDRESS

DM Yard Services
900 Main St.
Landscape, WI 53022

ITEM 8. Required - Monthly Employment Count
8. MONTHLY DATA SHOULD COUNT ALL FULL-TIME AND PART-TIME WORKERS IN COVERED EMPLOYMENT WHO WORKED DURING OR RECEIVED PAY FOR THE PAYROLL PERIOD WHICH INCLUDES THE 12TH OF THE MONTH. IF NONE, ENTER -0-

1st Month	Number of Employees	2nd Month	Number of Employees	3rd Month	Number of Employees
	2		3		3

9. TOTAL COVERED WAGE Must agree with total wages on Wage Report	7,455	75
10. LESS EXCLUSIONS FOR WAGES OVER $14,000 (See instructions on back of form.)		
11. DEFINED (TAXABLE) PAYROLL Item 9 minus Item 10 THIS LINE MUST BE COMPLETED	7,455	75
12. TAX RATE:	.0410	
13. TAX DUE: Multiply Item 11 by Item 12	305	69
14. INTEREST DUE: If filed after due date, compute interest on Item 13 above. (See instructions on back of form.)		
15. LATE FILING FEE: If Wage Report (UC-7823) is filed after due date, add fee. (See instructions on back of form.)		
16. LESS ELECTRONIC FUND TRANSFER PAYMENT		
17. LESS CREDIT AVAILABLE as of		
18. TOTAL AMOUNT ENCLOSED WITH THIS REPORT	305	69

The second page of UCT-101 (which is not shown here and does not need to be completed) is a list of total wages by employee for the quarter to tie to line 9 above. You would use your Payroll Summary for this to tie to the quarter's wages.

- Go to Pay Liabilities and make the 2nd quarter payment (check #1047). Review the transaction journal on the check for the correct journal entry.

- Pay 940 deposit *if required*; refer to instructions for IRS Form 940 to determine when 940 deposits are due.

Credit Card Services, Inc.

DM Yard Services

Statement Date: 7/5/2016

Last Payment: 6/15/2016 $581.70

Amount Due: $477.00

Due Date: 7/15/2016

Charge Summary:

- Gas to Go   82.00
- Gas to Go   130.00
- Cell World   60.00
- Gas to Go   55.00
- Utility Service Corp. 150.00

XYZ Bank

DM Yard Services

Acct. #745-1332									7/1/2016 thru 7/31/2016

Beg. Balance: $2,3678.08

Deposits & CM

7/10 $5,787.56

Checks & DM

#1033	$435.20	#1039	477.00
#1034	1,074.48	#1040	135.63
#1035	1,424.82		
#1036	1,000.00		
#1037	750.00		
#1038	1,000.00		

7/31   SC   15.00

Ending Balance: $2,3153.51

July Questions

1. As shown in April transactions, reconcile the QuickBooks sales tax reports (Sales Tax Revenue Summary *and* Sales Tax Liability) to their respective account balances per the Profit and Loss and trial balance to the Wisconsin ST-12. Use snips of reports.

2. Show reconciliation of the 2nd quarter Payroll Summary report to respective general ledger accounts and amounts on your WT-6, 941, and UCT-101. (Duplicate *your* reconciliations as shown in July transactions.) Document reconciliations in the monthly question Word document. (Note: Another approach would be to show all three parts for each reconciliation in an Excel worksheet. Ask your instructor which approach to use.)

3. Print (copy and paste or snip in Word document) the 940 deposit requirements per IRS. (Print *only* the deposit requirements.)

4. Complete a) the Monthly Task List and b) your To Do/Follow-up Question List with at least two items to be addressed by your "manager"/teacher.

CHAPTER PRINT/SUBMISSION SUMMARY

1. _____ Bank Account Reconciliation

2. _____ Trial Balance

3. _____ Question 1 — Reconciliations and ST-12

4. _____ Question 2 — Reconciliations for WT-6, 941, and UCT-101

5. _____ Question 3 — Support for answer

6. _____ Task List/To Do/Question List

JULY TASK LIST

Check here if completed	Task	Initials
	Review of Unpaid Bills Detail Report	
	Use of Payroll Summary report	
	Review check register for WT-6,941, and UCT-101 payments	
	Review financial statements for new accounts added (Are they on the correct financial statement?)	
	Verify cash balance on trial balance equals cash balance on bank reconciliation	
	Review trial balance for completeness and accuracy	
	Back up your monthly transactions to an external destination (e.g., flash drive), changing file name to the month	

To Do/Follow-up/Question List

August Transactions/Activities

Reminder: Complete monthly tasks!

8/6   Year-end close-out of bushes at JS Garden Supply, picked up 6 boxwood bushes at $6.50 each and 4 of the 5' pine trees at $12.50 each. (Do *not* change cost for these close-out items in the inventory items.) Invoice 872, terms 2/10, n/30.

8/7   In preparation for the start of school at Forest Hill School, reseeded areas laying 15 yards of topsoil, 2 bags of seed and 3 bales of straw, 5 yards of mulch, including general clean-up, 30 hours of landscaping services. Create invoice.

8/10   Received payment from July statements except for Brown's April invoice, Forest Hill School, and Jacksonville Industrial Park.

8/10   Completed lawn maintenance for *all* contracted customers; create invoices.

8/13   Planted 5 boxwood bushes and 5 tall (5') pine trees and spread 4 yards of topsoil and 10 yards of mulch, 20 hours of landscaping services, for Davidson Foods. Create invoice.

8/15   Review Unpaid Bills Detail; pay any amounts due, and apply an outstanding credit memo to the JS Garden Supply invoice. (Note: To agree with the check on the bank statement, calculate the discount on the whole amount before the credit, noting in business you would *not* be allowed this whole discount.)

8/15   Dave approved another $1,000 payment to ABC Equipment plus interest from July 15 through August 15 (should account for 31 days of interest using a 360-day year for calculation, interest = $28.68). Next payment will be made in November.

To account for the interest on this check, per QuickBooks Help Community, enter a bill for the vendor for the interest. Pay a partial on the regular invoice and the interest.

Pay both bills for ABC Equipment with check #1051.

8/22   Received payments from Davidson Foods for 8/13 work and from Forest Hill and Jacksonville Industrial Park for balances due from their July statements.

8/24   Completed lawn maintenance for *all* contracted customers; create invoices.

8/27   Ordered 20 bags of fertilizer at fall close-out price of $6/bag for fall applications from JS Garden Supply. Prepare purchase order 2. (Do not change item cost.)

8/31   Had a company picnic for employees and families at Dave's house. Cost of $122.86 paid from petty cash.

8/31   Perform month-end tasks.

Payroll:

Brian: 65 hours (#1052) (last payroll for Brian as he is returning to school)

Mary — salaried   (#1053)   Max: 150 hours due to seasonal/business needs (#1054)

- ➢ Reminders:
  - On Brian's check, you may have to zero out his state withholding; he is exempt from federal and state withholding.
  - On Mary and Max, you have to recalculate state withholding AFTER the 401k; and you may have to enter the health insurance *deductions* and *company contributions* for Mary and Max.

Credit Card Services, Inc.

DM Yard Services

Statement Date: 8/5/2016

Last Payment: 7/15/2016 $477.00

Amount Due: $612.85

Due Date: 8/15/2016

Charge Summary:

- Gas to Go   85.00
- Office City   65.63
- Cell World   60.00
- Gas to Go   125.00
- PP Equipment   43.05
- Utility Service Corp. 150.00
- ABC Food Store   84.17

XYZ Bank

DM Yard Services

Acct. #745-1332   8/1/2016 thru 8/31/2016

Beg. Balance: $23153.51

Deposits & CM

8/10 $3,487.22

8/22   2,828.55

Checks & DM

#1041	$281.20	#1047	305.69
#1042	965.39	#1048	750.00
#1043	1,231.69	#1049	612.85
#1044	1,000.00	#1050	61.32
#1045	539.48	#1051	1,028.68
#1046	1,304.72		
8/31	SC 15.00		

Ending Balance: $21373.26

Receipt 8/30 for petty cash disbursement

ABC Food Store $ 122.86

Disbursement should be noted on your petty cash sheet

August Questions

1. List three internal control procedures for petty cash.

2. Research the income tax treatment of entertainment expenses as it pertains to the company picnic, and copy and paste information in your Word document; highlight information if possible. Then state *your* conclusion as to the treatment based on information presented.

3. Complete: a) the Monthly Task List (note tasks for completion) and b) your To Do/Follow-up Question List with at least two items to be addressed by your "manager"/teacher.

CHAPTER PRINT/SUBMISSION SUMMARY

1. ____ Bank Account Reconciliation

2. ____ Trial Balance

3. ____ Questions 1 and 2

4. ____ Task List/To Do/Question List

AUGUST TASK LIST

Check here if completed	Task	Initials
	Review of Unpaid Bills Detail Report	
	Verify cash balance on trial balance equals cash balance on bank reconciliation	
	Review trial balance for completeness and accuracy	
	Back up your monthly transactions to an external destination (e.g., flash drive), changing file name to the month	

To Do/Follow-up/Question List

September Transactions/Activities

Reminder: Complete monthly tasks!

9/3 Planted 3 of the 36" pine trees and 3 boxwood bushes with 3 yards of mulch at the entrance to Nottingham Condominium complex, 16 hours of landscaping services. Create an invoice.

9/3 Spent 8 hours of landscaping services on general clean-up work at Davidson Foods. Create an invoice.

9/5 Placed an ad in the local newspaper advertising snowplowing services, charged $27.00 on the credit card.

9/7 Completed lawn maintenance for *all* contracted customers. Create invoices.

9/10 Received full payment from the August statements except for Brown's April invoice.

9/15 Make federal and Wisconsin estimated tax payments (checks #1058 and 1059). Prepare 1040-ES and WI 1-ES.

9/21 Completed lawn maintenance for *all* contracted customers. Create invoices.

9/26 Received and paid invoice #382 to American Insurance, $960 and $450 for workers compensation (comp) and business insurance for October 2016 through March 2016. *Edit date on memorized transaction. (See April transaction.)*

9/27 Received fertilizer ordered from JS Garden Supply; terms n/30, invoice #56. Do not change vendor terms.

9/30   Payroll: Mary (last month of full salary) (ck #1061)   Max: 120 hours (ck #1062)

Watch your Excel file for wage limits — Max goes over the federal unemployment wage limit this month.

9/30   Mary will return to part-time status for the remainder of year; hourly wage will be used starting in October.

9/30   Perform month-end tasks.

Credit Card Services, Inc.

DM Yard Services

Statement Date: 9/5/2016

Last payment: 8/15/2016 $612.85

Amount Due: $384.00

Due Date: 9/15/2016

Charge Summary:

- Gas to Go   120.00
- Cell World   60.00
- Gas to Go   54.00
- Utility Service Corp.   150.00

XYZ Bank

DM Yard Services

Acct. #745-1332   9/1/2016 thru 9/30/2016

Beg. Balance: $2,1373.26

Deposits & CM

9/10 $3,928.32

Checks & DM

#	Amount	#	Amount
#1052	$435.20	1057	384.00
#1053	965.39	1058	500.00
#1054	1,059.56	1059	150.00
#1055	1,000.00		
#1056	750.00		

9/30   SC   15.00

Ending Balance: $2,0042.43

September Questions

1. Prepare an Excel or Word report of wages for workers compensation audit: 1/1/16 through 9/30/2016.
   - ✓ List total gross wages *by employee* for the period.

   - ✓ List wages *by types*: office and landscaping/field labor.

   - ✓ Make sure the total per employee list equals the total per type list.

   - ✓ Wages are reported by type, because the workers comp rates are different for office versus field labor; list the workers comp codes per the Wisconsin Workers Comp Code Manual, and choose the best fit. All of Mary's wages should be classified as office here.

2. Quarterly Tasks:

   > Verify the A/R, Inventory, and A/P control account balances per the trial balance agree with one of the respective (A/R, Inventory, or A/P) detail reports; document this in your Word document.

   > As measures of internal control:

   a) Print a report of *quarterly* numerically sorted invoices to ensure all invoices are accounted for.

   b) Print a quarterly check detail report for Dave's review for reasonableness of payees and amounts; Dave initials report.

   c) Review the general ledger on screen *only* — no printing. The general ledger will be used extensively to reconcile differences in your accounts compared to "check figure" trial balances. Review the general ledger for information presented and note the review in your Word document for monthly questions.

3. Identify and list two managerial/business-related (e.g., address controls to safeguard inventory) and three financial-related (e.g., current ratio is …) observations through September for your landscaping business.

4. Complete a) the Monthly Task List and b) your To Do/Follow-up Question List with at least two items to be addressed by your "manager"/teacher.

CHAPTER PRINT/SUBMISSION SUMMARY

1. ____ Subsidiary ledger reports for A/R, A/P, and Inventory (if snips not included in question)

2. ____ Report of numerically sorted invoices for quarter

3. ____ Check Register for July – September with Dave's initials to indicate review

4. ____ Bank Account Reconciliation

5. ____ Trial Balance

6. ____ Questions 1 – 3

7. ____ Task List/To Do/Question List

SEPTEMBER TASK LIST

Check here if completed	Task	Initials
	Review of Unpaid Bills Detail Report	
	Compare A/R control account balance (A/R on trial balance) to a detail report of the A/R subsidiary ledger	
	Compare A/P control account balance (A/P on trial balance) to a detail report of the A/P subsidiary ledger	
	Compare Inventory control account balance (Inventory on trial balance) to a detail report of the Inventory subsidiary ledger	
	Prepare a report of numerically sorted invoices	
	Review check detail for July – September; Dave indicates review with his initials on report	
	Review year-to-date general ledger	
	Verify cash balance on trial balance equals cash balance on bank reconciliation	
	Review trial balance	
	Back up your monthly transactions to an external destination (e.g., flash drive), changing file name to the month	

To Do/Follow-up/Question List

October Transactions/Activities

Reminder: Complete monthly tasks!

10/3 Purchased a used heavy-duty dump truck with plow for snowplowing from PP Equipment for $20,000, $500 down payment, 5%, 5-year note for remaining balance.

> ➢ Prepare an amortization schedule in Excel; calculate monthly payment using the PMT function. Monthly payments start November 3, 2016.
>
> ➢ Use the write check function to record the *entire* entry; review the journal entry (Reports/Transaction Journal). We will classify the note as long-term (long-term liability) at this time and properly split it into short-term/long-term at year-end. The dump truck is not suited for personal use.
>
> ➢ Reminder: Enter the snowplow into Fixed Asset Manager (asset description, accounts, under book column cost, and date acquired); remember to back up Fixed Asset Manager.

10/5 Completed lawn maintenance for *all* contracted customers and performed leaf service (additional time incurred is noted below) for all contracted customers:

Brown/Calhoun/Laxson/Garrett: 2 hours for *each* customer of additional time

Forest Hill School: 4 hours additional

Jacksonville Industrial Park: 6 hours additional

Nottingham Condominium Complex: 6 hours additional

Also incurred 3 hours at Davidson Foods for fall clean-up.

Create invoices. Account for leaf service in Landscaping Services income, and enter the description of work for additional time.

10/5   Received invoices #278 and #1289 from Healthcare Insurance and Investors, Inc. respectively, for paying 3rd quarter health insurance of $1740 and 401k contributions of $321; terms: n/10 on both. We are recording the bills here; cancel the message regarding paying payroll liabilities. Payment will be made on the due date. Watch debit accounts! (Do not change vendor terms.)

10/10 Received full payment from all September statements except for Brown's April invoice.

10/12 Paid $27 to Girl Scouts, $12 for cookies, and $15 cash donation, with check #1066 to Ann Smith (new vendor), John Smith's daughter; charge to the drawing account. We will determine the income tax impact in the October questions.

10/15 Pay outstanding invoices *except* for ABC Equipment. (Reminder: Quarterly WT-6 payment is due. You will complete all payroll forms and reconciliations in the October questions.)

10/19 Completed lawn (Lawn Cutting and Trimming Income) and leaf (Landscaping Services) (see time incurred on October 5th) for *all* and *only* contracted customers (not Davidson Foods). Create invoices.

10/31 Prepare monthly payroll:

Mary: 32 hours (ck #1072)   Max: 150 hours (ck #1073)

Note: We will review Mary's wages for proper classification between office and field wages at year-end.

10/31 Perform month-end tasks:

> Reconcile sales tax reports, prepare ST-12, and pay 3rd quarter sales tax

- Note 1: ST-12 calculates .01 difference; enter -.20 on line 5 to reconcile to the Sales Tax Payable balance in the trial balance.

- Reconciling payroll reports, preparing 3rd quarter payroll reports (941 and UCT-101), and paying payroll liabilities. Refer to the July quarterly work if necessary.

    - Note 2: Watch the fraction of cents adjustment on 941; your check amount should agree with the total per the trial balance accounts.

- The draw will be check #1077.

Credit Card Services, Inc.

DM Yard Services

Statement Date: 10/5/2016

Last payment: 9/15/2016 $384.00

Amount Due: $576.24

Due Date: 10/15/2016

Charge Summary:

- Newspapers, Inc.   27.00
- Gas to Go   85.00
- ABC Food Store   117.24
- Cell World   60.00
- Gas to Go   95.00
- XYZ Drug Store   42.00
- Utility Service Corp. 150.00

XYZ Bank

DM Yard Services

Acct. #745-1332   10/1/2016 thru 10/31/2016

Beg. Balance: $2,0042.43

Deposits & CM

10/10 $3,372.70

Checks & DM

#1060	1,410.00	#1066	27.00
#1061	965.39	#1067	576.24
#1062	807.65	#1068	1,740.00
#1063	1,000.00	#1069	321.00
#1064	750.00	#1070	120.00
1065	500.00	1071	157.29

10/31   SC   15.00

Ending Balance: $1,5025.56

October Questions

1. Include an amortization schedule for the dump truck with snowplow in your monthly question Word document. Also for your own purposes, print on different color paper (if possible) as a carry forward schedule to refer to for each payment allocation between principal and interest.

2. Find the IRS publication that pertains to charitable contributions. Based on the guidelines, is the amount or part of the amount paid to the Girl Scouts tax deductible? Why or why not? Copy and paste support and *state* your conclusion.

3. Reconcile the QuickBooks sales tax reports (Sales Tax Liability and Sales Tax Revenue Summary) to their respective account balances (per Profit and Loss and trial balance) to the WI ST-12. Document the reconciliation in your monthly question Word document, using snips of reports.

4. Reconcile the 3rd quarter Payroll Summary report to its respective general ledger accounts and amounts on your WT-6, 941, and UCT-101. Document the reconciliation in your monthly question Word document, using snips of reports. Follow the reconciliations shown in July monthly transactions.

5. Complete a) the Monthly Task List and b) your To Do/Follow-up Question List with at least two items to be addressed by your "manager"/teacher.

CHAPTER PRINT SUMMARY

1. _____ Bank Account Reconciliation

2. _____ Trial Balance

3. _____ Question 1 – amortization schedule

4. _____ Question 2 – charitable contribution guidelines

5. _____ Sales Tax Reconciliations and ST-12 (question 3)

6. _____ Payroll reconciliations and reports: WT-6, 941, and UCT-101 (question 4)

7. _____ Task List/To Do/Follow-Up/Question List

OCTOBER TASK LIST

Check here if completed	Task	Initials
	Review of Unpaid Bills Detail Report	
	Verify cash balance on trial balance equals cash balance on bank reconciliation	
	Review trial balance for completeness and accuracy	
	Back up your monthly transactions to an external destination (e.g., flash drive), changing file name to the month	

To Do/Follow-up/Question List

November Transactions/Activities

Reminder: Complete monthly tasks!

11/1 *All* lawn maintenance customers and Davidson Foods have contracted for snowplowing and will be billed on a $45 per hour basis. Due to the varied numbers of hours for snowplowing, memorized invoices will not be used.

- In addition, DM has contracted with new snowplowing customers, Thrifty Outlet Mall and Memorial Hospital, from the newspaper ad. Add these customers.

- No invoicing will be done at this time.

11/3 The first payment on the note for the truck with snowplow is due today; for the split between principal and interest, refer to your amortization schedule. Both principal and interest are accounted for on check #1079.

11/5 Leaf service *only* (landscaping services); final maintenance of year for contracted customers.

Brown, Calhoun, and Laxson: 3 hours each

Garrett:	4 hours
Davidson Foods:	6 hours
Forest Hill School:	6 hours
Jacksonville Ind. Park:	8 hours
Nottingham Condo:	8 hours

11/6 Purchased printer paper, ink, and miscellaneous office supplies; charged $86.10 to the credit card.

11/10 Received full payment of the October balances from Davidson Foods, Forest Hill School, Jacksonville Industrial Park, and Nottingham Condominium Complex.

11/22 David attended a 3-day landscaping convention in Las Vegas. Sue (wife), Mason (son), and Jamie (daughter) went along to enjoy sightseeing and shopping.

> Total costs: Airfare: $1,200 (total for four people); hotel: $600 (a larger room for the family was *not* required); and food: $270 (total for four people). The entire trip charged to the credit card. Journalize all costs to drawing at this time; this will be adjusted in question 1.

11/28 Unexpected early snowstorm:

Brown/Calhoun/Laxson/Garrett:	1 hour each
Davidson Foods/Forest Hill School/Jacksonville Ind. Park:	2 hours each
Nottingham Condominium Complex:	4 hours
Thrifty Outlet Mall/Memorial Hospital:	6 hours each

Create invoices. Watch sales tax treatment of snowplowing!

11/30 Receipts in full from Brown (except April invoice), Calhoun, Laxson, and Garrett from the October statements.

> Since these are the first late payments, enter a reminder comment about payment terms in the footer on the DM Yard Services statement template for the November statements. See the March transactions for entering a dunning message on statements.

> Print/PDF YTD statement for Calhoun.

11/30   Perform month-end tasks (checks #1081 – 1084).

> ➢ Mary: 32 hours   Max: 80 hours

Reminder: Watch federal unemployment! Mary goes over the limit; year-to-date total should be $42.00.

> ➢ In addition, make a payment to ABC Equipment for another $1,000 plus interest since the last payment on August 15, 2016 (i.e., 107 days).

> ➢ Dave will take a $2,000 draw this month.

Credit Card Services, Inc.

DM Yard Services

Statement Date: 11/5/2016

Last payment: 10/15/2016 $576.24

Amount Due: $332.00

Due Date: 11/15/2016

Charge Summary:

- Gas to Go   82.00
- Cell World   60.00
- Utility Service Corp. 150.00
- Gas to Go   40.00

XYZ Bank

DM Yard Services

Acct. #745-1332   11/1/2016 thru 11/30/2016

Beg. Balance: $1,5025.56

Deposits & CM

11/10 $2,745.70

Checks & DM

#1072	$136.28	#1076	360.82
#1073	1,059.56	#1077	1,000.00
#1074	495.12	#1078	750.00
#1075	1,574.48	#1079	367.99
		#1080	332.00

11/30 SC   15.00

Ending Balance: $1,1680.01

November Questions

1. Research and copy and paste the support for the income tax treatment of convention costs as it pertains to the landscaping convention attended by Dave and his family. After your research, review and correct your accounting for the convention costs. Non-deductible costs should be accounted for in the drawing account and deductible costs in Travel Expense and Meals and Entertainment Expense accounts. *State* your conclusion.

2. Review financial statements, Profit & Loss Standard, and Balance Sheet Standard for correct classification of accounts added in the last months. State in your Word document this review was completed.

3. Complete a) the Monthly Task List and b) your To Do/Follow-up Question List with at least two items to be addressed by your "manager"/teacher.

CHAPTER PRINT/SUBMISSION SUMMARY

1. ____ Customer statement for Calhoun with dunning message (November 30th transaction)

2. ____ Bank Account Reconciliation

3. ____ Trial Balance

4. ____ Questions 1 and 2

5. ____ Task List/To Do/Follow-up/Question List

NOVEMBER TASK LIST

Check here if completed	Task	Initials
	Review of Unpaid Bills Detail Report	
	Prepare a customer statement with dunning message	
	Review financial statements	
	Verify cash balance on trial balance equals cash balance on bank reconciliation	
	Review trial balance for completeness and accuracy	
	Back up your monthly transactions to an external destination (e.g., flash drive), changing file name to the month	

To Do/Follow-up/Question List

December Transactions/Activities

Reminder: Complete monthly tasks!

12/3   Made payment on note for the truck with snowplow.

12/6   Received full payment from the November statements except for the following: Brown's April invoice, Jacksonville Industrial Park, and Larry Laxson.

12/11 Heavy snowstorm plowing:

Brown/Calhoun/Laxson:	3 hours each
Garrett:	4 hours
Davidson Foods/Forest Hill School:	6 hours each
Jacksonville Industrial Park/Nottingham Condo:	8 hours each
Thrifty Outlet Mall/Memorial Hospital:	8 hours each

Create invoices.

12/13 New customer, Memorial Hospital, complained about poor snowplowing job; issued a credit memo for 3 hours. Apply credit to the above invoice.

12/17 Purchased and received a pallet (quantity of 40 – 50# bags) of salt from JS Garden Supply. Invoice #919, $160 total amount, terms n/30. Salt, a new inventory item, will be used for sidewalks and entry ways and *billed* at $6/bag. Create Salt Income, a subaccount of snowplowing. Do not change vendor terms.

12/24 Purchased a ham and turkey for both Mary and Max from ABC Food Store as holiday gifts; charged the business credit card, $35.32.

12/31 Perform month-end tasks (checks: #1088 – 1091).

> ➢ Payroll: Mary: 24 hours   Max: 60 hours
>
>   ✓ These hours are through December 23; the remaining time for the year will be accounted for in a year-end accrual in the year-end tasks.
>
> ➢ Pay remaining balance to ABC Equipment with interest (31 days).
>
> ➢ Monthly draw to Dave, $1,000.

Credit Card Services, Inc.

DM Yard Services

Statement Date: 12/5/2016

Last payment: 11/15/2016 $332.00

Amount Due: $2,458.10

Due Date: 12/15/2016

Charge Summary:

- Office City — 86.10
- Gas to Go — 42.00
- Best Air — 1,200.00
- Cell World — 60.00
- Win Here Inn — 600.00
- Convention Food Serv. — 270.00
- ABC Food Store — 50.00
- Utility Service Corp. — 150.00

XYZ Bank

DM Yard Services

Acct. #745-1332   12/1/2016 thru 12/31/2016

Beg. Balance: $1,1680.01

Deposits & CM

| 12/1 | $1,323.00 |
| 12/6 | 2,094.51 |

Checks & DM

#1081	$136.28
#1082	471.76
#1083	1,072.23
#1084	2,000.00
#1085	750.00
#1086	367.99
#1087	2,458.10
12/31 SC	15.00

Ending Balance: $7,826.16

December Questions

1. Dave will make his last federal and Wisconsin estimated income tax payments on the January 17, 2017, due date.

    ➢ What impact does this have on this year's income tax return?
    - A) Will he be able to include the January *federal* estimate payment on his 1040 as a *payment*?
    - B) Will he be able to include the January Wisconsin estimate on his federal income tax return on Schedule A as an itemized deduction?
    - Research and copy and paste the IRS support. *State* your conclusion for *both* items.

2. Dave learns that Max has been doing snowplowing jobs on the side with company equipment. Address the financial and legal impacts of this situation. What controls would help detect this activity?

3. Dave also learns that Max has been plowing Mary's driveway. Address the impact on Mary's wages, noting the amount is deemed to be de minimis.

4. Per the Wisconsin Department of Revenue, snow removal services are non-taxable. In December, we purchased salt for the driveways and sidewalks as well; research the taxability of salt for DM Yard Services, and include a snip of the information found on the Wisconsin Department of Revenue website in your monthly questions Word document.

5. Dave provided holiday gifts to his employees; research and copy and paste the IRS guidelines of fringe benefits to employees. State your conclusion.

6. Two quarterly tasks: Only two of the quarterly tasks will be completed in December; the others will be completed as part of the year-end account reconciliation process.

    ➢ As measures of internal control:

    a) Print a report of *quarterly* numerically sorted invoices to ensure all invoices are accounted for.

    b) Print a quarterly check detail report for Dave's review for reasonableness of payees and amounts; Dave initials report.

7. Identify and list two managerial/business-related (e.g., internal controls and marketing) and three financial-related (e.g., current ratio currently in a good position) observations through December for your landscaping business.

8. Complete a) the Monthly Task List and b) your To Do/Follow-up Question List with at least two items to be addressed by your "manager"/teacher.

CHAPTER PRINT/SUBMISSION SUMMARY

1. _____ Customer Balance Detail with credit memo approval (export to Excel to note initials)

2. _____ Report of numerically sorted invoices for the quarter

3. _____ Check Register for October – December, reviewed and initialed by Dave

4. _____ Bank Account Reconciliation

5. _____ Trial Balance

6. _____ Questions 1 – 5 and 7

7. _____ Task List/To Do/Question List

DECEMBER TASK LIST

Check here if completed	Task	Initials
	Review of Unpaid Bills Detail Report	
	Credit memo prepared and approved	
	Quarterly invoice register reviewed for sequential invoices	
	Review check register for October – December and submit with Dave's initials	
	Verify cash balance on trial balance equals cash balance on bank reconciliation	
	Review balance for completeness and accuracy	
	Back up your monthly transactions to an external destination (e.g., flash drive), changing file name to the month	

To Do/Follow-up/Question List

Year-End Activities: Account Reconciliations and Year-End Analysis

Note: Use QuickBooks help where needed. *Add new accounts if needed.*

1. Balance Sheet Account Analysis, Adjusting Entries and Business Tax Forms:
    - ✓ Refer to the general ledger to help complete this analysis.

    - ✓ Memorize year-end trial balance and put in group (reports/memorized/accountant) to be able to refer to throughout these reconciliations:

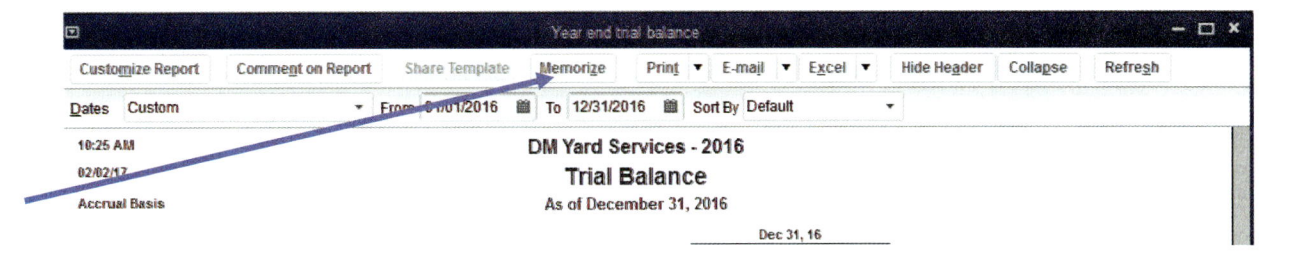

    ![Year end trial balance screenshot showing DM Yard Services - 2016 Trial Balance As of December 31, 2016, with arrow pointing to Memorize button]

    - ✓ *Use supplemental information provided on the following pages. (Look ahead at pages.)*

    - ✓ Use snips and provide full explanations of adjustments, comments, and reconciliations in one Excel file with multiple sheets or one large Word document with headings. Depending on your choice, there may be a few PDF files to submit as well, that is, 1096 and 1099s.

    - ➤ Cash: Verify/show cash balance in the general ledger (or trial balance, noting the source of the trial balance *is* the general ledger) agrees with reconciled balance on the December bank reconciliation. As explained above, use snips of each, enhance with highlighting/arrows, and then

        - o Comment on the cash position throughout the year.
        - o Make two suggestions to improve the cash position for 2017.

    - ➤ Petty Cash: Replenish fund; document (snip) journal entry for check written.

➢ Accounts Receivable: As we did each quarter, reconcile the subsidiary account balances to the A/R control account on the trial balance, showing the subsidiary ledger report and trial balance snips.

- o Review for past due invoices, noting the invoice date and our terms from the statement date (QuickBooks does not calculate the due dates correctly). Comment that you completed this task.

- o Prepare friendly collection letters for Jacksonville Industrial Park and Larry Laxson, who did not pay in December from their November statements.

Under Company, select Prepare Letters with Envelopes and then Collection Letters:

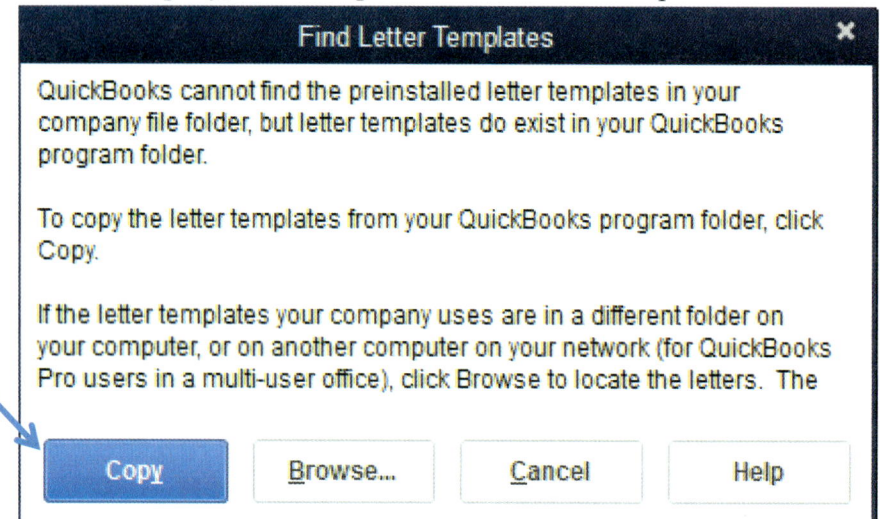

Find Letter Templates

QuickBooks cannot find the preinstalled letter templates in your company file folder, but letter templates do exist in your QuickBooks program folder.

To copy the letter templates from your QuickBooks program folder, click Copy.

If the letter templates your company uses are in a different folder on your computer, or on another computer on your network (for QuickBooks Pro users in a multi-user office), click Browse to locate the letters. The

[Copy] [Browse...] [Cancel] [Help]

Select Active-Customers-1 day or more. Select Jacksonville and Laxson. Select Friendly Collection and enter "your name" as Owner. Click Next, then click OK for *QuickBooks information is missing*. There is no need to prepare envelopes. Edit the letter to be a reminder of payment due. Note: If this function is not active in your QuickBooks, prepare your own simple, short, friendly collection letter.
Include letters in an Excel/Word file.

- Write off Brown's long outstanding uncollected April invoice using the *direct write-off method*.

    ✓ Review transactions to date:

    - April 2 invoice:

Type	Date	Num	Item	Account	Debit	Credit
Invoice	04/02/2016	3		Accounts Receivable	315.00	
			Mulch	Mulch Sales		230.00
			Mulch	Inventory Asset		192.50
			Mulch	Mulch Costs	192.50	
			Landscaping Services	Landscaping Services		70.00
			Wisconsin sales tax (Sales Tax)	Sales Tax Payable		15.00
					507.50	507.50

    - May 12 credit memo:

Type	Date	Num	Name	Item	Account	Debit	Credit
Credit Memo	05/12/2016	CM3	Walter Brown		Accounts Receivable		36.75
			Walter Brown	Landscaping Services	Landscaping Services	35.00	
			WI Dept of Revenue	Wisconsin sales tax (Sales Tax)	Sales Tax Payable	1.75	
						36.75	36.75

    ✓ First, write off the *entire balance ($278.25) in accounts receivable* (direct write-off method) using QuickBooks help.

    ✓ Next, a general journal entry is necessary to adjust for the sales tax portion ($13.25). Bad debt expense should only reflect the sale portion of entry. This write-off will be accounted for on your 4th quarter sales tax return. (Use Wisconsin Department of Revenue as the vendor.) Document in your file, including snips of the write-off and journal entry.

    ✓ Prepare your own short customer letter notifying Brown of this adjustment. As mentioned several times to this point, include *any and all* tasks in the Word/Excel file.

- On Company Snapshot, create a bar graph for Top Customer by Sales, and submit snip. (Note: QuickBooks will only prepare this graph for the current and prior year.)
    - If outside this time period, select Reports/Sales/Graph, edit the dates, sort by customer, and snip the *pie chart*.

- On Company Snapshot, determine the customer with shortest and longest average days to pay and then document the answer.

- Comment on receivable collection throughout the year.

- Make a suggestion relating to receivable management for 2017.

➢ Inventory: As we did each quarter, first, reconcile the inventory subsidiary ledger to the control account on the trial balance, showing the subsidiary ledger report and trial balance snips.

- Compare the inventory stock status report to the physical count listing (see listing on the following pages) and make any necessary adjustment(s) to the item's cost of goods sold account; include a snip of the adjustment. This is referred to as a book to physical adjustment.

- Comment on year-end inventory levels; be specific to inventory items.

➢ Supplies: Review supplies physical inventory listing (found on the following pages), make any necessary adjusting entry, and document or snip the entry. Explain why this adjusting entry is made.

➢ Prepaid Insurance: Reconcile unexpired insurance balance. Calculate the number of months of insurance for 2017 and compare to the prepaid insurance balance; make any necessary adjusting entry; document to show comparison.

➢ Security Deposit: Determine whether balance is correct; comment in the file.

➢ Equipment/Trucks/Computer/Leasehold Improvements: Calculate and record straight-line depreciation using IRS suggested lives. Use IRS Publication 946 as your guide), half-year convention with zero salvage values, *round to whole dollar*.

- o Update Fixed Asset Manager for Depreciation Method/Recovery Period and Convention for each asset.

- o In Fixed Asset Manager PDF report of depreciation
  - Reports/Display Report/Depreciation Schedule by G/L Account
  - Use Basis: Book
  - Print to PDF (found under Setup)
  - Include a snip of report in the file

- o In Fixed Asset Manager, record depreciation
  - QuickBooks/Post Journal Entry to QuickBooks
  - Basis to Post: Book
  - Make journal entry for depreciation rounded to *whole* dollar amount
  - Preview entry
  - Post entry to QuickBooks
  - Select File Backup/Asset Synchronization Log and click OK

- o In QuickBooks, review your journal entry:
  - Go to Accountant pull-down menu/Accountant/Make General Journal Entries, arrow to depreciation entry, noting FAM (Fixed Asset Manager) as entry no.
  - Snip the general journal entry into your document/file

➢ Equipment/Trucks/Computer/Leasehold Improvements Part 2: In Wisconsin, businesses are also subject to a personal property tax.
  - o Research to define "personal property." Document.

  - o Find the Wisconsin Statement of Personal Property return (PA-003), any year; copy and paste or include a snip of Schedule A of the return in your file.

➢ Accounts Payable: As we did each quarter, reconcile subsidiary account balances to the A/P control account on the trial balance, showing the subsidiary ledger report and trial balance snips.

- Research the requirements to determine which of our vendors would receive a 1099. (Hint: There are two of them!) Copy and paste this information in your file.

- Using QuickBooks help and 1099 Wizard, prepare the necessary 1099s with the amounts in the appropriate boxes and the 1096 summary page. (Hint: Tax IDs may be found in earlier transaction and invoice.) (Note: These will print as if printed on the actual 1096/1099 forms. Snip forms into your file or include a PDF file of 1096 and 1099s.)

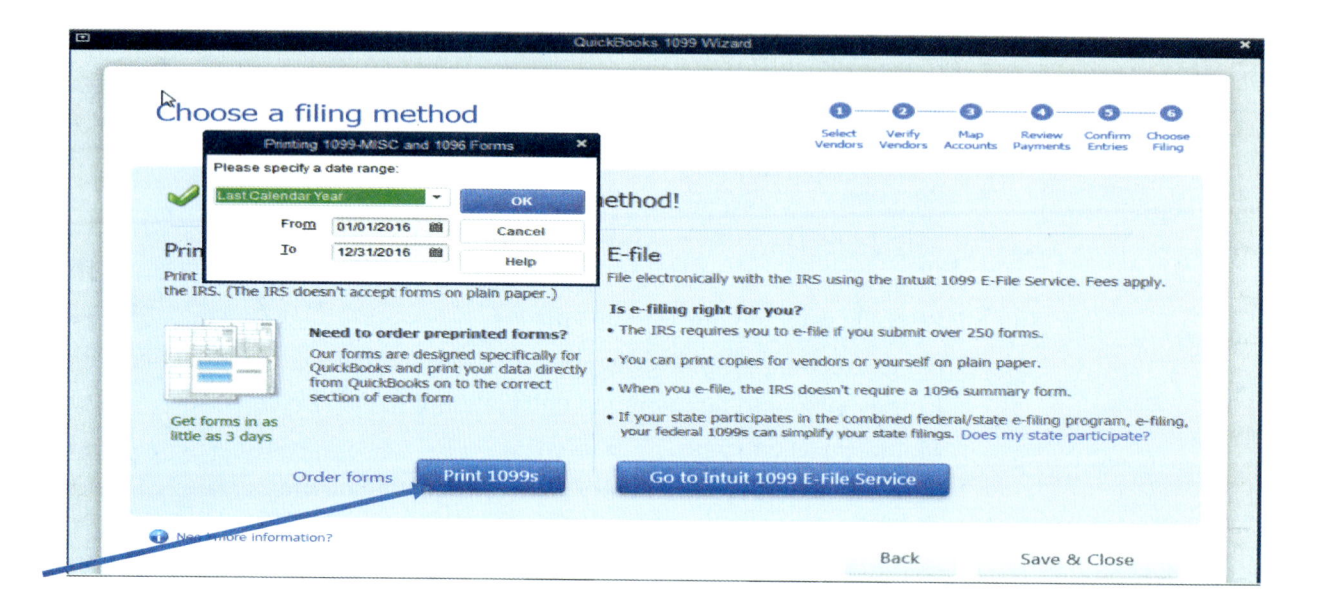

➤ Credit Card Payable: Reconcile balance in account per trial balance to December credit card statement owed in January 2017, found on the following pages; record any additional charges, noting all charges have been incurred at or prior to 12/31/2016. After adding charges, document using snips reconciliation, showing Credit Card Payable per the trial balance equals the credit card statement balance.

➤ Sales Tax Payable: Complete reconciliations of Sales Tax Revenue Summary and Sales Tax Liability Reports to Profit and Loss and trial balance and to ST-12.

- Prepare 4th quarter, ST-12, sales tax return. (Reminder: Account for Brown's write-off on the Sales Returns, Allowances, and Bad Debt lines.) Include a snip of the report.

- Payment is not due until January 2017.

> Notes Payable: Compare the balance in the account to the amortization schedule. Document the comparison in your file.

  o Record the general journal entry to properly classify the note between current and long-term liability accounts.

  o Accrue for *December* interest using your amortization schedule — use the interest amount for January 3, 2017, payment and account for 28 days in December.

All Payroll-Related Accounts:

  o First, make sure all of Mary's wages are accounted for in Office Wage Expense. Make a journal entry if necessary.

  o Complete all 4th quarter payroll reconciliations (as done in July and October) *and* year-end payroll reports. (Note: No payment of payroll liabilities is made at this time; these amounts are due and will be paid in January 2017.)

    ✓ Reconcile and complete 4th quarter 941 (Payroll Summary to Trial Balance to 941).

    ✓ Reconcile and complete 4th quarter state withholding WT-6 (Payroll Summary/Trial Balance/WT-6).

    ✓ Reconcile and complete 4th quarter WI unemployment UCT-101 (Payroll Summary for Wages and WI — Unemployment/Trial Balance/UCT-101).

    ✓ Reconcile and complete 2016 Annual 940 (use any year form) (Payroll Summary/Trial Balance/940). (Note: Include *employer* 401k payments in Total payments on line 3 as well as in Payments exempt on line 4.) See the screen shot below.

      o To reconcile to the FUTA Payable balance, plug in .01 on line 11.
      o Use the general ledger to complete Part 5.

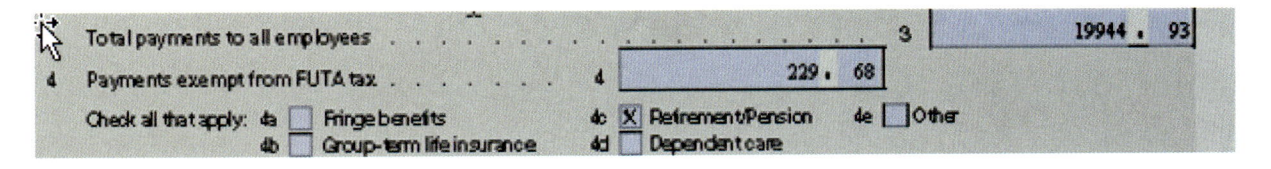

Total payments to all employees			3	19944 . 93
4 Payments exempt from FUTA tax		4	229 . 68	
Check all that apply: 4a ☐ Fringe benefits		4c ☒ Retirement/Pension	4e ☐ Other	
4b ☐ Group-term life insurance		4d ☐ Dependent care		

- 2016 W-2s and W-3: Go to Employees/Payroll Tax Forms and W-2s/Create Excel Tax Form Worksheet for Annual W-2/W-3. Compare the amounts on the worksheet to QuickBooks' Employee Earnings Summary. Show the comparison of box 1 amounts for Mary, Max, and Brian in your file.

- Reconcile and complete annual state withholding summary, WT-7 (Payroll Summary to trial balance to WT-7). Use any year form for WT-7.

- Accrue for payroll for the last week of year: Mary 8 hours, Max 12 hours. Include a snip of journal entry. (Note: Since these wages are not *paid*, they are not accounted for on any of the above payroll forms.)

- Research W-2 health insurance reporting requirements as pertains to DM Yard Services with three employees. Note your finding in your file.

- Compare balances of 401k and health insurance (employee and employer) on 4th quarter Payroll Summary Report to payable accounts on trial balance. Document the comparison.

➢ Dave Michaels, Capital: Review for any misclassified entries; include a comment that the task was completed.

➢ Dave Michaels, Drawing: Review for any misclassified entries; include a comment that the task was completed.

YEAR-END ANALYSIS

2. Prepare an edited 2016 Income Statement, Statement of Owner's Equity, Balance Sheet, and Statement of Cash Flows; reflect a proper presentation in accordance with GAAP and professional appearance, show only year-to-date numbers, and shade and bold headings.

   Hint: Use QuickBooks statements as your starting point, noting you do not have to use all of the same headings or subtotals. Use financial statements from your prior accounting courses as a guide.

   Note 1: You should have line items for Sales Discounts, Sales Returns and Allowances, Purchase Discounts, and Purchase Returns and Allowance.

   Note 2: QuickBooks' Statement of Cash Flows is not correct; QB cannot accurately account for all changes in the accounts, that is, truck and equipment accounts, capital, and so on.

   Use an Excel sheet or Word page for each statement.

3. Select five ratios; use only year-end balances when calculating ratios with "average" denominators, and *comment* on the results of each ratio. (Note: A ratio comparison of several years or to an industry standard would be most useful. Use a variety of liquidity and profitability ratios.)

4. Calculate the payroll to net sales ratio in two ways:
   - First, use the total of wage expense (Office and Field) as the numerator.

   - Second, use the total wage expense *and* employee benefits (health insurance and 401k expense, no payroll taxes) as the numerator.

   - Comment on the results of each ratio.

5. QuickBooks does not have a formal year-end closing process. On the first of the new fiscal year, QuickBooks automatically closes all income and expense accounts to the default equity account, "Capital/Retained Earnings." At year-end, an entry to close the drawing account to capital would have to be journalized.

Per the QuickBooks community help:

QuickBooks does not have the Closing Entries in the sense that you can pull up the Journal Entries on the screen and see the credits to expenses and debits to income and credit to the Retained Earnings. When you run a report that needs to show these entries, e.g., a QuickReport on Retained Earnings, QuickBooks calculates them and displays them in the report. But you cannot "QuickZoom" on them to bring them to the screen. The type will show as "Closing Entry" which is not a real transaction type in QuickBooks.

Since we are not using the "real" current year, we will *not* complete this process in QuickBooks, nor close the drawing account.

- o Print/snip a January 2017 Profit and Loss statement, noting zero balances.

6. List three suggestions for the 2017 business plan and explain the reasoning for your suggestions.
    - ✓ Consider using the above ratios as a basis for your suggestions.
    - ✓ Also consider using information from the company snapshot.

7. Using Word, Excel, or PowerPoint, prepare an organizational chart of the owner and current employees with a brief list of each of their duties under each name on the chart.

    Next, show a second chart with the addition of two office employees and how this affects the segregation of Mary's duties, keeping in mind good internal controls.

    Copy and paste or snip into your file.

8. Identify:
    a. Two internal controls in place

    b. Two current weaknesses in internal control, and suggest controls that should be implemented to address those weaknesses

    c. Three new internal controls that would need to be implemented if DM Yard Services expanded to 10 employees, additional inventory, and an increased client base.

YEAR-END PRINT/SUBMISSION SUMMARY

1. _____ Excel file/Word document of year-end activities with adjustments, comments, snips, and ratios

2. _____ Task List

ANY OF THE BELOW IF NOT INCLUDED AS SNIPS IN YOUR FILE ABOVE:

3. _____ A/R:

- Jacksonville Industrial Park and Laxson collection letters
- Brown's collection letter
- Top Customer by Sales Bar Graph

4. _____ Equipment/Trucks:

- Fixed Asset Manager Report
- WI Statement of Personal Property Tax Return

5. _____ A/P: 1099s and 1096

6. _____ ST-12

7. _____ Payroll-Related:

- Payroll Summary Report
- 4th quarter 941
- 4th quarter WT-6
- 4th quarter UCT-101
- Annual 940
- Annual WT-7
- Excel worksheet: W-2s and W-3

8. _____ Excel file of financial statements

9. _____ January 2017 Profit and Loss statement

YEAR-END TASK LIST

Check here if completed	Task	Initials
	Verify Cash balance in the general ledger agrees with reconciled balance on the December bank reconciliation	
	Record a journal entry to replenish a petty cash fund	
	Compare a total of A/R subsidiary ledger to the A/R control account balance	
	Write off Brown's account	
	Compare Inventory balance to the physical listing; make inventory adjustment	
	Record Supplies, adjusting entry	
	Reconcile Prepaid Insurance	
	Verify Security Deposit balance	
	Calculate and record depreciation	
	Complete fixed asset subsidiary ledgers	
	Compare balance of A/P subsidiary ledger to A/P control account balance	
	Prepare 4th quarter, ST-12; reconcile balance in Sales Tax Payable account to balance due on report	
	Classify Note Payable and accrue interest	
	Account for Office Wages; accrue for year-end payroll; prepare 4th quarter and year-end payroll reports; compare balances in employee benefit accounts	
	Review capital and drawing accounts for reasonableness of entries	

Credit Card Services, Inc.

DM Yard Services

Statement Date: 1/5/2017

Last payment: 12/15/2016 $2,458.10

Amount Due: $617.02

Due Date: 1/15/2017

Charge Summary:

- ABC Food Store   124.72
- Max's Drug Store   15.18
- Gas to Go   120.00
- Cell World   60.00
- Gas to Go   74.00
- ABC Food Store   35.32
- Utility Service Corp. 150.00
- PP Equipment   37.80   (charge to Repairs and Maintenance expense)

Physical Inventory List

Item ID	Item Description	Count	By
Pine trees 36"	Pine trees 36"	1	DM
Pine trees 5'	Pine trees 5'	0	DM
Boxwood bushes	Boxwood bushes	0	DM
Fertilizer	Fertilizer	20 bags	DM
Mulch	Bulk mulch	DNV*	DM
Salt	Salt	40 bags	DM
Seed	Grass seed	0	DM
Straw	Straw bales	0	DM
Topsoil	Screened topsoil	DNV*	DM

*DNV = did not verify due to bulk nature of item

Office Supply Physical Inventory List

Printer paper   2 reams at $10 each = $20

Printer ink   2 cartridges = $34

Miscellaneous $15

Income Tax Return Preparation

Prepare individual federal and Wisconsin Income Tax Returns for Dave and Sue Michaels; use YOUR NAME as the last name on returns using tax preparation software.

- ✓ If you do not have school-provided software, purchase the Tax Act software "ultimate bundle," which includes federal and state editions; the cost is approximately $25. Select the download version (see http://www.taxact.com).

- ✓ See the completed organizer and source documents on the next pages.

- ✓ Use MACRS depreciation
    a. Chevy truck GVWR is 6250# and 22,000 business miles, no personal miles.
       Reminder: This was not a new truck when placed into service.
    b. Note: No Sec. 179 or bonus depreciation will be taken.

- ✓ Reconcile the difference between the DM Yard Services net income (net loss) per QuickBooks Profit and Loss statement and the Schedule C net profit(loss), document on the QuickBooks statement or Word document, and submit with your return.

- ✓ Understand the income tax treatment of each item; upon completion of returns, your instructor may select each student to explain one item or area.

- ✓ Save the file and submit the federal and Wisconsin income tax returns.

2016 Client Tax Organizer (Prepared by Tax Client 2/20/2017)

★ Indicates source document attached.

1. Personal Information

	Name	Soc. Sec. No.	Date of Birth	Occupation	Work Phone
Taxpayer	David A. Michaels	388-22-6666	8/14/64	Self-employed	
Spouse	Sue G. Michaels	360-24-9781	6/26/66	Admin. Asst.	
Street Address 800 Main St.		City Landscape	State WI	ZIP 53022	County Winnebago

	Taxpayer	Spouse	Marital Status		
Blind	☐Yes ☒No	☐Yes ☒No	☒Married	Will file jointly	☒Yes ☐No
Disabled	☐Yes ☒No	☐Yes ☒No	☐Single		
Pres. Campaign Fund	☐Yes ☒No	☐Yes ☒No	☐Widow(er), Date of Spouse's Death _____		

2. Dependents (Children & Others)

Name (First, Last)	Relationship	Date of Birth	Social Security Number	Months Lived With You	Disabled	Full Time Student	Dependent's Gross Income
Mason Michaels	Son	5/21/02	550-65-9944	12		X	--
Jamie Michaels	Daughter	7/8/04	251-85-6333	12		X	--
Dolly Weatherspoon(1)	Sue's mother	8/12/30	397-82-5531		Blind		22,140 total

(1) Dolly lives in an assisted living facility. Dave & Sue provided over one-half of Dolly's support. (Determine Dolly's dependency status; no other income tax effect.)

Please provide all statements (W-2s, 1098s, 1099s, etc.)

Please answer the following questions to determine maximum deductions

1. Are you self-employed or do you receive hobby income?	☒Yes ☐No	9. Were there any births, deaths, marriages, divorces or adoptions to your related family?	☒Yes ☐No
2. Did you receive income from raising animals or crops?	☐Yes ☒No	10. Did you give a gift of more than $13,000 to one or more people?	☐Yes ☒No
3. Did you receive rent from real estate or other property?	☒Yes ☐No	11. Did you have any debts cancelled, forgiven, or refinanced?	☐Yes ☒No
4. Did you receive income from gravel, timber, minerals, oil, gas, copyrights, patents?	☐Yes ☒No	12. Did you go through bankruptcy proceedings?	☐Yes ☒No
5. Did you withdraw or write checks from a mutual fund?	☐Yes ☒No	13. If you paid rent, how much did you pay? Was heat included?	☐Yes ☒No
6. Do you have a foreign bank account, trust, or business?	☐Yes ☒No	14. Did you pay interest on a student loan for yourself, your spouse, or your dependent during the year?	☐Yes ☒No
7. Do you provide a home for or help support anyone not listed in Section 2 above?	☐Yes ☒No	15. Did you pay expenses for yourself, your spouse, or your dependent to attend classes beyond high school?	☒Yes ☐No
8. Did you receive any correspondence from the IRS or State Department of Taxation?	☐Yes ☒No		

16. Did you have any children under the age of 19 or 19 to 23 year old students with unearned income of more than $950? ☐ Yes ☒ No

17. Did you purchase a new alternative technology vehicle or electric vehicle? ☐ Yes ☒ No

18. Did you install any energy property to your residence such as solar water heaters, generators or fuel cells or energy efficient improvements such as exterior doors or windows, insulation, heat pumps, furnaces, central air conditioners or water heaters? ☐ Yes ☒ No

19. Did you own $50,000 or more in foreign financial assets? ☐ Yes ☒ No

3. Wage, Salary Income

Attach W-2s:

Employer	Taxpayer	Spouse
★General Manufacturing	☐	☒
	☐	☐
	☐	☐
	☐	☐

4. Interest Income

Attach 1099-INT, Form 1097-BTC & broker statements

Payer	Amount
★Educators Credit Union	754.08
★Winnebago Bank	30.89
Tax Exempt	

5. Dividend Income

From Mutual Funds & Stocks – Attach 1099-DIV

Payer	Ordinary	Capital Gains	Non-Taxable
★American Funds	169.98	40.00	1.00

6. Partnership, Trust, Estate Income

List payers of partnership, limited partnership, S-corporation, trust, or estate income – Attach K-1

_____
_____
_____

7. Property Sold

Attach 1099-S and closing statements

Property	Date Acquired	Cost & Imp.	Sold
Personal Residence			
Vacation Home			
Land –★WI Dells (See attorney stmt.)	1/2/2005	5,000	4/6/16
Other –Personal car, sold for $1,000	3/2/2008	7,600	10/5/16

8. I.R.A. (Individual Retirement Acct.)

Contributions for tax year income

	Amount	Date	√ for Roth
Taxpayer			
Spouse			

Amounts withdrawn. Attach 1099-R & 5498

Plan Trustee	Reason for Withdrawal	Reinvested?
		☐Yes ☐No
		☐Yes ☐No
		☐Yes ☐No
		☐Yes ☐No

9. Pension, Annuity Income

Attach 1099-R Payer*	Reason for Withdrawal	Reinvested?
		☐Yes ☐No
		☐Yes ☐No
		☐Yes ☐No
		☐Yes ☐No

* Provide statements from employer or insurance company with information on cost of or contributions to plan.

Did you receive	Taxpayer	Spouse
Social Security Benefits	☐Yes ☒No	☐Yes ☒No
Railroad Retirement	☐Yes ☒No	☐Yes ☒No

Attach SSA 1099, RRB 1099

10. Investments Sold

Stocks, Bonds, Mutual Funds, Gold Silver, Partnership Interest—Attach 1099-B & confirmation slips

Investment	Date Acquired/Sold	Cost	Sale Price
★Widget, Inc.	1/8/95 / 9/5/2016	1,090.00	1,100.00
★Standard Products	2/8/98 / 5/8/2016	5,526.00	3,822.00

11. Other Income

List all Other Income (including non-taxable)	
Alimony	
Child Support	
★Scholarship (Grants) (Sue)	500
★Unemployment Compensation (Sue)	1,825
Prizes, Bonuses, Awards	
★Gambling, Lottery (expenses _170_)	2,000
Unreported Tips	
Director / Executor's Fee	
Commissions	
Jury Duty	
Worker's Compensation	
Disability Income	
Veteran's Pension	
Payments from Prior Installment Sale	
★State Income Tax Refund	1,275
Other : Inheritance (Sue's uncle)	10,000

12. Medical/Dental Expenses

Medical Insurance Premiums (paid by you)	
Prescription Drugs	310
Insulin	
Glasses, Contacts	475
Hearing Aids, Batteries	
Braces	
Medical Equipment, Supplies	
Nursing Care	
Medical Therapy	
Hospital	
Doctor/Dental/Orthodontist	
Mileage (no. of miles)	
Miles after June 30	

13. Taxes

Real Property Tax 1)★Residence	4,045.46
2) Cabin in Northern WI	600.00
Other: -Telephone excise tax	100
- 2014 Federal Income Tax Refund	712
-WI sales tax not pd on out-of-state purchases	19

14. Interest Expense

★Mortgage interest paid (attach 1098)	5,000.59
Interest paid to individual for your home (include amortization schedule)	
Paid to:	
Name _____	
Address _____	
Social Security No. _____	
Investment interest	
Premiums paid or accrued for qualified mortgage insurance	
Other: _MasterCard_	150

15. Casualty/Theft Loss

For property damaged by storm, water, fire, accident, or stolen.
Location of Property _____
Description of Property _____

	Other	Federally Declared Disaster Losses
Amount of Damage		
Insurance Reimbursement		
Repair Costs		
Federal Grants Received		

16. Charitable Contributions

	Other	
★Church	705	
United Way	25	
Scouts	12	Cookies bought by D & M Yard Services
University, Public TV/Radio		
Heart, Lung, Cancer, etc.	30	(Includes $15 to Girl Scouts by D & M Yard Services)
Wildlife Fund		
★Salvation Army, Goodwill	350	See donation receipt.
Other: Political Party	300	
Non-Cash _____		
Volunteer (no. of miles) _____ @.14		

17. Child & Other Dependent Care Expenses

Name of Care Provider	Address	Soc. Sec. No. or Employer ID	Amount Paid

Also complete this section if you receive dependent care benefits from your employer.

18. Job-Related Moving Expenses

Date of move _____
Move Household Goods _____
Lodging During Move _____
Travel to New Home (no. of miles) _____
    Miles after June 30 _____

19. Employment Related Expenses That You Paid (Not self-employed)

Dues—Union, Professional (Sue)	240
Books, Subscriptions, Supplies	
Licenses	
Tools, Equipment, Safety Equipment	
Uniforms (include cleaning)	
Sales Expense, Gifts	
Tuition, Books (Sue —)	See #24

Began pursuing associates degree in accounting and took 1 evening class at Winnebago County Technical College
700 Main St., Landscape, WI 53022
39-0043212   SEE 1098-T

Entertainment _____
Office in Home:
In Square feet: a) Total Home _____
             b) Office _____
             c) Storage _____
Rent _____
Insurance _____
Utilities _____
Maintenance _____

20. Investment-Related Expenses

Tax Preparation Fee (300 for personal part of return; 200 for Schedule C/business; 100 for Schedule E/rental)	600
Mutual Fund Fee	
Safe Deposit Box Rental	120

21. Business Mileage

Do you have written records?   ☒Yes ☐No
Did you sell or trade in a car used for business?   ☐Yes ☒No
If yes, attach a copy of purchase agreement
Make/Year Vehicle: (Information in DM Yard Services)
Date purchased _____
Total miles (personal & business) _____
Business miles (not to and from work) _____
    Miles after June 30 _____
From first to second job _____
    Miles after June 30 _____
Education (one way, work to school) _____
Job Seeking _____
Other Business _____

Round Trip commuting distance _____
Gas, Oil, Lubrication _____
Batteries, Tires, etc. _____
Repairs _____
Wash _____
Insurance _____
Interest _____
Lease Payments _____
Garage Rent _____

22. Business Travel

If you are not reimbursed for exact amount, give total expenses.*
Airfare, Train, etc. _____
Lodging _____
Meals (no. of days _____) _____
Taxi, Car Rental _____
Other _____
Reimbursement Received _____

*Business Convention to Las Vegas (see DM Yard Services' financial statements)

23. Estimated Tax Paid

Due Date	Date Paid	Federal	State
	Apr 15, 2016	500	150
	June 15, 2016	500	150
	Sept 15, 2016	500	150
	Jan 16, 2017	500	150

24. Education Expenses

Student's Name	Type of Expense	Amount
Sue Michaels	Books	182
	Tuition	600

—— Note: Books are <u>not</u> required to be purchased from the

Mason Michaels (gr. 8)	Tuition**	2,800
Jamie Michaels (gr. 6)	Tuition**	2,300

**PRIVATE SCHOOL TUITION

**Divine Lutheran School 23-7246411

100 Main St.

Landscape, WI 53022

25. Other Deductions

Alimony /(Child Support) Pd. to David's ex-wife $3,600
(ex-wife claims dependent)
Social Security No. _____ $
Student Interest Paid $
Health Savings Account Contributions $
Archer Medical Savings Acct. Contributions $

26. Questions, Comments, & Other Information

See DM Yard Services for business income/expense

Residence:
Town _____   County _Winnebago_
Village _____   School District _1862_
City _Landscape_

27. Direct Deposit of Refund/or Savings Bond Purchases

Would you like to have your refund(s) directly deposited into your account?   ☒ Yes   ☐ No

ACCOUNT

Owner of account   ☐ Taxpayer   ☐ Spouse   ☒ Joint

Type of account   ☐ Checking   ☒ Traditional Savings   ☐ Traditional IRA   ☐ Roth IRA
☐ Archer MSA Savings   ☐ Coverdell Education Savings   ☐ HSA Savings   ☐ SEP IRA

Name of financial institution _Educators Credit Union_
Financial Institution Routing Transit Number (if known) _123456_
Your account number _120356_

Supplemental information:

```
                              RENTAL PROPERTY
    Address:  123 W. South St.
              Landscape, WI 53022
  Rents:         $12,000         Purchased property and placed into service on 4/1/2003
  Insurance:         159         for $80,000 total, $15,000 allocated to land
★ Mtg. Interest:  6,971.93
  Repairs:           242         Purchased refrigerator:  7/5/2016   $1,200
★ Real Estate Tax: 4,210.80
  Utilities:         182
                                 Vehicle info: 2004 Chevrolet Impala
                                 purchased on 7/8/2007
                                 10,000 total miles driven in 2017
                                 (700 rental-related miles)
```

To the best of my knowledge, the information enclosed in this client tax organizer is correct and includes all income, deductions, and other information necessary for the preparation of this year's income tax returns for which I have adequate records.

Dave Michaels	2/20/2017	_Sue Michaels_	2/20/2017
Taxpayer	**Date**	**Spouse**	**Date**

Self-employed		_Administrative Assistant_
Occupation		**Occupation**

★ Indicates source document attached.

FACTS ABOUT YOUR 2016 SOCIAL SECURITY BENEFIT STATEMENT

This is your 2017 Social Security Benefit Statement. Use it, along with the information below, to see if part of your Social Security benefits may be taxable.

What You Need to Do

Determine whether any of your Social Security benefits are taxable.

Box 2—"Social Security Number"—shows the Social Security number of the person shown in Box 1.

Box 3—"Benefits Paid in 2017"—shows the total amount paid to you in 2017.

SEE IRS PUBLICATION 915 FOR FULL DESCRIPTION OF BOXES ON SSA-1099.

Box 4—"Benefits Repaid to SSA in 2013""—shows the total amount of benefits you repaid us in 2017.

FORM SSA-1099—SOCIAL SECURITY BENEFIT STATEMENT

2016 — PART OF YOUR SOCIAL SECURITY BENEFITS SHOWN IN BOX 5 MAY BE TAXABLE INCOME. SEE THE REVERSE FOR MORE INFORMATION.

Box 1. Name	Box 2. Beneficiary's Social Security Number
Dolly Weatherspoon	397-82-5531

Box 3. Benefits Paid in 2017	Box 4. Benefits Repaid to SSA in 2017	Box 5. Net Benefits for 2017 (Box 3 minus Box 4)
21990.30	NONE	21990.30

DESCRIPTION OF AMOUNTS IN BOX 3	Description of Amount in Box 4
Paid by check or direct deposit $19,914.00 Medicare Part B premiums deducted from your benefits $2,076.30 Total Additions $21,990.30 Benefits for 2017 $21,990.30	NONE

Box 6. Voluntary Federal Income Tax Withheld
NONE

Box 7. Address

Box 8. Claim Number *(Use this number if you need to contact SSA.)*

Form SSA-1099-SM (1-2016)   DO NOT RETURN THIS FORM TO SSA OR IRS

☐ CORRECTED (if checked)

PAYER'S name, street address, city, state, ZIP code, and telephone no. Bank of America P.O. Box 2 Anywhere, CA 55222	Payer's RTN (optional)	OMB No. 1545-0112 2016 Form **1099-INT**	**Interest Income**
	1 Interest Income $150		
	2 Early withdrawal penalty $		

PAYER'S federal identification number 16-1234567	RECIPIENT'S identification number 397-82-5531	**3** Interest on U.S. Savings Bonds and Treas. Obligations $		Copy B For Recipient
RECIPIENT'S name Dolly Weatherspoon		**4** Federal income tax withheld $	**5** Investment expenses $	This is important tax information and is being furnished to the Internal Revenue Service. If you are required to file a return, a negligence penalty or other sanction may be imposed on you if this income is taxable and the IRS determines that it has not been reported.
Street address (including apt. no.) 800 Main St		**6** Foreign tax paid $	**7** Foreign country or U.S. possession	
City, state, and ZIP code Landscape, WI 53022		**8** Tax-exempt interest $	**9** Specified private activity bond interest $	
Account number (see instructions)		**10** Tax-exempt bond CUSIP no.	**11** State **12** State identification no.	**13** State tax withheld $

Form **1099-INT** (keep for your records) Department of the Treasury – Internal Revenue Service

22222	Void ☐	**a** Employee's social security number 360-24-9781	For Official use Only ▶ OMB No. 1545-0008	
b Employer identification number (EIN) 14-0689340			**1** Wages, tips, other compensation 76,707.24	**2** Federal income tax withheld 8,623.39
c Employer's name, address, and ZIP code General Manufacturing P.O. Box 60300 Ft. Myers, FL 33906			**3** Social security wages 83,869.53	**4** social security tax withheld 3,522.52
			5 Medicare wages and tips 83,869.53	**6** Medicare tax withheld 1,216.11
			7 Social security tips	**8** Allocated tips
d Control number			**9**	**10** Dependent care benefits
e Employee's first name and initial Sue G	Last name Michaels	Suff.	**11** Nonqualified plans	**12a** See instructions for box 12
800 Main St Landscape, WI 53022			**13** Statutory employee ☐ Retirement plan ☒ Third-party sick pay ☐	**12b** DD 12,910.16
			14 Other	**12c** C 171.93
				12d D 7,162.29
f Employee's address and ZIP code				

15 State WI	Employer's state ID number 761015	**16** State wages, tips, etc. 76,707.24	**17** State income tax 4,709.91	**18** Local wages, tips, etc.	**19** Local income tax	**20** Locality Name

Form **W-2** Wage and Tax Statement 2016

Copy C For Employee's Records.

Department of the Treasury—Internal Revenue Service
For Privacy Act and Paperwork Reduction Act Notice, see the separate instructions.

Cat. No. 10134D

Do Not Cut, Fold, or Staple Forms on This Page

☐ CORRECTED (if checked)

PAYER'S name, street address, city, state, ZIP code, and telephone no.		Payer's RTN (optional)	OMB No. 1545-0112	**Interest Income**
Educators Credit Union **1400 N Newman Rd** **Racine, WI 53406** **262-886-5900**		**1** Interest Income $ 754.08	**2016**	
		2 Early withdrawal penalty $ .00	Form **1099-INT**	
PAYER'S federal identification number **39-0555293**	RECIPIENT'S identification number **388-22-6666**	**3** Interest on U.S. Savings Bonds and Treas. Obligations $ .00		**Copy B** **For Recipient**
RECIPIENT'S name, street address (including apt. no.), city, state, and ZIP code **David and Sue Michaels** **800 Main Street** **Landscape, WI 53022**		**4** Federal income tax withheld $ .00	**5** Investment expenses $ .00	This is important tax information and is being furnished to the Internal Revenue Service. If you are required to file a return, a negligence penalty or other sanction may be imposed on you if this income is taxable and the IRS determines that it has not been reported.
		6 Foreign tax paid $ .00	**7** Foreign country or U.S. possession	
		8 Tax-exempt interest $ .00	**9** Specified private activity bond interest $ .00	
Account number (see instructions) 120356		**10** Tax-exempt bond CUSIP no. (see instructions)		

Form **1099-INT** (keep for your records) Department of the Treasury – Internal Revenue Service

QuickBooks

		Payer's identifying number	**1** Interest income not included in Box 3
Winnebago Bank		39-0734270	30.89
P.O. Box 648		Recipient's identifying number	**2** Early withdrawal penalty
Landscape, WI 53022		39-1212121	.00
		PAYER'S RTN (OPTIONAL)	**3** Interest on U.S. Savings Bonds and Treas. obligations
	CORRECTED (if checked) ☐	0759-01341	.00

If your taxpayer identifying number is not shown or is incorrectly shown, please furnish the correct number to the payer.

TO WHOM PAID ▶

OMB No. 1545-0112

2016

**Interest Income
Copy B
For Recipient
FORM 1099 INTEREST
SUBSTITUTE**

D & M Yard Services
900 Main Street
Landscape, WI 53022

4 Federal income tax withheld .00

5 Foreign tax paid .00

6 Foreign country or U.S. possession .00

This is important tax information and is being furnished to the Internal Revenue Service. If you are required to file a return, a negligence penalty or other sanction may be imposed on you if this income is taxable and the IRS determines that it has not been reported.

Keep this copy for your records

INTEREST STATEMENT FOR

TYPE	ACCOUNT NUMBER	INTEREST EARNED	FORFEITURE	FEDERAL TAX WITHHELD
STMT SUPER SAVER ACCOUNT		30.89	.00	.00

American Funds

PO Box 6007
Indianapolis IN 46206-6007

Recipient's name and address

David and Sue Michaels
800 Main Street
Landscape, WI 53022

Form 1099-DIV

OMB No 1545-0110

2016 Dividends and Distributions | **Copy B** For Recipient

Payer's name, address and telephone number
American Funds Service Company
PO Box 6007
Indianapolis IN 46206-6007
800-421-4225

Recipient's identification number:

388-22-6666

- This is important tax information and is being furnished to the Internal Revenue Service (IRS). Please keep for your records.
- If you are required to file a return, a negligence penalty or other sanction may be imposed on you if this income is taxable and the IRS determines that it has not been reported.

Payer's (Fund's) name and federal identification number	Recipient's account and fund number	1a	Total ordinary dividends	1b	Qualified dividends	2a	Total capital gain distributions	4	Federal income tax withheld	6	Foreign tax paid
The Investment Company of America 95-1426645			169.98		169.98		40.00		0.00		N/A

See Next Page for State Tax Exclusion

QuickBooks

229

American Funds

State tax exclusions for U.S. government income worksheet

Worksheet results

Fund name	Ordinary dividend	x	U.S. government factor	=	Your U.S. government income
The Investment Company of America®	$169.98		0.0043		$0.73

Your total state tax exclusion: $0.73

To determine your individual tax situation, please consult your tax adviser.

Legal Services of America

4/6/2016

TO: Dave and Sue Michaels
      800 Main St.
      Landscape, WI 53022

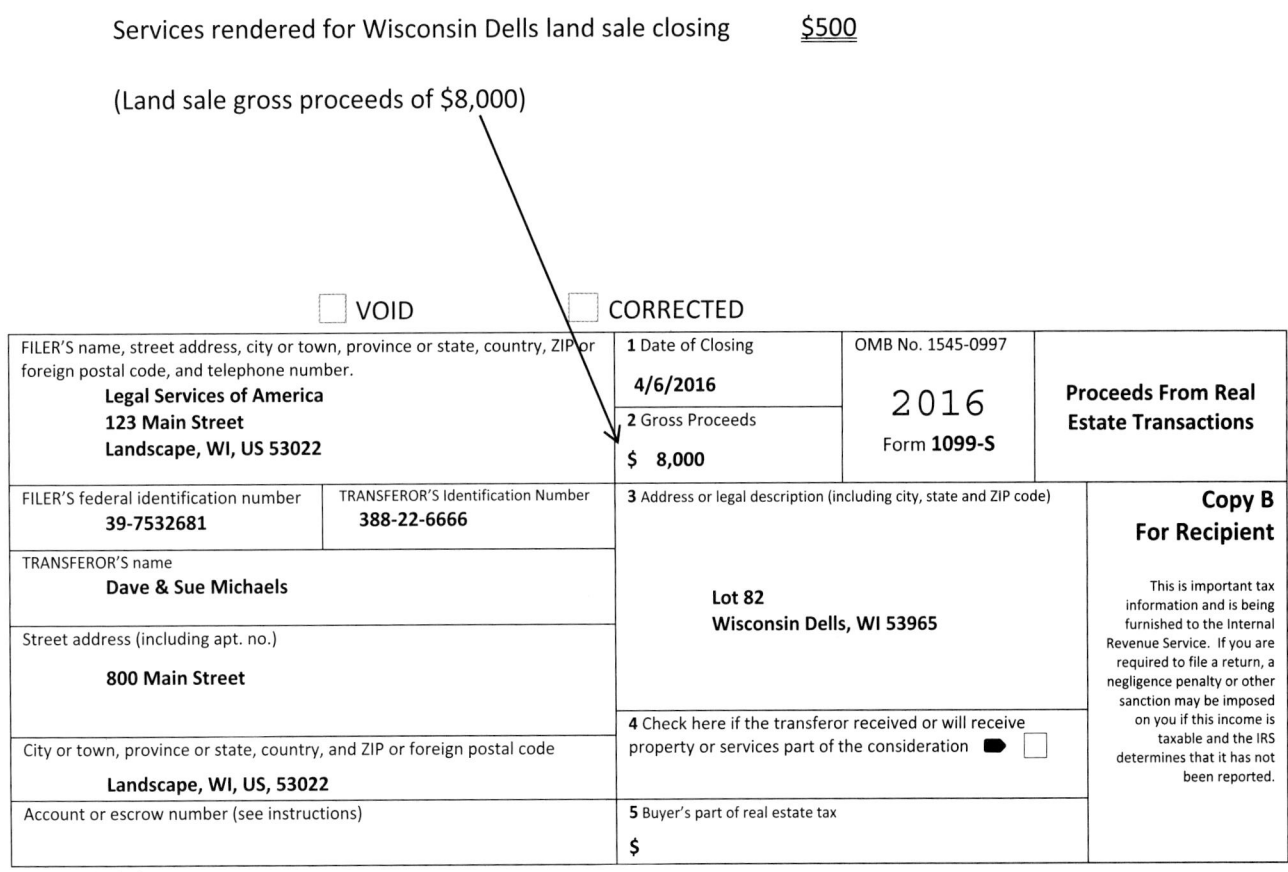

Services rendered for Wisconsin Dells land sale closing $500

(Land sale gross proceeds of $8,000)

☐ VOID   ☐ CORRECTED

FILER'S name, street address, city or town, province or state, country, ZIP or foreign postal code, and telephone number. **Legal Services of America** **123 Main Street** **Landscape, WI, US 53022**	**1** Date of Closing **4/6/2016**	OMB No. 1545-0997 **2016** Form **1099-S**	**Proceeds From Real Estate Transactions**
	2 Gross Proceeds $ 8,000		
FILER'S federal identification number **39-7532681**	TRANSFEROR'S Identification Number **388-22-6666**	**3** Address or legal description (including city, state and ZIP code)	**Copy B For Recipient**
TRANSFEROR'S name **Dave & Sue Michaels**		**Lot 82** **Wisconsin Dells, WI 53965**	This is important tax information and is being furnished to the Internal Revenue Service. If you are required to file a return, a negligence penalty or other sanction may be imposed on you if this income is taxable and the IRS determines that it has not been reported.
Street address (including apt. no.) **800 Main Street**			
		4 Check here if the transferor received or will receive property or services part of the consideration ▶ ☐	
City or town, province or state, country, and ZIP or foreign postal code **Landscape, WI, US, 53022**			
Account or escrow number (see instructions)		**5** Buyer's part of real estate tax $	

Form **1099-S**

NOTE: 1099-S is correct form for reporting; however, 1099-B will be used in Tax Act.

QuickBooks

3232 ☐ VOID ☐ CORRECTED

PAYER'S name, street address, city or town, province or state, country, and ZIP or foreign postal code	1 Gross winnings $ 2000.00	2 Date won 11/6/2016	OMB No. 1545-0238 **2016** Form **W-2G** Certain Gambling Winnings
Potawatomi Bingo Casino 1721 W. Canal St. Milwaukee, WI 53223	3 Type of wager slots	4 Federal income tax withheld $ 0.00	
	5 Transaction 1000275818	6 Race	
	7 Winnings from identical wagers $	8 Cashier Roaf	

PAYER'S federal identification number	PAYER'S telephone number	9 Winner's taxpayer identification no.	10 Window	For Privacy Act and Paperwork Reduction Act Notice, see the 2016 General Instructions for Certain Information Returns.
39-1693007	800-729-7244	360-24-9781	8	

WINNER'S name Sue Michaels	11 First I.D.	12 Second I.D.	
Street address (including apt. no.) 800 Main St.	13 State/Payer's state identification no. WI 036102042076003	14 State winnings $ 2000.00	
City or town, province or state, country, and ZIP or foreign postal code Landscape, WI 53022	15 State income tax withheld $	16 Local winnings $	File with Form 1096
	17 Local income tax withheld $	18 Name of locality	Copy A For Internal Revenue Service Center

Under penalties of perjury, I declare that, to the best of my knowledge and belief, the name, address, and taxpayer identification number that I have furnished correctly identify me as the recipient of this payment and any payments from identical wagers, and that no other person is entitled to any part of these payments.

Signature ▶ *Sue Michaels*   Date ▶ 11/6/2016

Form **W-2G**   Cat. No. 10138V   www.irs.gov/w2g   Department of the Treasury - Internal Revenue Service

Do Not Cut or Separate Forms on This Page — Do Not Cut or Separate Forms on This Page

| PAYER'S name, address, ZIP code
Wisconsin Department of Revenue
Mail Stop 5-77
PO Box 7878
Madison, WI 53708-7878

Payer's Federal Identification Number:
39-6006491

RECIPIENT'S name

David and Sue Michaels
800 Main Street
Landscape, WI 53022 | Form 1099-G **2016**
Certain Government Payments
Refund is for tax year: **2015**
Recipient's Tax Account Number: 001-1023698246-02   Recipient's Identification Number: 388-22-6666
Computation of State Tax Refund:
Refund Requested   1,275.00
• State Income Tax Refund: $1,275.00 |

This is important tax information and is being furnished to the Internal Revenue Service. If you are required to file a return, a negligence penalty or other sanction may be imposed on you if this income is taxable and the IRS determines that it has not been reported. Federal law requires all states to provide a Form 1099-G if you receive, or received the benefit of, a state income tax refund.

What is this form?
- This is information about your Wisconsin income tax refund for 2015.
- It is not a refund. This refund was already issued to you in 2016.
- It is not a bill. You do not owe the amount shown.
- If you use a tax preparer, give this form to him/her with all of your other tax documents. A tax preparer will know how to use this information when filing your federal income tax return.

Why did I receive this form?
- Your Wisconsin Income tax refund may be taxable income on your federal tax return, if you itemized deductions on Schedule A of a prior year federal tax return.
- Usually the refund in box 1 is the same as the refund that was issued to you. It may be different if:
  - All or part of your refund was used for next year's estimated tax,
  - You reported sales and use tax or donated all or part of your refund,
  - You received certain credits that are not refunds of income tax,
  - You were charged penalties, interest, or a late filing fee, or
  - All or part of your refund was used to pay a debt you owed.

What should I do with this form if I prepare my own tax returns?
- Use the instructions for federal Form 1040, line 10 to compute the taxable refund amount.
- This refund amount is not taxable on your Wisconsin tax return:
  - If you file Form 1, subtract this amount from your federal income on line 6.
  - If you file Form 1A, do not include this amount as income.

Go paperless
- This form is now available online from our confidential website. It's free, simple, and secure!
- Sign up at revenue.wi.gov – click "Form 1099-G." We will email you when the forms are posted

| Wisconsin Department of Revenue
• www.revenue.wi.gov – search 1099G
• Dor1099G@revenue.wi.gov
• (608) 266-2486 | Internal Revenue Service
• www.irs.gove
• 1-800-829-1040 toll-free |

(NOTE: This amount is fully taxable.)

Town of Landscape   Tear at Perforation; Return Top Portion with Payment   **2016 REAL PROPERTY TAX BILL**

Assessed Value Land 115,000	Assessed Value Improvements 185,000	Total Assessed Value 300,000	Ave. Assmt. Ratio 1.0063	Net Assessed Value Rate (Does NOT reflect Lottery Credit) 13.9704/M
Est. Fair Mkt. Land 114,300	Est. Fair Mkt. Improvements 183,800	Est. Fair Mkt. 298,100	A star in this box means unpaid prior year taxes.	School taxes reduced by school levy tax credit 433.18

Taxing Jurisdiction	Last Year Est. State Aids Allocated Tax District	This Year Est. State Aids Allocated Tax District	Last Year Net Tax	This Year Net Tax	% Tax Change
STATE OF WISCONSIN			50.53	50.59	.1
COUNTY OF WINNEBAGO	110,417	100,169	669.93	674.41	2.2
TOWN OF LANDSCAPE	319,200	269,609	776.27	777.93	.2
SCHOOL DISTRICT 1862	6,569,787	5,978,140	2,295.85	2,315.13	.8
WINNEBAGO TECH COLLEGE	106,176	79,552	367.31	373.06	1.6
Total	7,105,580	6,427.470	4,149.89	4,191.12	1.0
		First Dollar Credit	63.23	62.69	.9-
		Lottery and Gaming Credit	79.73	82.97	4.1
TAX KEY		Net Property Tax	4,006.93	4,045.46	1.0

Make Check Payable to: TOWN OF LANDSCAPE KATHY KARALEWITZ, TREASURER W320S8315 Beulah Rd Landscape, WI 53022	Full payment Due On or Before January 31, 2017 **$4,045.46**	O T H E R
	First Installment Due On or Before January 31, 2017 **$1,981.46**	
When paying after January 31, 2017 Make Check Payable to: WINNEBAGO COUNTY TREASURER 515 W MORELAND BLVD, ROOM 148 LANDSCAPE, WI 53022	Second Installment Due On or Before July 31, 2017 **$2,064.00**	
		TOTAL DUE FOR FULL PAYMENT PAY BY January 31, 2017 **$4,045.46** Warning: If not paid by due date, installment option is lost and total tax is delinquent and subject to interest and penalty (See Reverse).

Property Address:
800 Main Street
Landscape, WI 53022

PAID 12/29/2016 $4,045.46

RECIPIENT'S/LENDER'S name, address and telephone number 01/10/17	*Caution: The amount shown may not be fully deductible by you. Limits based on the loan amount and the cost and value of the secured property may apply. Also, you may only deduct interest to the extent it was incurred by you, actually paid by you, and not reimbursed by another person.	OMB No. 1545-0901 **2016** Substitute Form 1098	**MORTGAGE INTEREST STATEMENT** Copy B For *Payer*

Wells Fargo Bank, N.A.
Return Mail Operations
PO Box 14411
Des Moines, IA 50306-3411
 	
We accept telecommunications relay service calls.
Fax #: 1-866-278-1179 ☐ CORRECTED (if checked)
Phone #: 1-866-234-8271
PAYER'S/BORROWER'S name, street address, city, state, and ZIP code
 	
David and Sue Michaels
800 Main Street
Landscape, WI 53022
	RECIPIENT Federal identification no.
	  94-1347393
	
	PAYER'S SOCIAL SECURITY number
	  388-22-6666
	
	1. Mortgage interest received from Payer(s)/borrower(s) $5,000.59
	2. Points paid on purchase of principle residence (See Box 2 on back) $0.00
	3. Refund of overpaid interest (See Box 3 on back.) $0.00
	4. Mortgage Insurance Premiums $0.00
	Account number (optional) 5 Real Estate Taxes $0.00
			The information in boxes 1, 2, 3, and 4 is important tax information and is being furnished to the Internal Revenue Service. If you are required to file a return, a negligence penalty or other sanction may be imposed on you if the IRS determines that an underpayment of tax results because you overstated a deduction for this mortgage interest or for these points or because you did not report this refund of interest on your return.

Form 1098 Substitute SEE BACK SIDE FOR IMPORTANT INFORMATION (Keep for your records.) Department of the Treasury – Internal Revenue Service

Please consult a Tax Advisor about the deductibility of any payments made by you or others.

Principal reconciliation	Property Address
$87,082.35 Beginning balance $17,651.07 Principal applied $69,431.28 Ending balance	800 Main Street Landscape, WI 53022
	$1,198.86 Total current payment

---2016 INTEREST DETAIL--

TOTAL INTEREST APPLIED 2016 $5,000.59
2016 MORTGAGE INTEREST RECEIVED FROM PAYER/BORROWER(S) $5,000.59

If you have questions about your loan, you can use our automated "Personal Mortgage Information Line" at the toll free number listed at the top of this statement. By selecting one of the options listed, you can receive information regarding:

- Taxes paid year-to-date
- The amount and date of your last payment
- Interest paid year-to-date
- Other valuable information

Wells Fargo Home Mortgage, a division of Wells Fargo Bank, NA, believes customers come first. You can always count on us to provide the excellent service you've come to expect.

Goodwill NCW
Serving North Central Wisconsin Communities

Donor Name: _Sue Michaels_
Address: _800 Main St, Landscape, WI 53022_
Date: _06/19/16_ Attendant: _J. Gilson_

Your donations support our programs and services in your community

- ❏ Antigo
- ❏ Ashwaubenon
- ❏ Darboy
- ❏ Eau Claire
- ❏ Grand Chute
- ❏ Green Bay East
- ❏ Green Bay West
- ❏ La Crosse
- ❏ Manitowoc
- ❏ Marshfield
- ❏ Menasha
- ❏ Menomonie
- ❏ Onalaska
- ❏ Oshkosh
- ❏ Rhinelander
- ❏ Rice Lake
- ❏ Shawano
- ❏ Stevens Pt
- ❏ Tomah
- ❏ Waupaca
- ❏ Weston
- ❏ Wis Rapids
- ❏ E-Commerce

Thank you for increasing your Goodwill

Because Goodwill NCW is a not-for-profit, 501(c)(3) human services organization, your donation is tax deductible. Use this form as your donation receipt. *See back for guidelines.

$ _____	Clothing - men's	$ _____	Jewelry
$ _350_	Clothing - women's	$ _____	Books, toys, games
$ _____	Clothing - children's	$ _____	Sporting goods
$ _____	Shoes/boots/sandals	$ _____	Tools
$ _____	Housewares	$ _____	Small appliances
$ _____	Dishes and glassware	$ _____	Small furniture items
$ _____	Other _____		

Value (as determined by donor*) $ _____
*For more donation information ask for our Donating to Goodwill brochure, or see our Web site: www.goodwillncw.org

Note: This is confirmation that you did not receive any goods or services in exchange for this donation.

Goodwill NCW, 1800 Appleton Road, Menasha, WI 54952

Divine Lutheran Church
100 Main St.
Landscape, WI 53022

Printed on: 01/24/2017
Church Phone: 262-367-8400
Envelope Number: 7311
Federal ID: 23-7246411

David and Sue Michaels
800 Main Street
Landscape, WI 53022

Contributions for the period of 1/1/2016 through 12/31/2016
Total: $705.00

This is your 2016 Contribution Statement. No goods or services were provided to the donor other than intangible religious benefits. Please contact the business office at 262-367-8400 if you have any questions.

General Fund (1)   Fund Total: **$705.00**

Pledge: (None)

Date	Amount	Description	Date	Amount	Description
1/09/16	40.00		1/23/16	40.00	
2/06/16	25.00		2/20/16	40.00	
2/27/16	20.00		3/13/16	25.00	
3/27/16	40.00		4/10/16	30.00	
4/17/16	20.00		4/24/16	25.00	
5/01/16	25.00		6/05/16	40.00	
6/26/16	25.00		7/10/16	40.00	
7/17/16	20.00		7/31/16	30.00	
8/21/16	20.00		9/18/16	40.00	
9/25/16	20.00		10/02/16	20.00	
10/23/16	20.00		10/30/16	20.00	
11/27/16	20.00		11/27/16	20.00	
12/11/16	20.00		12/18/16	20.00	

QuickBooks

☐ VOID ☐ CORRECTED

RECIPIENT'S/LENDER'S name, address, and telephone number		OMB No. 1545-0901	**Mortgage Interest Statement**
Norwest Mortgage P.O. Box 2222 Chicago, IL 87211		**2016** Form **1098**	
RECIPIENT'S federal identification no. 95-2318940	PAYER'S social security number 388-22-6666	**1** Mortgage Interest received from payer(s)/borrower(s) $6,971.93	**Copy B** **For Payer**
PAYER'S/BORROWER'S name David and Sue Michaels		**2** Points paid on purchase of principal residence $	For Privacy Act and Paperwork Reduction Act Notice, see the 2013 General Instructions for Certain Information Returns.
Street address (including apt. no.) 800 Main Street		**3** Refund of overpaid interest $	
City, state, and ZIP code Landscape, WI 53022		**4** Property Address: 123 W. South St. Landscape, WI 53022	
Account number (see instructions)			

Form **1098** Department of the Treasury – Internal Revenue Service

238 QuickBooks

© 2018 Cengage. May not be scanned, copied or duplicated, or posted to a publicly accessible website, in whole or in part.

STATE OF WISCONSIN
2016 PROPERTY TAX BILL FOR REAL ESTATE

PAY 1ST INSTALLMENT OR IN FULL TO:

TOWN TREASURER
BORIS SABATKE

Correspondence should refer to tax number.
See reverse side for important information.

Assessed Value Land	Assessed Value Improvements	Total Assessed Value	Ave. Assmt. Ratio	Est. Fair Mkt. Land	Est. Fair Mkt. Improvements	Total Est. Fair Mkt.
25,000	130,000	155,100	78.32%	31,900	166,100	198,000

☐ A star in the box means unpaid prior year taxes.

Taxing Jurisdiction #3	Last Year Est. State Aids Allocated Tax Dist.	This Year Est. State Aids Allocated Tax Dist.	Last Year Net Tax	This Year Net Tax	% Tax Change
STATE OF WISCONSIN	223,330	218,039	36.98	39.67	7.3
WINNEBAGO COUNTY	258,580	246,225	799.40	850.55	6.4
TOWN OF LANDSCAPE	412,467	394,392	647.47	646.36	.2-
WINNEBAGO SCHOOL	27,773	26,484	1,894.44	2,091.66	10.4
TECH DIST			252.32	265.03	5.0
Total	922,150	885,140	3,630.61	3,893.27	7.2
	Lottery Credit		83.48	57.47	31.2-
	Net Property Tax		3,547.13	3,835.80	8.1

School taxes reduced by school levy tax credit: 386.28

Net Assessed Value Rate (Does NOT reflect lottery credit)
025101663

Net Property Tax	3,835.80
DELQ UTILITI	375.00

TOTAL DUE — FOR FULL PAYMENT
PAY BY JANUARY 31 NEXT YEAR TO LOCAL TREASURER
$ 4,210.80

Warning: If not paid by due dates, installment option is lost and total tax is delinquent subject to interest and, if applicable, penalty. (See reverse.)

Or Pay 1st Installment
TO LOCAL TREASURER
$2,264.80
BY: January 31, 2017

And Pay 2nd Installment
TO COUNTY TREASURER
$1,946.00
BY: July 31, 2017

IMPORTANT: Be sure this description covers your property. This description is for property tax bill only and may not be a full legal description.

Special Charge Paid		Special Tax Paid
Special Assessment Paid		Total Amount Paid
Property Tax Paid		Balance Due
Paid by	Rec'd by	Date

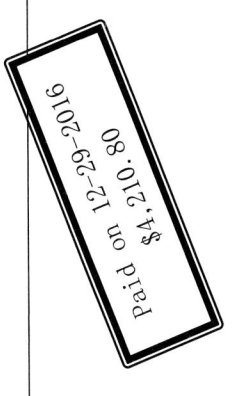

Property Address:
123 W. South St.
Landscape, WI 53022

Paid on 12-29-2016 $4,210.80

☐ VOID ☐ CORRECTED

PAYER'S name, street address, city, state, ZIP code, and telephone no. Wisconsin Dept. of Labor P. O. Box 89 Madison, WI 51160	**1** Unemployment Compensation $1,825	OMB No. 1545-0120 **2016**	**Certain Government Payments**
	2 State or local income tax refunds, credits, or offsets $	Form **1099-G**	
PAYER'S federal identification number 39-7654321	RECIPIENT'S identification number 360-24-9781	**3** Box 2 amount is for tax year $	**4** Federal income tax withheld $	**Copy 1**
RECIPIENT'S name Susan Michaels		**5** RTAA payments $	**6** Taxable grants $	
Street address (including apt. no.) 800 Main St		**7** Agriculture payments $	**8** Check if box 2 is trade or business income ▶ ☐	
		9 Market gain $		
City, state, and ZIP code Landscape, WI 53022				
Account number (see instructions)		**10a** State WI	**10b** State identification no.	**11** State income tax withheld

Form **1099-G**

CORRECTED (if checked)

FILER'S name, street address, city or town, state or province, country, ZIP or foreign postal code, and telephone number Winnebago County Technical College 1000 Main St. Landscape, WI 53022		**1** Payments received for qualified tuition and related expenses $600	OMB No. 1545-0112 2016 Form **1098-T**	**Tuition Statement**
		2 Amounts billed for qualified tuition and related expenses **$600**		
FILER'S federal identification number 14-0689340	STUDENT's Social Security number 360-24-9781	**3** Check if you have changed your reporting method for 2015 ☐		Copy B **For Recipient** This is important tax information and is being furnished to the Internal Revenue Service. If you are required to file a return, a negligence penalty or other sanction may be imposed on you if this income is taxable and the IRS determines that it has not been reported.

STUDENT name
   Sue G. Michaels
 	
Street address (including apt. no.)
   800 Main St
 	
City, state, and ZIP code
   Landscape, WI 53022
		4 Adjustments made for a prior year
		
		$
			5 Scholarships or grants
			
			$500	

		6 Adjustments to scholarships or grants for a prior year $	**7** Check this box if the amount in box 1 or 2 includes amounts for an academic period beginning January – March 2015 ☐	
Service Provider/Account number (see instructions)		**8** Check if at least half-time student. ☐	**9** Check if a graduate student ☐	**10** Ins. contract reimb./refund

Form **1098-T**   **(keep for your records)**   Department of the Treasury –
Internal Revenue Service

PAYER'S name, street address, city, state, ZIP code, and telephone no. **House Company, Inc.** **100 Franklin St.** **Cranston, RI**	Applicable check box on Form 8949 **1a** Description of property (Example 100 sh. XYZ Co.) **75 sh. of Widget Inc.**	OMB No. 1545-0112 **2016** Form **1099-B**	**Proceeds From Broker and Barter Exchange Transactions**
	1b Date Acquired 1/8/1995	**1c** Date Sold 9/5/2016	
PAYER'S federal identification number 12-3456789	RECIPIENT'S identification number 388-22-6666	**1d** Proceeds $ 1,100.00	**1e** Cost or Other Basis $ 1,090.00	
RECIPIENT'S name, street address (including apt. no.), city, state, and ZIP code **David and Sue Michaels** **800 Main Street** **Landscape, WI 53022**	**1g** Code if any	**1h** Adjustments $ .00	**Copy B** **For Recipient** This is important tax information and is being furnished to the Internal Revenue Service. If you are required to file a return, a negligence penalty or other sanction may be imposed on you if this income is taxable and the IRS determines that it has not been reported
	2 Type of Gain or Loss Short Term Long Term **XX**	**3** Check if basis reported to IRS	
	4 Federal Income Tax Withheld $ --	**5** Check if noncovered security	
	6 Reported to IRS: Gross Proceeds Net Proceeds **XX**	**7** Check if loss is not allowed based on amount in 1D	
	8 Profit or (loss) realized in 2015 on closed contracts	**9** Unrealized profit or (loss) on open contracts—	
	10 Unrealized profit or (loss) on open contracts—	**11** Aggregate profit or (loss) on contracts	
Account number (see instructions)	**12**	**13** Bartering	
14 State name WI	**15** State identification no	**16** State Tax Withheld	
CUSIP number			

Form **1099-B** (keep for your records) Department of the Treasury – Internal Revenue Service

PAYER'S name, street address, city, state, ZIP code, and telephone no. **House Company, Inc.** **100 Franklin St.** **Cranston, RI**	Applicable check box on Form 8949	OMB No. 1545-0112	Proceeds From Broker and Barter Exchange Transactions
	1a Description of property (Example 100 sh. XYZ Co.) **300 sh. of Standard Products**	**2016** Form **1099-B**	
	1b Date Acquired 1c Date Sold 2/8/1998 5/8/2016		
PAYER'S federal identification number 12-3456789	RECIPIENT'S identification number 388-22-6666	1d Proceeds $3,822.00	1e Cost or Other Basis $5,526.00	
RECIPIENT'S name, street address (including apt. no.), city, state, and ZIP code **David and Sue Michaels** **800 Main Street** **Landscape, WI 53022**	1g Code if any	1h Adjustments $ .00	Copy B For Recipient This is important tax information and is being furnished to the Internal Revenue Service. If you are required to file a return, a negligence penalty or other sanction may be imposed on you if this income is taxable and the IRS determines that it has not been reported
	2 Type of Gain or Loss Short Term Long Term **XX**	3 Check if basis reported to IRS ☐	
	4 Federal Income Tax Withheld $ --	5 Check if noncovered security ☐	
	6 Reported to IRS: Gross Proceeds Net Proceeds **XX**	7 Check if loss is not allowed based on amount in 1D	
	8 Profit or (loss) realized in 2015 on closed contracts	9 Unrealized profit or (loss) on open contracts—	
	10 Unrealized profit or (loss) on open contracts—	11 Aggregate profit or (loss) on contracts	
Account number (see instructions)	12	13 Bartering	
14 State name WI	15 State identification no	16 State Tax Withheld	
CUSIP number			

Form **1099-B**   (keep for your records)   Department of the Treasury –
Internal Revenue Service

PAYER'S name, street address, city, state, ZIP code, and telephone no. Jacksonville Industrial Park 504 Norton Dr. Landscape, WI 53022	**1** Rents **2** Royalties $	OMB No. 1545-0115 **2016** Form **1099-MISC**	**Miscellaneous Income**
PAYER'S federal identification number 39-1231234	RECIPIENT'S identification number 39-1212121	**3** Other Income $	**4** Federal income tax withheld $	**Copy B** **For Recipient**
RECIPIENT'S name DM Yard Services Street address (including apt. no.) 900 Main St City, state, and ZIP code Landscape, WI 53022		**5** Fishing Boat Proceeds $ **7** Nonemployee compensation $7437.58 **9** $	**6** Medical and Health Care Payments $ **8** Substitute payments in lieu of dividends or interest	This is important tax information and is being furnished to the Internal Revenue Service. If you are required to file a return, a negligence penalty or other sanction may be imposed on you if this income is taxable and the IRS determines that it has not been reported.
Account number (see instructions)		**10a** State WI	**10b** State identification no. 036-0000036666-04	**11** State income tax withheld	

NOTE: This is just ONE of the 1099-MISC forms DM Yard Services would have received; account for this on Schedule C.